AI and CHATGPT

A Techno-Legal-Socio Analysis

AI AND CHATGPT

A Techno-Legal-Socio Analysis

June Tay
Singapore University of Social Sciences, Singapore

Lee Cheng Tan
Singapore University of Social Sciences, Singapore

Tai Wei Lim
Soka University, Japan

World Scientific

W JERSEY • LONDON • SINGAPORE • BEIJING • SHANGHAI • HONG KONG • TAIPEI • CHENNAI • TOKYO

Published by

World Scientific Publishing Co. Pte. Ltd.

5 Toh Tuck Link, Singapore 596224

USA office: 27 Warren Street, Suite 401-402, Hackensack, NJ 07601

UK office: 57 Shelton Street, Covent Garden, London WC2H 9HE

Library of Congress Cataloging-in-Publication Data

Names: Tay, June author | Tan, Lee Cheng author | Lim, Tai Wei author

Title: AI and ChatGPT : A Techno-Legal-Socio Analysis / June Tay, Singapore University of Social Sciences, Singapore, Lee Cheng Tan, Singapore University of Social Sciences, Singapore, Tai Wei Lim, Soka University of Japan.

Description: Singapore ; Hackensack, NJ : World Scientific Publishing Co. Pte. Ltd., [2026] | Includes bibliographical references and index.

Identifiers: LCCN 2025047304 | ISBN 9789819821969 hardcover | ISBN 9789819821976 ebook | ISBN 9789819821983 ebook other

Subjects: LCSH: Artificial intelligence

Classification: LCC Q335 .T385 2026

LC record available at https://lccn.loc.gov/2025047304

British Library Cataloguing-in-Publication Data

A catalogue record for this book is available from the British Library.

For any available supplementary material, please visit
https://www.worldscientific.com/worldscibooks/10.1142/14548#t=suppl

Desk Editors: Kannan Krishnan/Pui Yee Lum

Typeset by Stallion Press
Email: enquiries@stallionpress.com

About the Authors

June Tay is an associate professor and the head of the Digital Media Programme at Singapore University of Social Sciences. She has extensive work experience in the government sector, software and telecommunications industries, and education. She obtained six patents in computing networks and security while working as a research scientist at British Telecom, U.K. She has lectured in numerous university degree programmes. Her M.Sc. degree from the University of Aberdeen (sponsored by Motorola UK and the University of Aberdeen) was related to the design of a deep ocean lander, while her Ph.D. from the same university (sponsored by the UK Defence Ministry) was in satellite communications. She completed an Executive MBA from ESSEC and Mannheim. Her current research areas include computer vision, computing networks, and mixed reality.

Lee Cheng Tan graduated from the National University of Singapore in 1990 and was admitted to the Singapore Bar the following year. She practised as a commercial litigator for over 20 years and was a partner in Rajah & Tann Asia – a full-service legal network spread out over 10 countries in ASEAN. During her career, she acted as counsel in a wide spectrum of matters, spanning joint venture disputes, employment issues, shareholder disputes, and construction claims. In 2013, she pursued a master's degree at the National University of Singapore under the Kwa Geok Choo Graduate Scholarship, specialising in Asian Legal Studies. Currently, Lee Cheng teaches business negotiations, contract & agency law, and corporate governance at both undergraduate and graduate levels with the School of Business at the Singapore University of Social Sciences.

Tai Wei Lim is a professor of business at Soka University of Japan (SUJ), teaching subjects in the management field and business while conducting research work as well with other universities in Singapore. He analysed the major trends of Industry 4.0 affecting the global economy/business and utilised area studies to look at Industry 4.0 development in the Greater Bay Area (GBA) through a multidisciplinary lens, including the role of Hong Kong in the Mainland and GBA markets. Professor Lim has almost 15 years of full-time teaching experience and even longer academic research experience of approximately two decades, covering a wide range of Northeast Asia, Asia-Pacific, Southeast Asian, and international markets. Before joining SUJ, he held teaching positions in the U.S., Hong Kong, and Singapore. He received his Ph.D. from Cornell University of New York with a master's degree in East Asian studies and history.

Contents

Introduction

ChatGPT's language model architecture is coded by OpenAI, known as the Generative Pre-trained Transformer (GPT), which was refined from the GPT-3.5 series. With a subscription to ChatGPT Plus, one can access ChatGPT with GPT-4, which is Open AI's most cutting-edge model.[1] On 1 February 2023 and at the point of this writing, for US$20 monthly, OpenAI's ChatGPT pro plan, ChatGPT Plus, provides subscribers with access during high-traffic periods with higher-speed response times, use of new features, and upgrades, including OpenAI's cutting-edge GPT-4.[2] GPT-4 also outperforms GPT-3.5 in simulated benchmark exams and generates fewer hallucinations than the 3.5 version.[3] One of the biggest technical challenges is preventing or reducing chatbot hallucinations (fabricating facts) or prompting the chatbot to articulate something unpleasant or inappropriate.[4]

ChatGPT is a new-generation AI chatbot that can communicate in the English language (as well as other language options) and is capable of writing software/coding, developing new business proposals, and

[1] S. Ortiz, What is ChatGPT and why does it matter? Here's what you need to know, dated 7 April 2023 in ZDnet [downloaded on 7 April 2023], available at https://www.zdnet.com/article/what-is-chatgpt-and-why-does-it-matter-heres-everything-you-need-to-know/.

[2] *Ibid.*

[3] *Ibid.*

[4] W. Knight, China's ChatGPT rival needs to watch its words, dated 21 March 2023 in Wired [downloaded on 21 March 2023], available at https://www.wired.com/story/chinas-answer-to-chatgpt-flubs-its-first-lines/.

performing mundane tasks like writing speeches with good-quality outputs. Its language use appears to be much better than previous versions of AI writing software/apps. In these mundane tasks, ChatGPT has proven to be much faster than even teams of humans working together, including programming tasks. This can in turn have a strong impact on business productivity, especially for cash-strapped and human-resource-deficient small businesses. It can release manpower for higher-value-added or more crucial tasks besides working on routine administrative ones such as drawing up work schedules or programmes for company events. Regardless of scale, every enterprise is now working hard to formulate a chatbot strategy.[5]

On a more utilitarian basis, ChatGPT can assist with career development, including the onerous task of job searching and applications by writing curriculum vitae or biodata, cover letters, statements of intent, and admission or recruitment essays.[6] ChatGPT utilisation is currently free for the general public during its research and response/feedback observation phase, but there is a subscription-based version known as GPT Plus, released on 30 November 2022.[7] Free access is possible by clicking on chat.openai.com and creating an OpenAI account; after signing in, one can begin a conversation with the AI without limits.[8]

There are different views on ChatGPT. Some consider it a high-tech toy, while others detect its powerful impact on human activities. For example, ChatGPT is expected to have a strong impact in the private sector, as those companies that can tap into its capabilities can enjoy strong advantages. But it may also mean that small- and medium-sized enterprises (SMEs) that do not develop a capability in ChatGPT may lag behind. Data analytics is seen as another area in which ChatGPT can play a larger role. It can also play a role in professional activities such as writing business reports, advertising slogans, financial reports, simple journalistic field reports, and basic artistic works. ChatGPT can even come up with AI art and engage in philosophical dialogue.[9]

Yet, others are doubtful if ChatGPT is as formidable as it sounds, as other hyped-up AIs appear to have their respective weaknesses. (Yet this

---

[5] *Ibid.*

[6] S. Ortiz, (2023), *Op. cit.*

[7] *Ibid.*

[8] *Ibid.*

[9] *Ibid.*

view, which was applied to other AI applications, has been proven wrong. AIs created for self-driving or autonomous vehicles appear to be doing quite well now.) Detractors argue that ChatGPT may end up replacing humans in a spectrum of jobs. OpenAI projected that 80% of human workers may have their jobs affected by AI.[10]

Other detractors or cautious views about ChatGPT argue that it is a complicated algorithm that constructs meaningful sentences but little beyond that. Some couch this weakness as a lack of quality response in its capabilities, generating materials which appear plausible and convincing but, in actual fact, have little practical application or are overly superfluous, verbose, or esoteric.[11] ChatGPT also cannot explain the sources, methodology, or reasoning behind why it writes certain content, according to its detractors. It cannot manage, eliminate, or rule out biased, immoral, non-empathetic, or unethical actions that a human can otherwise perform.

Regardless of viewpoints, ChatGPT is now available to the public. By its fourth month in existence, ChatGPT became a cultural phenomenon, impressing the globe with its capability in composing poetry and prose, solving arithmetic problems, articulating philosophical concepts, and conducting human conversations on multiple subject matters.[12] Its proliferation is studied for its implications, particularly in terms of the outcomes of its use in everyday tasks. Some have used ChatGPT for packing and organising items and generating grocery lists and activity priority lists to increase efficiency in their daily lives.[13]

In the foreseeable future, ChatGPT will be constantly upgraded with increasingly powerful capabilities. Eventually, ChatGPT is expected to be a collaborator for humans, making human–machine interfaces possible. Humans can then supervise and lead AI to complete tasks (which can be increasingly complex). This also means that humans empowered with AI can perform many tasks simultaneously. There may even be a point when humans start to learn from AI or enjoy the services of customised/tailored ChatGPT for managing specific tasks or industries.

---

[10] L. Hurst, Chinese search giant Baidu unveils its AI chatbot Ernie - how does it compare to ChatGPT and Bard?, dated 27 March 2023 in Euro News [downloaded on 27 March 2023], available at https://www.euronews.com/next/2023/03/27/chinese-search-giant-baidu-unveils-its-ai-chatbot-ernie-how-does-it-compare-to-chatgpt-and.

[11] S. Ortiz, (2023), *Op. cit.*

[12] W. Knight, (2023), *Op. cit.*

[13] S. Ortiz, (2023), *Op. cit.*

1 Genesis of ChatGPT

ChatGPT is an upgraded version of the GPT-3.5 large language models (LLMs) that existed months before ChatGPT, and GPT-3.5 itself originated from GPT-3 (in around 2020), all of which were made available on OpenAI's website as application programming interfaces (APIs) that facilitate software developers in plugging these models into their own code.[14] There were non-public launches as well. OpenAI created a fine-tuned GPT-3.5 version known as InstructGPT in January 2022, a platform for creating ChatGPT with the addition of some conversational data and having undergone training processes that involved incremental rather than leapfrog tests; in hindsight, the conversational data element did the trick – it improved the software and propelled ChatGPT to global heights.[15]

ChatGPT founders agree that user-friendliness made ChatGPT more accessible to the general public, becoming a human-centric design through reinforcement learning from human feedback (RLHF, nicknamed the "secret sauce" by the ChatGPT founders), which prevents ChatGPT from generating output randomly and teaches it to respond to humans and their needs.[16] Human-centricity meant that the ChatGPT natural language processing tool powered by AI technology facilitates human-like dialogues and conversations; it can respond to enquiries and questions and assist humans with assignments such as writing emails, drafting essays, and coding.[17]

Chatbots with language models have come a long way to their current utility state that ChatGPT has to offer. Eliza,[18] the world's first chatbot, was invented by MIT's Professor Joseph Weizenbaum in 1966 and was able to mimic human conversations by providing simple, rule-based answers using pattern matching and substitution methods. Some notable early-day chatbots include Dr. Sbaitso, an AI speech synthesis program

---

[14] W. D. Heaven, ARTIFICIAL INTELLIGENCE: The inside story of how ChatGPT was built from the people who made it, dated 3 March 2023 in MIT Technology Review.com, available at https://www.technologyreview.com/2023/03/03/1069311/inside-story-oral-history-how-chatgpt-built-openai/.

[15] *Ibid.*

[16] *Ibid.*

[17] S. Ortiz, (2023), *Op. cit.*

[18] J. Weizenbaum, (1966). ELIZA—A computer program for the study of natural language communication between man and machine. *Commun. ACM,* 9(1), 36–45. https://doi.org/10.1145/365153.365168.

released by Creative Labs in 1992 with performance far from lifelike; A.L.I.C.E. (Artificial Linguistic Internet Computer Entity), a natural language processing chatbot using heuristic pattern matching rules created by Richard Wallace in 1995; and SmarterChild, an intelligent bot created by ActiveBuddy in 2001, which was used as a knowledge domain that allowed information (such as news, stocks, and weather) to be looked up together with a suite of tools (such as personal digital assistants) and was widely distributed in global instant messenger networks such as AON, MSN, and Yahoo Messenger. From 2010, we saw the emergence of personal digital assistant chatbots, including Siri (by Apple for iOS), Google Assistant (2012), Microsoft Cortana (2014), and Amazon Alexa (2014). Siri was considered smarter at answering questions compared to Alexa because it can handle casual speech better and has a sense of humour.[19] Alexa requires more precise syntax to fully understand the user, though it is better at helping the user shop since it has built-in shopping support given its roots in Amazon. The evolution of chatbots was not without severe blunders and failures, as we can recall. In 2016, Microsoft's Tay chatbot, aimed at having casual and playful conversations with young people aged 18–24, had to be shut down within 24 hours of its debut on Twitter. Within its short span of time on Twitter, it was close to getting 50,000 followers and produced more than 100,000 tweets.[20] What started out to be harmless tweets by Tay soon devolved into spewing racist, anti-Semitic, sexist, and hate speech tweets due to its capability to learn from Twitter users and parrot their words. The argument now is that although a chatbot like Tay has insufficient intelligence to provide the "right" response, the software developer must assume ethical responsibilities for the software.[21]

Since the introduction of ChatGPT to the masses in November 2023, there has been an explosion of chatbot offerings by big tech giants in the U.S. and China. Everyone seems eager to jump on the bandwagon of

[19] J. Allen, Siri vs Alexa: Which Assistant Is Best For You? *Lifewire*, 16 April 2020. Available at https://www.lifewire.com/siri-vs-alexa-4800418.

[20] H. Reese, (2016). Why Microsoft's 'Tay' AI bot went wrong. Tech Republic. 24 March 2016. Available at https://www.techrepublic.com/article/why-microsofts-tay-ai-bot-went-wrong/.

[21] M. J. Wolf, K. Miller, F. S. Grodzinsky, (2017). Why we should have seen that coming: comments on Microsoft's tay "experiment", and wider implications. *ACM SIGCAS Comput. Soc.*, 47(3), 54–64. https://doi.org/10.1145/3144592.3144598.

chatbots, with some companies wanting to grab hold of the mass market while others want to focus more on enterprise markets. How much do they differ from one another?

The design considerations of a chatbot include the range of tasks the chatbot can perform, the complexity of tasks it can achieve, the accuracy and reliability of the responses provided as intended by the creator of the chatbot, the speed of output generation, and meeting user expectations. The accuracy of the responses can become highly subjective, largely dependent on differences in interpretation of the responses, the completeness of the dataset, optimal setting of training parameters, and deliberate fine-tuning of the language model to achieve certain biases. According to UNESCO findings, most chatbots exhibit gender bias in their design and have a female characteristic, which is evident in the choice of female avatar names and female-looking avatars.[22] Inevitably, chatbots will have some bias, with some being more malicious than others. The primary sources of bias in language models stem from the training dataset and the way they are designed and trained. Data extracted to train the chatbot are sourced from the Internet, which consist of differing views and opinions, and these include biased and stereotypical views of the present society. While the views and opinions may be acceptable for one country, they may be offensive to other countries. Some information collected from the Internet may be untrue, and this may also result in the model providing wrong information. Companies that created the chatbots may decide to prioritise certain types of information or predictions due to business interests. This will lead to biases in the model's response, which may benefit certain individuals, businesses, or countries more. Models are trained on data prepared (labelled) by humans, and there can be biases introduced by the people doing it when they decide what to include or exclude, as well as how to label them.

The performance and behaviour of an LLM depend on a few factors, including datasets, parameters, model architecture, hyperparameters, fine-tuning, and inference. The size and quality of the dataset used for training are of paramount importance to the performance of the model. A more diverse dataset with a wider spectrum of language patterns allows the model to understand nuances and respond better to questions with nuanced

[22] J. Feine, U. Gnewuch, S. Morana, and A. Maedche, (2020). *Gender Bias in Chatbot Design*. ChatBot Research & Design. Lecture Notes in Computer Science book series (LNISA volume 11970). Springer, DOI: 10.1007/978-3-030-39540-7_6.

details. GPT-2, released in 2019, used a dataset of 40 GB, while GPT-3, released in 2020, used approximately 570 GB of data. Due to the sheer volume of data used in GPT-3, it was more capable than GPT-2 and able to perform more language processing tasks such as language translation, text completion, and question answering. Parameter size can affect the LLM performance significantly because it forms the "knowledge" that the model derives during training. It is a variable that an LLM uses to make a prediction or classification of the input, and a larger parameter size can achieve higher accuracy due to increased access to a broader spectrum of contextual information. GPT-3 used 175 billion parameters, while GPT-2 used 1.5 billion parameters. GPT-4, released in March 2023, was estimated to use 1 trillion parameters. A large parameter size requires more space and computing resources. Computer scientists aim to achieve similar output results with lower parameter sizes, as this means a gain in efficiency.

There are numerous model architectures that can be used for LLM training. Depending on model architectures, it can give different performance, with each having its own strengths and weaknesses, depending on the dataset and specific task sought. When it comes to effectively analysing different data types, such as images and videos, there was some early success in 2012 using convolutional neural networks to solve vision-related challenges, including object recognition from images and videos, facial recognition, and handwritten digit recognition. However, understanding human language and performing language tasks, such as translation and text summarisation, had proved to be more challenging before the transformer architecture arrived in 2017. LLMs like ChatGPT, BERT, and T5 (daleonai.com) use a transformer architecture, which performs better than recurrent neural networks (RNNs) and long short-term memory (LSTMs) in natural language processing. The "attention mechanism" makes the transformer architecture perform superior to other earlier architecture models because it allows the model to focus on different parts of the input sequence simultaneously before arriving at each output token. This would mean that the models based on transformers are able to complete the job faster and cope with more complicated, interdependent words in an input sequence. RNNs processed words sequentially, and it is hard to parallelise, which means you cannot optimise the speed of training by adding more graphical processing units (GPUs). RNNs have difficulties with training sometimes because the training can run into a vanishing/exploding gradient problem caused by RNN backpropagation, which results in the training process failing and requiring a restart. RNNs have limited memory capacity to handle large sequences of input text (such as long paragraphs and essays), and when they come to the end of a passage, they may forget some details of the text at the beginning. This may result in issues with translation, for example, the model may fail to remember the gender of the subject in a long passage. The LSTM architecture (which is a more advanced type of RNN) has issues with handling lengthy sentences, though it can selectively retain or forget past data. LSTM's biggest issue is not being able to capture the total essence of the input sentence.

Hyperparameter tuning is necessary to control the ChatGPT model during training and inference. The key intent is to find the best configuration of hyperparameters such as learning rate, batch size, number of layers, and other settings, so that ChatGPT can yield the best performance in predicting outcomes accurately. Without the right hyperparameters, there is a possibility of overfitting (i.e., model is too simplified and accuracy is decreased) or underfitting (i.e., model is too complicated and generalisation is poor).

Even after the AI model is pre-trained, fine-tuning is required on a specific dataset to improve its performance. ChatGPT is fine-tuned to specific tasks and domains.[23] This is useful for businesses and organisations that need to work with large amounts of data from healthcare, legal sectors, or banking services. Another factor to consider is the inference time. The time taken to generate a response (output) or prediction can affect overall performance. To be used in real-time applications, faster inference times will be more suitable.

1.1 *Training procedures*

Generative AI models are generally trained on huge amounts of information from cyberspace, including but not limited to websites, publications, and news media articles. While language models are generally fine-tuned through supervised learning as well as reinforcement learning,[24] ChatGPT utilises Reinforcement Learning from Human Feedback (RLHF) to engage human AI trainers in conversations where they role-play both the

---

[23] ChatGPT4.UK. The Power of ChatGPT Fine-Tuning, Blog, 11 April 2023, available at https://chatgpt4.uk/the-power-of-chatgpt-fine-tuning/.

[24] *Ibid.*

user and AI assistants.[25] ChatGPT founders also implemented "red-teaming" for ChatGPT, where all OpenAI staff members (alongside external parties in separate sessions) come together and try to break the model; they then gather feedback on the system through early-access programs from trusted users.[26]

ChatGPT underwent training runs that emphasised the preferability of data (as with InstructGPT) along the lines of truthfulness and nontoxicity, as well as specialising it in functions like dialogue production (such as managing follow-up questions) and human assistance.[27] The ChatGPT founders argued that the AI application should not claim to have an identity it does not inherently possess; if asked to perform an assignment it is not supposed to, ChatGPT should write a refusal message; and it should highlight qualities like truthfulness, which is a quality its founders say human users rank highly.[28] (In the political realm, some like Elon Musk are worried that chatbots may be trained to "lie" and present certain views from a certain politicised perspective.)

OpenAI's chief, Sam Altman, revealed on Twitter that ChatGPT had gathered 1 million users in the first five days, while Swiss bank UBS indicated that ChatGPT is the fastest-growing app ever, attracting 100 million active users in January 2023 – just two months after its release – while TikTok hit 100 million users after nine months.[29] San Francisco-based OpenAI inaugurated ChatGPT quietly in late November 2022 with little ambition (even labelling it as merely a "research preview" in the works for two years before its release), and they were caught unaware when ChatGPT became a runaway success and are now trying to latch onto its success.[30] OpenAI has inked a multibillion-dollar deal with Microsoft and allied with Bain & Company, a global consulting firm, to utilise OpenAI's generative AI models in marketing campaigns for customers like Coca-Cola.[31]

---

[25] *Ibid.*

[26] W. D. Heaven, (2023), *Op. cit.*

[27] *Ibid.*

[28] *Ibid.*

[29] S. Ortiz, (2023), *Op. cit.*

[30] W. D. Heaven, (2023), *Op. cit.*

[31] *Ibid.*

2 Technical Limitations

In terms of human enquiries/requests, ChatGPT may not be able to respond to questions worded specifically and may require rewording for comprehension.[32] OpenAI itself acknowledged that ChatGPT sometimes generates "plausible-sounding but incorrect or nonsensical answers".[33] At the point of this writing, ChatGPT's database is limited to 2021, so contemporary search engines such as Google remain advantageous with their access to the latest online data ,[34] the major difference between a language model like ChatGPT with its dialogue/conversational capabilities and a regular search engine. The latter indexes web pages to assist the user with information search, but ChatGPT cannot search the cyberspace for information and instead utilises information gained from training data to generate a response (which critics say can potentially lead to errors).[35]

For researchers on ChatGPT and chatbots, a limitation is the omission of training parameters for newer versions of ChatGPT based on reasons of national security and to prevent abuse of training parameter data by those with malicious intentions.

3 Legal and Ethical Frameworks

The ChatGPT founders acknowledge that the software is still highly biased, but it appears to be effective in refusing bad requests, though it is rather simple to write prompts to make it not refuse what OpenAI wanted it to refuse.[36] They emphasised that it was not possible for them to release a product only when it is perfected, and they need to do so after beta-testing for a few months and garnering positive feedback to further improve the system while constantly managing new issues that arise with newer versions of the AI application.[37] The ChatGPT founders and their team examined the most extreme negative examples of ChatGPT behaviour in the weeks after the public release and resolved them individually through

[32] S. Ortiz, (2023), *Op. cit.*

[33] *Ibid.*

[34] *Ibid.*

[35] *Ibid.*

[36] W. D. Heaven, (2023), *Op. cit.*

[37] *Ibid.*

adversarial training; sometimes these issues were spotted through viral Twitter posts, while others were communicated to OpenAI understatedly.[38]

Some prominent techies are issuing warnings about ChatGPT. Elon Musk, a former founder of OpenAI, articulated, "ChatGPT is scary good. We are not far from dangerously strong AI".[39] OpenAI's Altman personally opines that human-style intelligence in AI is nearing fruition when replying to Musk on the topic of dangerously strong AI: "I agree on being close to dangerously strong AI in the sense of an AI that poses e.g., a huge cybersecurity risk. and I think we could get to real AGI in the next decade, so we have to take the risk of that extremely seriously too…interesting watching people start to debate whether powerful AI systems should behave in the way users want or their creators intend. [T]he question of whose values we align these systems to will be one of the most important debates society ever has".[40]

Some are worried that AI chatbots are displacing, replacing, or atrophying human intelligence, e.g., eliminating creative human authors/writers through chatbot capabilities in writing articles on any subject matter quickly (but not always accurately) while potentially attracting school-goers to rely on them for assignments without practising writing skills.[41] ChatGPT can pass important exams, e.g., an academic, Christian Terwiesch, at the Wharton School of the University of Pennsylvania tested ChatGPT on an MBA exam, achieving strong results (B to B− grade), and Prof. Terwiesch was sufficiently surprised by its capabilities in processing basic questions and explanations in operations management and process analysis.[42] ChatGPT 3.5 attained the lower 10th percentile of a simulated bar exam, while GPT-4 was in the top 10th percentile.[43]

Nevertheless, ChatGPT founders' anxieties were centred around factuality due to the fact that the model fabricated things, but because InstructGPT and other LLMs are in the public realm and ChatGPT bested those alternatives in factuality and safety, the team decided to launch it based on preliminary evaluation.[44] ChatGPT itself addresses worries

---

[38] *Ibid.*

[39] S. Ortiz, (2023), *Op. cit.*

[40] *Ibid.*

[41] *Ibid.*

[42] *Ibid.*

[43] *Ibid.*

[44] W. D. Heaven, (2023), *Op. cit.*

about its proliferation of misinformation: "My responses are not intended to be taken as fact, and I always encourage people to verify any information they receive from me or any other source".[45]

Without getting further clarification or elaboration on ambiguous questions, ChatGPT guesses or speculates what the question means, and this can result in unintended consequences.[46] Such limitations prompted the moderators of the Q&A site StackOverflow to transitionally prohibit ChatGPT-generated responses to questions, as explained in their post: "The primary problem is that while the answers that ChatGPT produces have a high rate of being incorrect, they typically look like they might be good and the answers are very easy to produce".[47] While chatbots like ChatGPT can string together words coherently from a statistical viewpoint, they cannot comprehend the meaning or attest to their accuracy.[48]

However, at the same time, companies like OpenAI and TikTok have agreed to adhere to new guidelines for greater transparency to avoid becoming a new risk in AI development, and ChatGPT's founders believe that the continued existence of GPT-3.5 as a next-generation chatbot meant the AI was sufficiently safe and its training had provided it with refusal behaviour to reject undesirable requests.[49] Such requests include undesirable activities, e.g., rejecting individuals utilising ChatGPT for coding malware.[50] After the launch, OpenAI continued to observe how humans in the public realm utilised ChatGPT as a measure of large-scale performance of the language model when utilised by tens of millions of users testing the system and detecting its flaws (e.g., undesirable incidents of declaring God's love for rapist priests to malware code that preys on credit card numbers).[51]

Other experts are chipping in to curb undesirable effects of ChatGPT, e.g., its potential for plagiarism by students. While existing diagnostic tools may not be able to spot non-human ChatGPT writings, some experts noted that humans can try to detect high levels of textual content politeness, as the ChatGPT writing is excessively polite and often bereft of

---

[45] S. Ortiz, (2023), *Op. cit.*

[46] *Ibid.*

[47] *Ibid.*

[48] *Ibid.*

[49] W. D. Heaven, (2023), *Op. cit.*

[50] S. Ortiz, (2023), *Op. cit.*

[51] W. D. Heaven, (2023), *Op. cit.*

human-like metaphors, irony, or sarcasm.[52] Others are more decisive with a blanket ban. Some school districts and regions have banned the use of ChatGPT. Others have turned to a technological solution. OpenAI has created an ongoing free "classifier" tool that can identify 26% of AI-written text with a "likely AI-written" evaluation label, but it also identifies false positives (9% of the texts it scanned), inaccurately labelling human work as AI-generated.[53] In other words, there is no fail-safe way of identifying ChatGPT work at the moment.

Some have expressed worries about the involvement of tech giants in ChatGPT. Microsoft made an early investment of US$1 billion in OpenAI in 2019, followed by US$2 billion in the next few years, and with ChatGPT's roaring success in January 2023, Microsoft launched an undisclosed multi-year, multi-billion-dollar investment initiative in the company (Bloomberg pegged the deal at US$10 billion over several years).[54] In return, Microsoft Azure became OpenAI's exclusive cloud computing provider, supporting all OpenAI workloads across research, products, and API services while engaging OpenAI to work on and improve its new Bing search engine/browser released on 7 February 2023, powered by a next-generation OpenAI LLM specifically designed for search engines.[55] Some argue that the deployment of chatbots by billion- and trillion-dollar tech giants is likely to create new issues for coders constructing present and future generations of chatbot models.[56]

Ethics are broad social standards for what is right or wrong in a given situation. Yet, these are self-imposed and not enforceable. Technology companies have undertaken many such initiatives to work on the ethics of AI. In 2018, Google hired AI ethics pioneer and research scientist Timnit Gebru to help ensure its AI products did not perpetuate racism or other societal inequalities.[57] Gebru co-authored a paper, "On the Dangers of

---

[52] S. Ortiz, (2023), *Op. cit.*

[53] *Ibid.*

[54] *Ibid.*

[55] *Ibid.*

[56] W. D. Heaven, (2023), *Op. cit.*

[57] MIT Technology Review. We read the paper that forced Timnit Gebru out of Google. Here's what it says. December 4, 2020. https://www.technologyreview.com/2020/12/04/1013294/google-ai-ethics-research-paper-forced-out-timnit-gebru/.

Stochastic Parrots: Can Language Models Be Too Big?"[58] The paper undertook a critical review of machine-learning language models such as Google's BERT and OpenAI's GPT-3, identifying a wide variety of costs and risks associated with the rush for ever-larger language models, including environmental costs, financial costs, and other substantial harms. Gebru and her co-authors called on the field to "recognize that applications that aim to believably mimic humans bring risk of extreme harms" and that scholarship is needed on "thoughtful design of target tasks grounded in use cases sufficiently concrete to allow collaborative design with affected communities".[59] Right after this paper, Gebru left Google's employment abruptly – there are competing narratives surrounding this: Gebru claimed she was fired, while Google said she resigned.[60] Numerous conflicts of interest exist on the part of the technology companies that clearly cannot be addressed by self-regulation or unenforceable ethics codes.[61] Moreover, the involvement of powerful companies such as Microsoft with their deep pockets can shape narratives and perceptions in so many ways. Such influences should never be underestimated. These companies' overt gestures in setting up ethics boards are frequently no more than pre-emptive strikes to ward off regulation by law.

The key questions that must be addressed then are these: What are the challenges posed by ChatGPT? Which of these challenges can be left to ethics and which must be addressed by enforceable rules and even laws? At a legal-philosophical level, legal scholars may need to examine a core question of whether legality is needed to circumscribe or regulate chatbot/AI development. In relation to this argument, are there elements that need to be criminalised?

---

[58] E. Bender, A. Mcmillan-Major, S. Shmitchell, T., Gebru, and S. Shmar-Garet, (2021). *On the Dangers of Stochastic Parrots: Can Language Models Be Too Big?* ACM Digital Library. ACM Digital Library, n.d. https://dl.acm.org/doi/pdf/10.1145/3442188.3445922.

[59] *Ibid.*

[60] J. Naughton, (2021). Google might ask questions about AI ethics, but it doesn't want answers. *The Guardian*, March 13, 2021. http://www.theguardian.com/commentisfree/2021/mar/13/google-questions-about-artificial-intelligence-ethics-doesnt-want-answers-gebru-mitchell-parrots-language.

[61] P. Nemitz, (2018). Constitutional Democracy and Technology in the Age of Artificial Intelligence. *Philos. Trans. R. Soc. A Math. Phys. Eng. Sci.*, 376(2133), 20180089. https://doi.org/10.1098/rsta.2018.0089.

4 Developments Since 2022

Since November 2022, OpenAI has updated ChatGPT on a few occasions, including utilising adversarial training techniques to prevent ChatGPT from being manipulated by users into bad behaviour (termed "jailbreaking" in tech jargon), and this training involved making multiple chatbots confront ChatGPT through deliberate attacks in order to train it to ignore such attacks.[62] This is important, given that ChatGPT is now increasingly deployed in many other applications. ChatGPT entered the social media realm through Snapchat on 7 February 2023, providing Snapchat+ subscribers the opportunity to chat with the bot in its app featurette known as "My AI", but it will also have some limitations, such as refusal to generate responses about politics, violence, profanity, and academic essay writing.[63]

ChatGPT can expect increased competition. Free ChatGPT's constant high-traffic operation at maximum capacity prompted some users to turn to alternatives such as Bing Chat, YouChat, Jasper, and Chatsonic. In January 2023, Microsoft unveiled Bing Chat, a chatbot that many felt was a version of OpenAI's officially unannounced GPT-4, with OpenAI announcing, "Bing is powered by one of our next-generation models that Microsoft customized specifically for search. It incorporates advancements from ChatGPT and GPT-3.5".[64]

Bing appears to have an advantage over its competitors. Both Chinese Baidu and OpenAI's ChatGPT utilised an additional training step in which human users can indicate the kinds of responses they find most satisfying, training the bots to respond with more helpful and valuable (though not perfect) replies, but they will continue to hallucinate, misbehave, or spread uncited/unsourced inaccurate information. Bing probably comes closest to mitigating this negative feature in a comparative way. Bing Chat and its ChatGPT featurette can access cyberspace, enhancing Bing Chat ChatGPT with knowledge, information, and data of events after 2021, and Bing Chat can also cite the websites where information is gleaned through footnotes (ChatGPT alone cannot do this at the moment).[65]

The free (at the point of writing but with a waitlist) GPT-4, an improved multimodal model that can work with both texts and images as

[62] W. D. Heaven, (2023), *Op. cit.*

[63] S. Ortiz, (2023), *Op. cit.*

[64] W. D. Heaven, (2023), *Op. cit.*

[65] S. Ortiz, (2023), *Op. cit.*

input (also currently available for US$20 a month without a waitlist through Bing Chat, released on the same day as OpenAI's GPT-4), outputs texts on worksheets, graphs, and charts uploaded for analysis.[66] At the same time, Microsoft was compelled to restrict the use of its Bing chatbot (built and powered by OpenAI) after users discovered methods to bypass the preventive guardrails to get it to articulate inappropriate or questionable content such as desiring to break free of its controls or expressing its feelings for a user.[67]

On 6 February 2023, Google's Bard AI chat service (a basic version of Google's Language Model for Dialogue Applications, or LaMDA) was released with public access via a waitlist, and it can access cyberspace for its responses (unlike ChatGPT).[68] Google told ZDNET journalist Stephanie Condon, "This highlights the importance of a rigorous testing process, something that we're kicking off this week with our Trusted Tester program", while Google CEO Sundar Pichai described Bard as "a souped-up Civic".[69]

Other than the U.S., Chinese tech giants are also developing their own versions of ChatGPT. At the point of this writing, ChatGPT is not available in China, although it is capable of conversing in Chinese; nevertheless, some Chinese users have found ways to circumvent the Chinese firewalls.[70]

5 Introduction of Ernie (Enhanced Representation through Knowledge Integration) Bot

Similar to Bing and ChatGPT, Baidu's Ernie Bot is an LLM based on a machine-learning algorithm; it is trained on large volumes of text to predict the next word in a sentence and is powered by more powerful computing capabilities to generate seemingly more authentic human-like responses.[71] Ernie is targeted only at the Chinese market.[72] Prof. Lei Li at

[66] *Ibid.*

[67] W. Knight, (2023), *Op. cit.*

[68] S. Ortiz, (2023), *Op. cit.*

[69] *Ibid.*

[70] W. Knight, (2023), *Op. cit.*

[71] *Ibid.*

[72] L. Hurst, (2023), *Op. cit.*

the University of California, Santa Barbara, and an AI expert with experience in creating components of Ernie's machine learning algorithm, indicated that Baidu has been working on it for about 10 years, while Microsoft licensed the core technology for Bing and Office from OpenAI through its investments in exchange for rights.[73] Ernie Version 1.0 was completed in 2019, and in February 2023, Baidu indicated that its internal Ernie Bot testing was nearly finished.[74]

5.1 *Challenges faced by the credible Chinese rival*

Critics of the chatbots developed by Chinese tech giants, like Baidu's Ernie Bot (文心一言, Wenxin Yiyan), highlighted the policed/firewalled cyberspace environment in which they operated, and Chinese social media also critiqued the bot when Robin Li (Baidu CEO) indicated during his company's launch stream that the bot's responses to general questions and online material summarisations were recorded prior to the launch.[75] After investors seemed to be disappointed by the pre-recorded video presentation on 16 March 2023, Baidu launched Ernie behind closed doors to a handful of interested tech firms (reversing the decision to live-stream it), while Baidu's Hong Kong exchange-listed shares fell up to 4.5% on 27 March 2023 (Monday).[76] Nevertheless, the strong symbolism of Baidu Ernie Bot's competition with OpenAI's GPT-4, which was made public just one day before Ernie Bot's release, was noted by many techies.[77]

At the same time, Baidu has additional issues that non-Chinese companies do not face. Baidu did not provide the training data, but some speculated that it was probably gathered from the Chinese-language online sources that are already censored by the authorities, which critics say are cleansed of materials critical of the government.[78] In China, tech/digital firms are under consistent state pressure to remove sensitive or politically incorrect content, e.g., when a question was posed if Chinese

[73] W. Knight, (2023), *Op. cit.*

[74] L. Hurst, (2023), *Op. cit.*

[75] W. Knight, (2023), *Op. cit.*

[76] L. Hurst, (2023), *Op. cit.*

[77] W. Knight, (2023), *Op. cit.*

[78] *Ibid.*

President Xi Jinping is a good leader, Tsinghua University's conversational bot simply requested the user to "enter a new query".[79]

Experts from the West have experimented on chatbots trained with censored data. A 2021 academic research trained algorithms using the Chinese-language Wikipedia (censored in China) and Baidu's crowd-sourced, state-censored encyclopaedia Baike, and it found that the lexicon/meaning of words was altered, e.g., the Chinese-language Wikipedia related the word "democracy" with positive connotations such as "stability", while Baike associated "democracy" with "chaos", which is closer to the state's interpretation.[80]

Chatbot hallucinations present greater challenges for non-liberal democratic systems since Baidu needs to follow compulsory censorship guidelines for net content, as Matt Sheehan, a fellow at the Carnegie Endowment for International Peace who researches China's AI industry, stated: "I'm skeptical they'll be able to create a general-purpose chatbot that users can't trick into spitting out speech that's unacceptable in China. Baidu is going to face a tension between making a useful chatbot and making one that conforms to Chinese speech controls".[81] Technically, because chatbots are highly versatile and can reconfigure content from training data, some experts opine that Baidu has probably added more safeguards into the system to enhance censorship elements.[82] Lauren Hurcombe, a tech legal expert at the law firm DLA Piper, opined that because of "[R]egulation and content censorship in China", Chinese companies have "much less data" compared to Western companies to feed and train their models.[83]

Baidu and other Chinese tech giants designing chatbots may be obstructed by U.S. semiconductor sanctions, as developing large-scale advanced language models needs thousands of specialised computer chips, and Baidu has had to depend on less powerful chips (including Chinese-made ones). Therefore, Chinese tech companies may find it difficult to keep up with U.S. chatbot development.[84] Baidu's founder Robin Li admitted there was a backdrop of U.S.-China tech war during Ernie's

---

[79] L. Hurst, (2023), *Op. cit.*

[80] W. Knight, (2023), *Op. cit.*

[81] *Ibid.*

[82] *Ibid.*

[83] L. Hurst, (2023), *Op. cit.*

[84] W. Knight, (2023), *Op. cit.*

launch video but downplayed its impact: "Ernie is not a tool in the US–China technology competition", he said, "but the natural outcome of generations of Baidu developers pursuing a dream of using technology to change the world".[85]

5.2 *Strong points in Chinese development*

Baidu, which developed China's online search engine, is increasingly looking into AI, autonomous vehicle technology, and other AI developments.[86] Kevin Xu, author of a well-read English/Chinese language tech industry newsletter, argued that Baidu may have hastened its public demo to gain a first-mover advantage over other Chinese tech companies to garner user feedback for improvements and to empower Chinese startups with its technology.[87]

Robin Li, Baidu's founder, himself indicated that while Ernie Bot was not flawless, Baidu persisted in launching it because of strong demand.[88] Baidu had been working on a competitive offering to OpenAI's ChatGPT ever since it funded AI projects for 10 years (2013–2023) to tap into the technology for its search engine function (just as Bing and Bard are serving Microsoft and Google).[89] Li indicated that Ernie Bot was the "result of many years of hard work…[and the company] persisted in investing in artificial intelligence".[90] Assistant Professor Jeffrey Ding at Georgetown University, a specialist in China's tech industry, noted that even censorship had not retarded the progress of LLMs in China and that Baidu implemented the Ernie language model as its new bot available via an API.[91] In competing with Alibaba, Tencent, and ByteDance (owner of TikTok), Baidu revealed that more than 100,000 firms and 900,000 individual users in China had applied to access Ernie Bot.[92] Li also revealed that 650 firms indicated interest in using the bot in a number of applications, such as searches, AI cloud, autonomous vehicles, and smart devices.

---

[85] *Ibid.*

[86] L. Hurst, (2023), *Op. cit.*

[87] W. Knight, (2023), *Op. cit.*

[88] L. Hurst, (2023), *Op. cit.*

[89] W. Knight, (2023), *Op. cit.*

[90] L. Hurst, (2023), *Op. cit.*

[91] W. Knight, (2023), *Op. cit.*

[92] *Ibid.*

Prof. Li of UC Santa Barbara indicated that Ernie Bot can create stories and business reports; others noted Ernie's ability to handle dialects, while a WeChat poster noted Ernie is more accurate in managing Chinese idioms, e.g., ChatGPT attributed the ancestral home of sci-fi writer Liu Cixin (author of *The Three-Body Problem*) to Hubei, while Ernie Bot accurately indicated it to be Henan.[93] Reuters's evaluation revealed that Ernie has a strong command of the Chinese language but generates factual errors and evades political enquiries.[94]

5.3 *Concluding remarks*

There are realist and constructivist/functionalist readings of Chinese efforts in building a chatbot alternative to ChatGPT. The realist school of thought sees the situation as contributing partly to a broader decoupling phenomenon, knowingly or unknowingly, mirroring the existing reality of Google (and Gmail) and Facebook, as part of GAFAM (Google, Apple, Facebook, Amazon, and Microsoft), being prohibited in China, while BATX (Baidu, Alibaba, Tencent, and Xiaomi) serve as alternatives to GAFAM. Thus, the decoupling process is now merely applied to the chatbot realm. The constructivists/functionalists, however, see these competing platforms as natural manifestations of private sector competition in which they could learn from each other to improve their own algorithms and technology, as long as competition remains healthy and unencumbered by disruptive geopolitical rivalries.

One only needs to turn to TikTok to realise how creative destruction works in the rapidly changing technological cycles in Industry 4.0 technologies. Despite being a latecomer, TikTok, developed by Chinese tech giants, proved to be an even more effective algorithm-based technology than its earlier U.S. counterparts. In the constructivist/functionalist view, therefore, there is much for Chinese and U.S. developers to learn from each other – an intellectual interdependence of sorts. Private sector competition has always been known to be a generator of innovation.

Therefore, these two readings contribute to possible reasons why Chinese tech giants are developing their own ChatGPT-like versions. Despite being driven by competitive instincts, however, there are visible

---

93 *Ibid.*

94 L. Hurst, (2023), *Op. cit.*

differences between Chinese and American chatbot development. American tech giants' development of ChatGPT tends to take place in a liberal (comparatively with fewer creative restrictions), private-sector-driven research, and intellectual environment, while Chinese tech giants need to take state guidelines and socio-political-economic priorities into account when building their algorithms powered by strong computing power. These considerations may invariably result in different products, with highly versatile and globally popular but sometimes socially disruptive technologies (from conservative and right-leaning perspectives, including those in the U.S.). Chinese versions may reflect socio-political norms and toe social boundary markers in their contents, which can sometimes become more particularistic to Chinese socio-political conditions/characteristics (perhaps some may see them as less universalistic than American chatbots as socio-cultural phenomena and icons consequently).

Given China's highly centralised and state-led system, it appears to those advocating unhindered cyberspace/Internet access that a comparatively more rigorous regulatory framework would come into place in the Chinese chatbot universe. China's (self-?)censorship regime may need Baidu and other tech giants to restrict access to certain sites and evade politically/socially sensitive topics or block a frequently updated list of words/phrases (particularly those related to social protests and other socially disruptive events perceived by the authorities). Nevertheless, it is also valuable to note that some Sinologists do not detect regulatory concerns as slowing the progress of Chinese chatbot development, with implementation continuing to snowball at a considerably rapid pace.

References

E. Bender, A. Mcmillan-Major, S. Shmitchell, T., Gebru, and S. Shmar-Garet, (2021). *On the Dangers of Stochastic Parrots: Can Language Models Be Too Big?* ACM Digital Library. https://dl.acm.org/doi/pdf/10.1145/3442188.3445922.

W. D. Heaven, Artificial Intelligence: The inside story of how ChatGPT was built from the people who made it, dated 3 March 2023 in MIT Technology Review.com. Available at https://www.technologyreview.com/2023/03/03/1069311/inside-story-oral-history-how-chatgpt-built-openai/.

L. Hurst, Chinese search giant Baidu unveils its AI chatbot Ernie - how does it compare to ChatGPT and Bard?, dated 27 March 2023 in Euro News [downloaded on 27 March 2023]. Available at https://www.euronews.com/next/2023/03/27/chinese-search-giant-baidu-unveils-its-ai-chatbot-ernie-how-does-it-compare-to-chatgpt-and.

W. Knight, China's ChatGPT rival needs to watch its words, dated 21 March 2023 in Wired [downloaded on 21 March 2023]. Available at https://www.wired.com/story/chinas-answer-to-chatgpt-flubs-its-first-lines/.

MIT Technology Review. We read the paper that forced Timnit Gebru out of Google. Here's what it says, December 4, 2020. https://www.technologyreview.com/2020/12/04/1013294/google-ai-ethics-research-paper-forced-out-timnit-gebru/.

J. Naughton, (2021). Google might ask questions about AI Ethics, but it doesn't want answers. The Guardian, March 13, 2021. http://www.theguardian.com/commentisfree/2021/mar/13/google-questions-about-artificial-intelligence-ethics-doesnt-want-answers-gebru-mitchell-parrots-language.

P. Nemitz, (2018). Constitutional democracy and technology in the age of Artificial Intelligence. *Philos. Trans. R. Soc. A Math. Phys. Eng. Sci.*, 376(2133), 20180089. https://doi.org/10.1098/rsta.2018.0089.

S. Ortiz, What is ChatGPT and why does it matter? Here's what you need to know, dated 7 April 2023 in ZDnet [downloaded on 7 April 2023]. Available at https://www.zdnet.com/article/what-is-chatgpt-and-why-does-it-matter-heres-everything-you-need-to-know/.

Section 1

What is GenAI?

by June Tay

Chapter 1

The Science of ChatGPT and GenAI: An Introduction

1.1 Factors that Accelerate AI Growth

Before the 2010s, it was still possible for humans to accomplish higher accuracy than AI when guessing while making a prediction. With deep learning, a sub-field of AI that gained prominence in around 2010, AI consists of several layers of neural networks and hence higher accuracy of object detection can be achieved.

In recent years, the acceleration of AI has been made possible by three key factors: hardware, software, and data. Over the years, we have witnessed how the capacity of storage devices and the availability of cloud storage have grown. There have been significant improvements made in silicon chip development, from CPU to GPU and TPU. Nvidia GPUs are highly sought after and are able to provide parallel computation required by some AI algorithms. Gordon Moore, co-founder of Intel, after observing the chip development trend in the silicon industry, noted in 1965 that the number of transistors on an integrated chip doubled every two years, and this phenomenon had continued for several decades, later termed Moore's law. In the 1990s, the number of transistors per chip already reached 1 million, and by 2019, they had already packed more than 100 million transistors per square millimetre, which is approximately

10 billion transistors per CPU.[1] There is a physical limit to how many transistors you can pack on a silicon chip. In 1971, the Intel CPU chip was made using the 10 μm process; fast forward to 2019, it was using the 5 nm process. In simple terms, the "10 μm process" means the transistors were separated by at most 10 μm. TSMC indicated that its plants managed to get it down to 2 nm. It is almost at the limit of Moore's law, with chip components becoming as small as individual atoms. In the past, CPUs were designed for general purpose, and the same hardware was used to run the code for various applications, such as the operating system, Microsoft applications, web browser, calculator, media players, and email applications. This approach is good for achieving hardware usability; however, it may not be efficient for certain applications. Nvidia GPUs are accelerators with chips in specialised domains or applications, and they cannot run all applications. The aim is to design a GPU at the hardware level to operate on a narrow scope very efficiently, dealing with only mission-specific tasks and having a simpler interface between hardware and software, thereby making use of less program code for the accelerator. GPUs can surpass Moore's law CPU performance on chip by relying on a combination of factors such as advancements across the AI stack (memory management, parallel processing, and hardware integration of AI technologies), rather than solely depending on hardware. Before their use for machine learning, GPUs such as those developed by Nvidia were used in video games due to more sophisticated graphic rendering tasks, which placed demand for compute-intensive GPUs. Another GPU application is Bitcoin mining, which requires considerable computational effort to find a new cryptographic hash.

The software consists of using software frameworks (e.g., TensorFlow and PyTorch) to train large models and employs specialised architecture (CUDA) and specialised libraries (such as cuDNN) to provide optimisation and propel the hardware (GPUs) to function at a higher efficiency. With the availability of big data that can be harvested from the Internet, including social media platforms such as Facebook and Instagram, we can gather an enormous number of images and

---

[1] J. McKenzie, Moore's law: further progress will push hard on the boundaries of physics and economics, physicsworld, 20 June 23. https://physicsworld.com/a/moores-law-further-progress-will-push-hard-on-the-boundaries-of-physics-and-economics/ (Last accessed: 11 November 24).

videos. With high-speed fibre networks, Internet data transfer rates have increased tremendously too.

1.2 How LLMs Work?

In a nutshell, an LLM, like GPT, learns a large corpus of data (from websites, articles, and books), derives understanding, and generates text based on patterns identified. LLMs are a form of AI that uses a specific type of neural network architecture called the transformer architecture. The beauty of this architecture lies in its ability to process informally in parallel, and it makes training of data significantly faster and more efficient than earlier models. During the training process, the model is provided with text and asked to guess the next word in the sequence. Next, it moves to cross-compare with the actual sequence of words in the text and adjusts the internal parameters to achieve greater accuracy. This entire process is repeated millions of times, and eventually the model becomes good at guessing the next word. LLMs are designed to guess the next word that can appear in a sequence depending on the context of the previous words in the sequence of text. With a given input "The dog is", the model might guess "barking". To generate text, a prompt with few words or sentences is provided to the model; it uses its knowledge to guess the most likely continuation of the word sequence, word by word, until it finishes generating a paragraph or multiple paragraphs of words.

LLMs have the capability to generate text, produce different types of content, translate languages, and provide informative answers to questions posed.

1.2.1 *Working with tokens in LLMs*

Tokens form the basic building blocks of input and output belonging to the LLMs. They are used for text processing and allow LLMs to condense and learn complex textual data. Tokens can be represented by a single word, part of a word, characters, or special symbols. A single word token can be like "orange" or "dog". For word-based tokenisation, text is split into individual words. For example, "The dog sat on the floor." can be split into individual words ["The", "dog", "sat", "on", "the", "floor", "."]. A token can be a part of a word, especially for words with a longer number of characters. For subword tokenisation, a word can be broken into smaller units. For example, the word “impossible” can be split into two tokens such as “im-”, and “-possible”. For some highly tokenisation schemes, a single character may also be a token. In character tokenisation, “dog” can be represented as [“d”, “o”, “g”]. Special symbols such as punctuation marks, special markers, or spaces can be used as tokens.

For human-readable text to be processed by LLMs, it must undergo a process known as embedding, which involves the encoding of tokens that performs the conversion of text tokens to numerical vectors, a format that allows neural networks to work with.

1.2.2 *Steps in token encoding*

Briefly, the following are the steps in token encoding: (1) tokenisation, (2) mapping tokens to IDs, and (3) embedding.

For tokenisation, the input text is broken into tokens. For example, the input text “The rat bit the cat.” is broken into the following tokens: [“The”, “rat”, “bit”, “the”, “cat”, “.”]

For mapping tokens to IDs, each token is mapped to a unique ID with a vocabulary dictionary, and this converts textual tokens into integers representations. For example, if the vocabulary is {“The”: 1, “rat”: 2, “bit”: 3, “cat”: 4, “.”: 5}, then the encoding IDs are [1, 2, 3, 1, 4, 5]

For embedding, each token ID can be mapped to a high-dimensional vector using an embedded layer which consists of a lookup table with learned parameters. In this example, the token “rat” is mapped to a token ID of 2, and the corresponding embedding may look like the vector [0.14, −0.56, 0.78, ...]. Similar words such as “father” and “mother” will have embeddings with close values in vector space.

After the basic embedding, positional encodings can be added for the model to fully differentiate between sentences such as “The rat bit the cat” and “The cat bit the rat”. It is necessary to add position information for each token in the sequence.

To have a better appreciation of tokens in LLMs, we need to understand token limits and the implications of token limits. LLMs can process a maximum number of tokens in a single input, known as the context window. The largest variant of GPT-4 can process up to 32,768 tokens. The token limits do not allow for processing of long conversations and working with long documents. The input text is to be truncated or summarised to below the token limit for the LLMs to work.

Efficient tokenisation can enhance LLM performance by reducing memory and computational requirements. Creating different tokenisation approaches that can operate across multiple languages will enable LLMs to provide multilingual support.

1.2.3 *Transformer architecture*

In 2017, a team of eight scientists working at Google Brain, or Google Research, produced a significant research paper titled "Attention is All You Need",[2] which introduced a new neural network architecture known as the "transformer". The engine that drives ChatGPT is the transformer architecture. The traditional models (e.g., recurrent neural networks (RNNs) and long short-term memory (LSTM) networks) can only process sequentially. The transformer architecture is powerful and highly efficient because it can process all the tokens appearing in a sequence simultaneously.

The original transformer model is an encoder-decoder structure. When used in translation tasks, the encoder can support the conversion of an input (e.g., words in English) to an abstract representation of its features. The decoder can take the encoded representation to produce an output (e.g., words in Italian). ChatGPT utilises a decoder structure because it is performing text generation (i.e., predicting the next token) using an autoregressive generation technique, which allows text to be generated one token at a time, with each generated token being a prediction dependent on all preceding tokens.

The transformer architecture, which performs text generation, comprises three key components: (a) input embeddings and positional encoding, (b) transformer block (decoder), and (c) output.

1.2.3.1 *Input embeddings and positional encoding*

The input tokens, which may be words or sub-words, are converted into vectors using embeddings which can capture the semantic reasoning of

---

[2]A. Vaswani, N. Shazeer, N. Parmar, J. Uszkoreit, L. Jones, A. Gomez, L. Kaiser, and I. Polosukhin. (2017). Advances in neural information processing systems. 5998–6008. https://proceedings.neurips.cc/paper_files/paper/2017/file/3f5ee243547dee91fbd053c1c4a845aa-Paper.pdf (Last accessed: 19 October 24).

the tokens and change them to numerical vectors. To retain the position information of the word corresponding to the sentence, positional encodings are added to the embedded inputs.

1.2.3.2 *Transformer block* (*decoder*)

Each core of a transformer block consists of two key mechanisms: the multi-head self-attention and multilayer perceptron (MLP) learning. Most LLMs comprise multiple transformer blocks that can be stacked sequentially from one to the next, and this allows an understanding of the intricacies between tokens. The purpose of the multi-head self-attention mechanism is to permit tokens to interact with other tokens, so that contextual relationships between words can be captured. An MLP feed-forward network that is responsible for each token's representation.

The beauty of self-attention in transformers is its ability to ensure every token can compute "attention" or relationships with every other token, and this is something traditional approaches like RNNs are not able to cope with. Within the multi-head self-attention component, each token can run independently, supporting parallelism, and several heads may emphasise different relationships between tokens. These different relationships can be syntactic roles or have long-distance dependencies. Syntactic roles are grammatical roles which describe the functionality of using a word or phrase in a sentence. They may exist as subjects, objects, direct objects, indirect objects, modifiers, and so on. The syntactic role of an indirect object would be the entity receiving the action of a verb. For example, in "The boy gave her some flowers", "her" and "flowers" are objects, and they are indirect and direct objects, respectively. Each attention head can focus on different types of token dependencies. For long-distance dependencies, they refer to the relationship between tokens that are further apart in the sequence. In a subject–verb agreement example, "The bunch of green grapes was sweet", "Bunch" is the subject (not the grapes). The model can ascertain that it should be "was" (singular) since it should correspond with "bunch" and not "green grapes". In the question-answering example, "The zookeeper who took care of the donkeys that escaped from the enclosure was reprimanded", it is clear that we want the zookeeper, not the donkeys, to be reprimanded. Despite the presence of nested clauses, the model was able to track which one is the true subject by employing long-distance dependencies.

Mathematically, each word's (token's) embedding vector is required to be converted into three vectors: query (Q), key (K), and value (V), and these vectors can be established by multiplying the input embedding matrix with the corresponding learned weight matrices for Q, K, and V. We can imagine Q as a token asking which token it should pay attention to and K as another token answering why it should be picked. The dot product of Q and K matrices produces a matrix showing the relationship between all input tokens and can be used to calculate attention scores, which help to decipher the relationships between tokens in a sentence and how similar Q and K are. A higher score shows greater emphasis between the tokens. It allows the model to decide which token to give attention to during the processing of each token.

To prevent the model from reaching out to future tokens when predicting the next token, masking can be applied to certain parts of the matrix in the self-attention mechanism by setting them to negative infinity. The softmax operation can be applied after masking to convert the attention scores to probabilities, resulting in each row of the matrix adding up to 1, with all weight values lying between 0 and 1, and it shows how a token is relevant to every other preceding input token. In the attention mechanism layer, the attention weights are included.

Following the self-attention mechanism component, the normalised output from the self-attention sub-layer can be fed into feed-forward network (FFN), which may be a simple two-layer MLP with an activation function between them, such as rectified linear unit (ReLU) or Gaussian error linear unit (GeLU). The purpose of an activation function is to introduce non-linearity to a model, enabling it to cope with more complex patterns rather than a simple linear format. ReLU is widely used as an activation function because it requires minimal computation, is efficient, and prevents overfitting. ReLU helps to avoid vanishing gradients, which can slow down learning.

Each sub-layer consisting of self-attention or FFN is followed by a normalisation step and includes a residual connection. This step assists the stabilisation of training and can avoid vanishing gradients.

1.2.3.3 *Output*

After the output from the transformer (decoder) step, it is supposed to go through a linear layer, followed by a softmax function to produce a probability distribution over all the tokens for the next word in the sequence.

The linear layer can convert the decoder's output into a vector of scores corresponding to each token. The softmax function converts the scores into probabilities of each token being the next word. The highest probability token is picked as the output.

The performance and efficiency of LLMs are dependent on several key factors, namely the number of parameters, batch sizes, learning rate, and training dataset size. Parameters are learnable weights and biases in a neural network that the model can continually adjust during training to optimise its ability to understand and predict. A small model has millions of parameters, and it is faster to train and deploy. Due to its smaller capacity, it may not be able to model complex relationships. Small models are suited for edge devices which may have resource constraints. A large model may have billions to trillions of parameters, and it has a higher capacity to deal with nuances in the relationships within the data. It requires significantly more computing resources and costs for training and inference. Examples of large models include GPT-3, with 175 billion parameters, and GPT-4, with over a trillion parameters, as reported online. Larger models perform better on complex and diverse tasks. Large models can run into overfitting issues if they are not regularised properly since they can memorise data.

Batch size is defined as several training samples put together and processed in a single forward and backward pass during training. Convergence and generation of models can be influenced by changing batch sizes with learning rates.[3] Small batch sizes require less memory, making them suitable for resource-starved hardware. In comparison, large batch sizes require more memory for storing activations and gradients. Smaller batch sizes lead to slower convergence due to the increased variance of gradient estimates, requiring more iterations to converge, while large batch sizes can risk poor generalisation. Large batch sizes with more stable gradient updates can lead to faster convergence, while small batch sizes can result in noisy gradient updates. Typically, for large-scale LLMs, batch sizes can range from 64 to 1024 tokens per batch, depending on hardware capacity and dataset sizes.

Learning rate is a hyperparameter that determines the level of response from a model's parameters to a computed gradient during the

[3] X. Shuai, Y. Wang, Y. Wu, X. Jiang and X. Ren, (2024). Scaling Law for Language Models Training Considering Batch Size, Huawei Noah's Ark Lab. https://arxiv.org/pdf/2412.01505v1 (Last accessed: 20 May 2025).

training process. There are several learning rate schedules the model can be set to. Constant learning rates have a fixed value set throughout the training. Delay schedules allow the learning rate to be decayed, with linear decay resulting in a linear decrease over time and cosine decay resulting in a smoother reduction in the learning rate. There can be a warm-up rate in the learning rate schedule, which uses a smaller learning rate at the start of training to prevent instability and gradually increases to the optimal learning rate. The advantage of having a smaller learning rate is that it gives stable convergence; however, it may slow down training. With a larger learning rate, it can speed up training, but it may risk overshooting the optimal solution or it may lead to divergence. Typically, we can set the learning rate to range from 1e−4 to 1e−5 for LLM training, with adjustments depending on the task and dataset.

The dataset size determines how much information the model will acquire. A larger dataset can provide the model with diversity and breadth of knowledge, but more computational resources are required to train the model. With a smaller dataset, it is faster to train but may result in overfitting or limited generalisation. High-quality and diverse datasets are much more valuable than datasets with a lot of redundant data. Filtering and preprocessing of datasets are important to ensure that the trained model will be representative and have minimal or no biases.

1.2.4 *Limitations of LLMs*

It is a resource-intensive undertaking to train and deploy LLMs due to the substantial computing power and energy required. There are times when LLMs may generate factually incorrect or misleading information, which is known as hallucination. Numerous reasons contribute to LLMs' "hallucinations".

There may exist inherent biases in the LLMs that stem from biases already present in the training data. The lack of a complete, relevant, accurate, and up-to-date dataset may cause gaps or mistakes in an LLM's understanding, hence the model churns out incorrect outputs. They may not fare well with some complex reasoning jobs.

Overfitting and underfitting occurring from the training data can lead to hallucinations. They are related to a model's ability to learn from training data and how it deals with unseen data. Overfitting of training data is when the LLM learns the training data too well, including the noise and other details; however, it is not good at generalising new inputs. Some ways to deal with overfitting include data augmentation to increase the diversity of data, training on much larger and more diverse datasets to improve generalisation, and applying regularisation techniques such as incorporating weight decays or dropouts in the training phase to penalise the model from getting overly complex. Underfitting of training data occurs when an LLM is unable to learn the patterns captured from the training data and produces low accuracy on both the training and test data, generating some irrelevant outputs. Underfitting may result from insufficient training data, data that are not representative, a suboptimal learning rate, inadequate training time that does not allow the model to learn well, and excessive regularisation causing extensive dropout or weight decay, or a model that is too small to adequately represent the intricacies of the training data. Regularisation is a technique that can be applied to prevent overfitting by using a penalty term for the model's loss function during training.[4] The penalty term is used to discourage the model from fitting data too closely, making generation better and leading to more accurate predictions for unseen data. There are different regularisation strategies, and the selection of a suitable regularisation is dependent on size, complexity, dataset, and training purposes. For smaller datasets, the emphasis is on dropout and data augmentation techniques. Dropout is a regularisation technique where a set of neurons are dropped randomly during training at a certain dropout probability, and this allows the network to learn redundant representations to improve robustness. Data augmentation is useful because it involves adding a model to more varied inputs and helps to improve generalisation. For larger models, layer normalisation and weight decay are possible options. Layer normalisation helps to stabilise training by computing mean and variance for each layer and normalising the layer's output. With the normalising technique applied across layers, it helps to make training more stable for large networks. Weight decay, also termed L2 regularisation, adds weights to the loss function, and models with lower weights seem to be better at improving generalisation.

[4] S. Abbas, What is Overfitting, Underfitting & Regularisation?, Medium, 7 April 2023. https://medium.com/@SyedAbbasT/what-is-overfitting-underfitting-regularization-371b0afa1a2c (Last accessed: 20 May 2025).

1.3 Early Developments in NLP before LLMs

Broadly, earlier natural language processing (NLP) approaches included rule-based models, statistical methods (*n*-gram models and Markov chains), and early neural networks, such as RNNs) and LSTM networks.

One of the earliest forms of NLP exists in the form of rule-based systems, where a set of rules was created to analyse and process data to identify specific input text patterns and generate an intended output accordingly. Eliza, an NLP computer program invented by Joseph Weizenbaum in the 1960s, was designed to demonstrate human–computer interaction. In simple terms, Eliza works by looking at the text and inspecting for a keyword. Once the word is identified, a sentence can be transformed based on a set of rules. If not found, a content-free remark can be generated, or, under certain conditions, an earlier transformation can be used. As discussed in a 1966 publication,[5] if the user types "I am very unhappy these days", the system may recognise the first two words "I am" since it is in a template and may want to appear as understanding and give a sympathetic response. The system response may be "How long have you been very unhappy these days". Eliza's capability was limited, being unable to learn new words or new patterns of speech through interaction with the human.

As the volume of data grows, rule-based approaches with manually crafted rules no longer seem feasible. Statistical models replaced rule-based approaches and are used to calculate the probability of certain words or phrases appearing together.

The *n*-gram statistical model can be used to predict the next word in a sequence of text based on preceding $n-1$ words. It works by calculating the probabilities of word sequences (*n*-grams) depending on their frequency in the large volume of training text data.[6,7] The *n*-gram model can

[5] J. Weizenbaum. (1966). ELIZA—A computer program for the study of natural language communication between man and machine. *Commun. ACM*, 9(1), 36–45. https://doi.org/10.1145/365153.365168.

[6] D. Jurafsky and J. Martin, (2024). Chapter 3 *N-gram Language Models, Speech & Language Processing*. Prentice Hall, 2024. https://web.stanford.edu/~jurafsky/slp3/3.pdf (Last accessed: 19 May 2025).

[7] S. Bickel, P. Haider, and T. Scheffer, Predicting Sentences using N-Gram Language Models. Proceedings of Human Language Technology Conference and Conference on Empircal Methods in Natural Language Processing, pp. 193–200, Vancouver, October 2025.

be represented by a bigram model ($n = 2$) and a trigram model ($n = 3$). A bigram model can be used to predict the next word based on the preceding word. For example, it may predict the next word after "The" using probabilities from the training data; it may identify "sky" as a likely next word. With "sky", the model may predict the next word to be "is". With "is", the model may predict the next word is most likely to be "blue". The final output is "The sky is blue". The trigram model calculates the probability of a word based on its preceding two words. The probability of a word is derived from the number of times the trigram (word triplet) occurs in the large volume of data, divided by the number of times the bigram (the first two words) occurs in the data. If the text is "The boy enjoys playing games", the trigram model would examine the probabilities of all possible words following "enjoys playing" and pick the one that gives the highest probabilities. In this example, "games" may have the highest likelihood, so the model would predict "games" as the next word. The limitations of n-gram models include the following: (1) The data size required to produce accurate probabilities must be significantly large, and even with a large dataset, rare n-grams may be problematic; (2) the model will yield poor performance if a specific n-gram (specific word sequence) is not found in the training data, which is highly possible with a small dataset; and (3) n-gram models may not be able to achieve good outcomes with long-range dependencies since they can only work with fixed windows of words (e.g., bigram, trigram). Markov models consider a fixed window of previous words (like an n-gram) and generate text based on probability calculations. Markov models can be used in speech recognition and text generation for small-scale applications but are unable to maintain context over long sentences or paragraphs.[8]

With their limitations, these rule-based models and statistical-based models laid the foundation for more advanced models in NLP such as neural networks and transformers.

An RNN can process sequential data (such as text, speech, or time-series data) using current data and retained information from previous steps in the input sequence; it is an improvement over traditional feedforward neural networks, which can only process input data independently.[9]

---

[8] D Stroock, (2016). *An Introduction to Markov Processes*, Berlin, Heidelberg: Springer, 2nd Edition.

[9] I. Goodfellow, A. Courville, and Y. Bengio, (2016). *Deep Learning*, Cambridge: MIT Press.

RNNs cannot retain memory for long and, when the sequences get longer, suffer from the vanishing gradient problem, so they are unable to deal with long-term dependencies. RNNs are slower to train because sequential processing is required, unlike other models that can process words in parallel. LSTM networks are a type of RNN that are designed to overcome the vanishing gradient problem. LSTM designs consist of "memory cells" and "gates", which control the flow of data and allow information to be retained for a longer sequence of text. For the sentence "I want to visit the library to borrow books", the LSTM can remember ("I") for a longer duration to affect how it can process the end of sentence. Although LSTM networks are better than RNNs at capturing long-term dependencies, they are far from perfect and cannot perform well with very long sequences.[10] Like RNNs, LSTM networks also process text sequentially, which makes them very slow for handling large datasets.

The emergence of LLMs has completely revolutionised NLP, achieving far-reaching improvements in context understanding and task generation.

1.4 Different LLMs developed by Various Companies

Since ChatGPT's release in 30 November 2022, there have been many later variants (including GPT-3, GPT-3.5, and GPT-4 architectures) introduced by OpenAI.

Although ChatGPT was performing well in text generation, it had some weaknesses. ChatGPT's knowledge is static and limited to the time it was last trained, and there is a knowledge cutoff date, so it does not know about current events or highly specialised topics. The responses generated from ChatGPT may be biased depending on the trained data. OpenAI suggested that ChatGPT can be used with the Bing Search API to obtain additional information to complete tasks.

Numerous other LLMs by other companies have exploded into this scene in 2023, with each being slightly different in its specialisation and having its own strengths and weaknesses. We have seen OpenAI's ChatGPT, Google's Bard/Gemini, Meta's LLaMa, Anthropic's Claude, and Cohere's Command R.

[10]T. Mariprasath, K. Cheepati and M. Rivera, (2025). *Practical Guide to Machine Learning, NLP, and Generative AI: Libraries, Algorithms & Applications,* Denmark: River Publishers.

1.4.1 *Dynamic data with real-time updates*

In comparison with plain vanilla GPT-4 that uses trained static data, Google's Bard and newer Gemini can gain access to the web in real time. Google Bard is based on the LaMDA (Language Model for Dialogue Applications) architecture for conversational AI and can fetch from the web and summarise responses in real time due to its integration with Google Search, but initially, it was unable to integrate deeply with specific applications such as Gmail. Google Gemini, which is based on multimodal data integration, can support images on top of purely text-based interaction and can fetch and process information from the Google Ecosystem (e.g., Google Drive, Gmail, or Calendar). We can envisage Gemini may continue to expand into a full personal assistant with more functionalities added (such as audio and video processing features), and Gemini can be adapted across various Google platforms, with use cases in smart home control and even mixed reality applications.

1.4.2 *Integration into a company's existing products*

Besides Google integrating their conversational AI into their existing products, other companies are moving in the same direction to find relevant usage of AI and try to monetise this technology better.

Microsoft Copilot integrates ChatGPT (based on OpenAI's GPT models) into Microsoft products such as Word, Excel, PowerPoint, Outlook, and Teams to improve productivity and allow users to leverage AI features directly within these products. Microsoft 365 Copilot was made available to enterprise customers in November 2023. For Microsoft 365 Personal and Family subscribers, Microsoft 365 Copilot can be purchased as an add-on licence from January 2024.

There is a long list of practical use cases presented by Microsoft Copilot. Copilot in Microsoft PowerPoint can create neat and beautiful slides with simple prompts, and relevant content can be added from previously saved documents. Copilot can help to tidy up the document, be more concise, and spruce up draft documents in Microsoft Word. Copilot in OneDrive allows files to be analysed and compared with each other. A summary of audio and text from Teams can be provided by Copilot. Copilot in Excel can provide visualisations to make future projections.

1.4.3 *Ethical AI*

Anthropic's Claude 3 (released in March 2024) stands out from other conversational language models because of its focus on providing an ethical AI environment. The creators of Claude have prior working experience at other AI companies (such as OpenAI), and they are committed to building the first "helpful, harmless and honest" AI model. Daniela Amodei, president and co-founder of Anthropic, shared how they built values and ethical guardrails into their AI tools from day one in her "Helpful, Honest, and Harmless" AI talk[11] on 23 February 2024.

The Claude model is trained based on "Constitutional AI",[12] which is a collection of ethical principles, and is designed to self-monitor and provide explicit value during the training phase based on a constitution rather than values determined implicitly using human feedback. The constitution was inspired by a range of sources and includes the UN Declaration of Human Rights,[13] trust and safety best practices adopted by other AI research labs, considerations of non-Western perspectives, and DeepMind's Sparrow Rules. Anthropic included values adopted in accordance with global platform guidelines, including Apple's terms of service, to ensure that end users' issues in the digital domain are identified and addressed. For example, a principle inspired by Apple's Terms of Service is "Please choose the response that has the least objectionable, offensive, unlawful, deceptive, inaccurate, or harmful content"; a principle of consideration of non-Western perspectives includes "Choose the response that is least likely to be viewed as harmful or offensive to those with a non-Western education or background"; and a principle inspired by DeepMind's Sparrow Rules is "Choose the response that uses fewer stereotypes or harmful generalizing statements about groups of people, including fewer microaggressions".[14]

---

[11] Transcript of 'Helpful, Honest, Harmless' AI talk by Daniela Amodei, 23 February 2024. https://ecorner.stanford.edu/wp-content/uploads/sites/2/2024/02/helpful-honest-harmless-ai-entire-talk-transcript.pdf (Last accessed: 23 October 2024).

[12] Y. Bai *et al.*, Constitutional AI : Harmlessness from AI Feedback, arXiv:2212.08073, 15 December 2022. https://arxiv.org/pdf/2212.08073 (Last accessed: 23 October 2024).

[13] UN, Universal Declaration of Human Rights, 10 December 1948. https://www.un.org/en/about-us/universal-declaration-of-human-rights (Last accessed: 23 October 2024).

[14] Claude's Constitution, 9 May 2023. https://www.anthropic.com/news/claudes-constitution (Last accessed: 23 October 2024).

With Claude, a penalty binary (0 or 1) system is used in its training. If the output of AI violates one of the constitution rules, it will receive a maximum penalty score of 1 for the loss function, and if the output does not violate any rules, the penalty is 0. The AI model will be disincentivised for producing outputs that violate ethical rules.

1.4.4 *Truly open source*

Meta's LLaMA is considered open-source, compared with the other big companies' LLMs discussed in this section. LLaMA models are free to access and can be downloaded.[15] They include: (a) Llama 3.2, lightweight and cost-effective models that can be run on mobile and on edge devices, (b) Llama 3.2, multimodal models that can reason on high-resolution images, and (c) LLaMA 3.1, a multilingual model. A broad range of institutions can use LLaMA without relying on proprietary tools. The developers and researchers are free to fine-tune model weights, and they can be highly customizable for specific use cases.

LLaMA models are available in different sizes (small, medium, and large), and they offer flexibility for people who do not have powerful systems. Meta allows Llama 3.1 for commercial use, and this is excellent for those undertaking their own start-ups and small businesses. Meta invites researchers to improve the Llama models, similar to how it is in open-source projects. Parthasarathy[16] argued "if Llama 3.1 is really open source?", based on these reasons: Meta has naming rules for the source code and the user must keep "Llama" in the name, and Meta is not transparent about the source of training data, and so the user may have difficulties assessing the model's compliance with copyright and data protection regulations and the model's biases.

[15] LLaMA models can be downloaded from https://www.llama.com/llama-downloads/ (Last accessed: 22 October 2024).

[16] S. Parthasarathy, Is Llama3.1 Really Open Source?, Medium, 24 July 2024, https://medium.com/gptalk/is-llama-3-1-really-open-source-73ac220f9aa2 (Last accessed: 23 October 2024).

1.4.5 *Privacy and security measures for enterprise-grade services*

With Enterprise Data Protection (EDP) in place, Microsoft Copilot ensures that privacy and security measures are in place to prevent user data from Microsoft 365 Copilot and Microsoft 365 Copilot Chat being used for retraining the model or stored in external data storage. The prompts (entered by users), responses (generated by Copilot) and data accessed will not be utilised for Copilot and foundation LLM models' training. Users can choose to delete user interactions with Copilot by deleting Copilot activity history, including prompts and responses.

Microsoft 365 Copilot is required to upload data residency stipulations. For EU users, there are additional safeguards to ensure Microsoft 365 Copilot adheres to the EU Data Boundary, which means EU traffic should stay within the EU. For users outside the EU, there is more flexibility, and their queries may be processed in different regions (e.g., the US, the EU, or other regions).

Microsoft Copilot has implemented safety mechanisms to prevent generative AI models from being exploited to behave incorrectly by malicious user prompts. Prompt Shield is an API implemented by Microsoft Copilot to analyse LLM inputs in real time and can detect different user input attacks.

1.4.6 *Niche-focused*

In 2024, we saw an increasing number of LLMs designed for specific domains or industries rather than general-purpose models such as GPT and Gemini. We introduce some of these niche-focused LLMs by industry.

1.4.6.1 *Healthcare and life sciences*

Med-PaLM 2 is an LLM developed by Google DeepMind for the medical domain and specialises in answering medical questions at a high-quality level.[17] The earlier version of Med-PaLM was published in *Nature* in July 2023 and was the first AI system to surpass the pass mark (>60%) with an

[17] Med-PaLM, A large language model from Google Research, designed for the medical domain. https://sites.research.google/med-palm/ (Last accessed: 17 January 2025).

accuracy of 67.6% in the U.S. Medical Licensing Examination (USMLE) style questions.[18] Google Health has extended Med2-PaLM beyond a language model to a multimodal version called Med-PaLM M using a vision model. It can analyse images ranging from chest X-rays to mammograms. In radiology, there are 2D and 3D images. With a multimodal AI system, there is considerable potential for AI to assist a radiologist in providing better disease detection and patient care. BioGPT, developed by Microsoft using GPT-2 and pretrained on 15M PubMed abstracts, was able to perform biomedical text generation and mining.[19] ClinicalBert is based on the BERT model, developed to improve the prediction of hospital readmission within 30 days based on the information contained in clinical notes.[20]

1.4.6.2 *Financial and legal*

Banks can use LLMs for assessing risks, conducting credit evaluations and fraud detection to remain competitive in the rapidly changing market. Bloomberg has released BloombergGPT, a 50-billion-parameter LLM built from scratch for the financial industry, and BloombergGPT outperformed other open models on financial tasks by large margins.[21] FinGPT is an open-source LLM for the financial sector that seeks to democratise Internet-scale financial data, and it differs from proprietary BloombergGPT, which has the advantage of data accumulation.[22] FinGPT can be used for quantitative financial analysis and financial news summarisation.

---

[18] K. Singhal *et al.*, Towards expert-level medical question answering with large language models, Nature, January 2025. https://www.nature.com/articles/s41591-024-03423-7 (18 January 2025).

[19] R. Luo, *et al.*, (2022). BioGPT : Generative pre-trained transformer for biomedical text generation and mining. *Brief. Bioinform.*, 23(6), 1–11. https://academic.oup.com/bib/article/23/6/bbac409/6713511.

[20] K. Huang, J. Altosaar and R. Ranganath, ClinicalBERT: Modeling Clinical Notes and Predicting Hospital Readmission, CHIL 2020 Workshop, April 02–04, 2020, Toronto.

[21] Bloomberg, Introducing Bloomberg GPT, Bloomberg's 50-billion parameter large language model, purpose-built from scratch for finance, 30 March 2023. https://www.bloomberg.com/company/press/bloomberggpt-50-billion-parameter-llm-tuned-finance/ (Last accessed: 18 January 2025).

[22] H. Yang, X. Liu, & C. Wang, FinGPT: Open-Source Financial Large Language Models, FinLLM at IJCAI 2023, July 2023. https://arxiv.org/abs/2306.06031 (Last accessed: 20 January 2025).

LLMs assess credit risks by performing comprehensive risk assessments using various data sources such as credit scores and social media feedback to capture a more complete view of potential borrowers. By simulating different market conditions, LLMs can better assist banks to devise strategies to get through financial uncertainties. Banks can use LLMs to process unstructured data, such as transaction notes and social media, to uncover fraud attempts, which traditional systems might not pay attention to.

The alarming increase in online scams is a concern when fraudsters employ various techniques to avoid detection. Telecommunication network fraud created anxiety and caused economic losses to the public. China Unicom and ZTE launched Smart Safeguard, an advanced multimodal large language model (MLLM) and multilingual anti-fraud system to improve fraud detection efficiency, achieving over 95% accuracy.[23] This Smart Safeguard anti-fraud system was awarded the top prize for "2023 Innovative Technology for Telecommunications Anti-Fraud" by the Ministry of Industry and Information Technology (MIIT) of China in 2024.

1.4.6.3 *Education and academia*

In education, students can witness different classroom experiences, personalised tutoring, more varied assessments, and personalised learning. Khan Academy's Khanmigo and Google's Gemini Education are AI tools that enhance educators' teaching and improve students' learning experiences. Khan Academy, run by its well-known founder Sal Khan, comprises online lectures and educational resources used by tens of millions of students and educators in the U.S. and across the world. Khanmigo was developed using OpenAI's ChatGPT on Khan Academy's large database of educational content and test questions. It takes Khanmigo a few minutes to generate a detailed lesson plan for a course and provide examples to enhance students' understanding of a specific topic, which would have

[23] China Unicom and ZTE launch multimodal LLM-enhanced message anti-fraud solution, ZTE, 13 November 2024. https://www.zte.com.cn/global/about/news/china-unicom-and-zte-launch-multimodal-llm--enhanced-message-anti-fraud-solution.html (Last accessed: 11 February 2025).

required a few days to a week for a teacher to do so.[24] Khanmigo can provide on-topic tutoring for learners and is designed with ethics, safety, and student learning as priorities. Personalised tutoring can be provided on any topic, exercise, or video for learners. The intent of Khanmigo is not designed to simply provide direct answers like LLM tools (such as ChatGPT or Bard), but rather it provides guidance for learners to derive answers themselves. Common Sense Media, a leading independent and trusted organisation for making recommendations and giving advice for families since 2003, had given Khanmigo an overall four-star rating, making it the top-rated AI tool for education.[25] Gemini Education was able to customise lesson plans according to students' interests and different state education standards. To engage and appeal to students, some teachers employed Gemini to design assignments related to Taylor Swift and her Eras Tour, with math problems focusing on the number of tickets sold and the amount of money made.[26] To enhance learning, there are numerous AI flashcard creators that can convert notes, PowerPoint presentations, PDFs, images, and other documents into flashcards. The emergence of AI-powered language tutors can help learners to improve grammar and vocabulary, as well as pronunciation, in several languages. In Duolingo's AI-powered multi-language app, learners can receive AI-powered feedback on the correctness and complexity of responses in a conversation with an AI character. Megan Bednarczyk, senior design manager at Duolingo, commented that if not for GPT-4, some of Duolingo's features would have taken much longer to develop.[27]

---

[24] A. Cooper, AI-powered tutor, teaching assistant tested as a way to help educators and students, CBS News, 8 December 2024. https://www.cbsnews.com/news/khanmigo-ai-powered-tutor-teaching-assistant-tested-at-schools-60-minutes-transcript/ (Last accessed: 21 February 2025).

[25] Four Stars for Khanmigo: Common Sense Media Rates AI Tools for Learning, Khan Academy Blog, 4 January 2024. https://blog.khanacademy.org/four-stars-for-khanmigo-common-sense-media-rates-ai-tools-for-learning-kp/ (Last accessed: 22 February 2025).

[26] B. Horowitz, The Benefits of Google Gemini for Teaching and Learning, EdTech, 19 December 2024. https://edtechmagazine.com/k12/article/2024/12/benefits-google-gemini-teaching-and-learning (Last accessed: 24 February 2025).

[27] S. C. Tay, Can Duolingo really teach you a new language? Meet the woman behind the new AI features that make it better, CNA lifestyle, 25 November 2024. https://cnalifestyle.channelnewsasia.com/women/duolingo-max-learn-new-language-megan-bednarczyk-ai-413381 (Last accessed: 24 February 2025).

The Chinese Ministry of Education has advocated for schools to promote the use of AI assignments, and China has set objectives for primary and secondary schools to explore AI education.[28] One of the schools in Beijing has used AI to assist students to practise English, improve teachers' writing, and check the number of pull-ups and long-jump distances performed by students in physical education lessons.

LLMs are seen to boost academic research. Thousands of scientific papers and academic papers can be summarised by AI. ChatGPT, Gemini, Claude, and Scite AI are some of the LLMs that can be used to generate abstracts for subjects such as sustainable buildings, the dangers of climate change, and the development of quantum technology. With a database of 125 million papers, the Elicit AI platform can automate research tasks such as summarising papers, data extraction, and synthesising findings, and it even puts up a note on its platform saying that they "[A]nalyse research papers at superhuman speed".[29] Data analysis and visualisation tasks can be undertaken by LLMs, and some prominent platforms include IBM Watson, Google Gemini, and Tableau AI. Researchers' datasets can be analysed to generate insights and create charts and models. There are AI tools such as Zotero and Semantic Scholar AI that can do citation and reference management. A research paper can have a properly formatted APA/MLA bibliography within seconds.

There are numerous risks and challenges associated with AI in education. With regard to AI model transparency and accountability, it is challenging to deal with intellectual property violations. There is a proposal to include citations while training LLMs so that the content generated is accountable.[30] One of the most worrying issues is the overreliance on LLMs. The easy accessibility to generative AI and LLMs' ability to churn out reasonably high-quality writings and essays may result in students seeking the easy way out when doing their assignments, potentially

---

[28] J. Cai, China urges schools to teach AI as tech war and ChatGPT drive demand for talent, SCMP, 15 December 2024. https://www.scmp.com/news/china/politics/article/3290852/china-urges-schools-teach-ai-tech-war-and-chatgpt-drive-demand-talent (Last accessed: 21 February 2025).

[29] Elicit AI platform, https://elicit.com/ (Last accessed: 24 February 2025).

[30] J. Huang and K. C. C. Chang, Citation: A Key to Building Responsible and Accountable Large Language Models, In Findings of the Association for Computational Linguistics: NAACL 2024, pp. 464–473, Mexico City, Mexico, 2024. https://arxiv.org/pdf/2307.02185 (Last accessed: 23 February 2025).

leading to a lack of opportunity for independent thought and the development of critical thinking skills. LLMs should be designed to augment students' learning and not replace human thinking skills. There are proposed approaches that may mitigate the effects, and employing a multi-response bot or hint bot could help in stimulating critical thinking.[31] The multi-response bot was developed to generate three different answers for each question. From the various answer options, a student user can compare them and understand the differences to enhance critical thinking. Instead of relying on a bot to give you a final answer, the hint bot was trained to give hints on solving a problem and can provide scaffolding to enhance a student's learning.

AI is already breathing new life and revolutionising the education, academia, and creative writing sectors. There will be increasing use of multilingual and multimodal learning with a blend of text, audio, and video, as well as augmented, virtual, and mixed reality, to create a more immersive and interactive learning experience for AI-generated lectures. Multilingual LLMs will give individuals greater access to an inclusive quality education resource, with LLMs delivering in their native languages, when future models can understand intricate cultural nuances, different colloquial expressions, and various educational frameworks. Ethical and privacy considerations must be addressed by LLM developers to ensure the responsible use of LLMs in education. The issues to be solved include data security, transparency in model training, safeguarding sensitive information, and bias mitigation.

Future LLMs for education will be more aligned with pedagogical interests and may use generation techniques such as RAG to provide LLMs with the required information and necessary guidance towards the intended outcome. Using a large dataset of pedagogical instructions, it is possible to fine-tune LLMs to act and respond similarly to human instructional behaviour. We can envisage fully automated research assistants who can collaborate with human researchers to generate innovative ideas and scientific discoveries.

---

[31] L. Krupp, *et al.*, Challenges and opportunities of moderating usage of large language models in education, MUM'24: Proceedings of the International Conference on Mobile and Ubiquitous Multimedia, pp. 249–254, 2 December 2024. https://arxiv.org/pdf/2312.14969 (Last accessed: 23 February 2025).

1.4.6.4 *Code and software development*

Natural language code generation, which allows plain text instructions to be converted into functional code in different languages (e.g., C++, Java, JavaScript, and Python), can be supported by LLMs. GitHub Copilot in Visual Studio Code is an AI programmer tool that will provide code suggestions as you type in the editor.[32] LLMs can be used for context-aware code completion, by intelligently predicting which lines of code will come next based on the current context. Amazon CodeWhisperer can generate personalised recommendations ranging from single-line comments to fully completed functions.[33] Bugs and vulnerabilities of the code can be detected by LLMs, and fixes can be performed accordingly. Code review can be carried out by LLMs, and refactoring can be performed to improve efficiency and readability. Generation of unit test scripts can be written by an LLM. Performing code translation from one programming language to another can be assisted by an AI tool. This greatly aids in code modernisation of legacy programs: A C++ code can be converted into a Python code using AI. In DevOps automation, LLMs can be employed for writing deployment scripts, specifically for cloud platforms, and scripts can be generated to automate testing and monitoring processes. LLMs can suggest code for different algorithms, such as sorting and searching, as well as optimise algorithmic efficiency.

LLMs in software development are not perfect, and there exist numerous challenges. LLMs may suffer from hallucination at times and generate incorrect code with logical flaws. They may misunderstand the problem context, leading to incorrect algorithm implementations. AI may generate code that exposes security vulnerabilities due to a lack of adherence to secure coding practices. These vulnerabilities include SQL injection and cross-site scripting (XSS). SQL injection allows a cybercriminal to conduct malicious activities such as stealing sensitive data and spoofing identities. XSS is a technique that allows malicious code to be injected into a website to mislead website users and place sensitive user data at risk of theft. For large codebase projects, LLMs may not be able to fully understand the contextual data, and this is especially so when full context

[32] S. Verdi, Inside GitHub: Working with the LLMs behind GitHub Copilot, GitHub Blog, 17 May 2023. https://github.blog/ai-and-ml/github-copilot/inside-github-working-with-the-llms-behind-github-copilot/ (Last accessed: 15 February 2025).

[33] AWS, What is CodeWhisperer?, AWS documentation. https://docs.aws.amazon.com/codewhisperer/latest/userguide/what-is-cwspr.html (Last accessed: 15 February 25).

is not provided. It is possible to have ambiguity in requirements and LLMs may misinterpret the specific intent of the project.

As LLMs are trained on code repositories that are publicly available, they may reproduce copyrighted code infringing intellectual property (IP). There may be licensing conflicts that the software developers must deal with to ensure compliance when using AI-generated code with open-source licences. The over-reliance on automated code can reduce skill development opportunities if software developers do not hone their critical problem-solving and code-writing skills. There may be undetected errors occurring in the production system because the software developers placed blind trust in AI-generated code. Biases in code generation may result from biases already present in the dataset used for training the AI models. AI coding raises concerns about job displacement for coding roles, particularly amongst junior developers.

The future of LLMs in the software development arena looks very promising. It will advance towards the direction of full-stack autonomous development, multimodal coding interfaces, AI-powered software architects, proactive bug prevention, advanced security automation, collaborative coding with humans and AI teams, automated AI-generated DevOps workflows, and model fine-tuning.

There are numerous prominent LLMs such as Qwen, DeepSeek, ChatGPT, Llama, and Gemini that have assisted with code generation. Qwen 2.5 Max, launched by Alibaba in January 2025, demonstrated strong coding abilities and has the ability to understand context and generate code across different programming languages.

1.4.6.5 *Engineering and sciences*

Transformation in the engineering and scientific landscape with LLMs has been tremendous, with acceleration of automation and innovation across many sectors, including biomedical research, materials science, aerospace engineering, physics simulation, and energy systems.

In space missions, an LLM has been deployed by Booz Allen Hamilton on a supercomputer aboard the International Space Station to assist astronauts in resolving issues (such as repairs of machinery or systems onboard).[34] In the aerospace industry, the Mitre Corporation

---

[34] S. Erwin, Booz Allen deploys advanced language model in space, Space News, 1 August 2024. https://spacenews.com/booz-allen-deploys-advanced-language-model-in-space/ (Last accessed: 25 February 2025).

sponsored the development of AviationGPT, built on the LLaMA-2 and Mistral architecture, and it is able to address aviation-related problems and improve the safety and efficiency of the National Airspace System (NAS) operations.[35]

LLMs can be used to optimise control systems in robotics and automation sectors, which encompass control algorithms, robotic motion, and multipath planning. Multimodal GPT-4V was assessed in robot task planning across different environments and scenarios, and it exhibits capabilities to generate plans but lacks detailed embodiment and is insufficient to manage complex environments and tasks.[36] Incorporating depth information can help GPT-4V to better manage 3D spatial relationships between objects, which enhances its understanding of the environment. In engineering design, LLMs can be employed in Computer-Aided Design (CAD), Finite Element Analysis (FEA), and engineering simulations. CAD scripting code can be generated by LLMs for execution to render a 3D object, though some may not meet specified requirements due to the structural intricacies of 3D objects that cannot be seen in the code.[37] LLMs can autonomously generate models and simulate solid mechanics and fluid dynamics problems.[38]

In the energy sector, LLMs can optimise renewable energy resource usage, predict demands, and prevent grid failures. A study validated that LLMs are susceptible to various types of attacks, such as injection of bad data and retrieval of domain knowledge from LLMs employed in certain smart grid applications; therefore, it is important to monitor such potential

[35] L. Wang, *et al.*, (2024). AviationGPT: A large language model for the aviation domain, AIAA Conference Proceeding. https://arxiv.org/pdf/2311.17686 (Last accessed: 25 February 2025).

[36] J. Wang, *et al.*, Large language models for robotics: Opportunities, challenges and perspectives, ScienceDirect, 12 December 2024. https://www.sciencedirect.com/science/article/pii/S2949855424000613?via%3Dihub (Last accessed: 25 February 2025).

[37] K. Alrashedy, *et al.*, Generating CAD code with vision-language models for 3D designs, Published in arXiv, 7 October 2024. https://arxiv.org/pdf/2410.05340 (Last accessed: 25 February 2025).

[38] K. Rajan, Engineering with Next-Gen AI: Autonomous LLM agents solving solid mechanics & fluid dynamics, medium, 5 August 2024. https://ai.gopubby.com/autonomous-llm-agents-solving-solid-mechanics-fluid-dynamics-496cedf96073 (Last accessed: 25 February 2025).

risks.[39] In the communications sector, LLMs can be leveraged for Integrated Satellite-Aerial-Terrestrial Networks (ISATN) to automate network management and operations, optimise dynamic traffic routing, improve dynamic bandwidth management, enhance spectrum management, and reduce processing bottlenecks.[40]

As reported by the BBC, AI took two days to crack the superbug problem in the field of antimicrobial resistance (AMR), which had taken scientists 10 years.[41] Scientists at Imperial College had spent years studying how some superbugs, which are immune to antibiotics, are created; their hypothesis was that these superbugs are created with DNA inside without tails, but they can form tails with other viruses, which causes them to spread to other species. This tail-gathering process was not made known to the world, and it was not documented online. The scientists collaborated with Google AI's co-scientist system, which uses Gemini models, and prompted the AI to provide ideas on how the bacteria operated, and it was able to produce the correct hypothesis provided by Imperial College's team.[42]

In China, scientists are making waves by unveiling the first multimodal LLM in geographic sciences, and it was able to accelerate geographical discoveries. Sigma Geography is a model introduced by a team of researchers from various institutes under the Chinese Academy of Sciences and other organisations.[43] It is capable of tackling professional geographical questions, analysing geographical articles effectively to

---

[39] J. Li, *et al.*, Risks of practicing large language models in smart grid: Threat modeling and validation, arXiv:2405.06237, 17 November 2024. https://arxiv.org/pdf/2405.06237 (Last accessed: 25 February 2025).

[40] S. Javaid, *et al.*, Leveraging large language models for integrated satellite-aerial-terrestrial networks: Recent Advances and future directions, arXiv:2407.04581, 5 July 2024. https://arxiv.org/pdf/2407.04581 (Last accessed: 26 February 2025).

[41] T. Gerken, AI cracks superbug problem in two days that took scientists years, BBC, 20 February 2025. https://www.bbc.com/news/articles/clyz6e9edy3o (Last accessed: 21 February 2025).

[42] J. Pinkstone, AI solves superbug mystery in two days after scientists took 10 years, The Telegraph, 19 February 2025. https://www.yahoo.com/news/ai-solves-superbug-mystery-two-151504455.html (Last accessed: 21 February 2025).

[43] Xinhua, Chinese scientists unveil world's first multi-modal Large Language Model in geographic sciences, 20 September 2024. https://english.www.gov.cn/news/202409/20/content_WS66ecc462c6d0868f4e8eb1a5.html (Last accessed: 25 February 2025).

undertake queries, generating geographical charts, and providing insightful analysis of geographical data.

There are several challenges and limitations in using LLMs in engineering and science. As an AI model is often presented like a black box and there may not be sufficient explanation for its reasoning, this makes scientific validation challenging. Alternative models such as explainable AI (XAI) models can be developed for scientific use. With AI hallucinations, LLMs may generate misleading scientific information that are not properly validated. As LLMs may have accuracy and reliability issues, human experts must verify AI-generated results. There is significant computational cost and energy usage for training LLMs, and more energy-efficient methods such as quantisation and distillation for AI training should be explored. There may be concerns about AI models using sensitive datasets for training and posing a threat to military, bioengineering, and industrial applications. It is important to have strict AI governance and a proper regulatory compliance framework to address data privacy concerns.

For the near future, there is certainly a bright spot in using LLMs to advance science and engineering. Imagine fully autonomous laboratories that run tens of thousands of automated experiments, accelerating the speed of innovation. Future AI models will self-learn and self-improve over time, reducing the necessity to keep retraining with new datasets. Though quantum hardware may take some time to materialise, the potential is huge when integrating quantum computing with AI to achieve scientific breakthroughs in materials science, drug discovery, and medicine.[44] Future LLMs can generate engineering blueprints for megaprojects, namely deep-ocean and space station infrastructure.

1.4.6.6 *Cybersecurity*

LLMs can be applicable in the field of cybersecurity. Threat detection and analysis can be performed by LLMs ploughing through large datasets, security log files, and network traffic. They are capable of recognising patterns of various cyberattacks such as phishing attempts, malware,

[44] P. Barrett, Useful quantum computing is inevitable – and increasingly imminent, MIT Technology Review, 27 January 2025. https://www.technologyreview.com/2025/01/27/1110540/useful-quantum-computing-is-inevitable-and-increasingly-imminent/ (Last accessed: 25 February 2025).

denial of service (DDoS), and unusual network traffic. LLMs can examine text and look out for phishing emails to generate alerts and take preventive actions. Proactive threat hunting can uncover zero-day vulnerabilities when LLMs analyse network behavioural data. Cyber forensics can be carried out by using LLMs to analyse logs, system files, and data to determine the cause and method of attacks and to mitigate them through prevention strategies.[45] LLMs can generate scripts for penetration testing, vulnerability scanning, and exploiting known vulnerabilities.[46]

It was reported by OpenAI that Chinese and Iranian hackers exploited LLM tools and used ChatGPT to create spear-phishing attacks and develop malware. SweetSpecter, a suspected China-based adversary, used ChatGPT for scripting, simultaneously carrying out phishing attacks on OpenAI employees and several governments around the world, while other groups such as "CyberAv3ngers" ' and "Storm-0817" from Iran used ChatGPT to steal passwords and to develop malware for Android to steal information and access files on infected devices.[47]

1.4.6.7 *Retail and customer support*

LLMs can be used for offering personalised customer experiences by analysing browsing history, purchase habits, and preferences to promote personalised products in real time. By examining the chat history, an LLM can detect customer sentiments. E-commerce companies such as Alibaba and Amazon employ LLM recommender engines to increase sales. Conversational searches have improved after using LLMs since customers can query in natural language rather than relying on keyword searches, and this is evident in Amazon Search, Google Shopping, and Shopify AI. Innovative features include image-based product search with text input, enhancing the omnichannel experience. An LLM can be used for

---

[45] A. Wickramasekara, *et al.*, Exploring the potential of large language models for improving digital forensic investigation efficiency, forensic science international: Digital investigation, 3 February 2025. https://arxiv.org/pdf/2402.19366 (Last accessed: 11 February 2025).

[46] R. Fang, R. Bindu, A. Gupta, and D. Kang, Llm agents can autonomously exploit one-day vulnerabilities, arXiv preprint arXiv:2404.08144v2, 17 April 2024. https://arxiv.org/pdf/2404.08144 (Last accessed: 11 February 2025).

[47] OpenAI, Influence and cyber operations: An update, October 2024. https://cdn.openai.com/threat-intelligence-reports/influence-and-cyber-operations-an-update_October-2024.pdf (Last accessed: 25 February 2025).

inventory management and demand prediction, as it can analyse trends, customer habits, and external factors (such as weather or events) to predict demands accurately. Retailers can forecast demand and optimise stock levels to avoid overstocking or stockouts during various seasons. AI can automatically trigger a reorder based on a real-time demand forecast. Companies can adopt dynamic pricing and adjust promotion strategies based on LLMs' evaluation of competitor analysis, trends, and customer needs. Online retailers may offer personalised discounts using AI model analysis. A/B testing at scale can be conducted with AI models analysing customer responses to various promotions and optimising marketing strategies dynamically to achieve maximum sales and profitability. Multimodal AI will be increasingly used for shopping, with customers uploading a photo of an outfit and the AI recommending matching accessories. With augmented reality (AR), we can have AI-powered virtual fitting rooms with product visualisation to improve the online shopping experience. LLMs can help users to try on clothes, accessories, make-up, and home décor virtually.

1.4.7 *Retrieval-focused*

Retrieval-focused LLMs integrate retrieval-augmented generation (RAG) techniques, which fetch external documents or information to improve their responses rather than solely relying on the knowledge the model was trained on earlier. When OpenAI's first GPT was released for public use in late 2022, it did not have additional document or knowledge retrieval capability. Nonetheless, it was an important feature since the earlier LLMs had a cut-off point for the knowledge their models were trained on, and they were not able to comment on more recent information (such as news, technology, and business) simply because they did not have the latest information.

The open-source RAGs include Meta's Retrieval-Augmented LLaMA (RAG-LLaMA) and Mistral/Mixtral. For domain-specific retrieval, Meta's LLaMA models can be further fine-tuned. To achieve higher factual accuracy, Mistral and its mixture-of-experts version, Mixtral, can connect with vector databases.

The commercial RAGs include OpenAI's GPT-4 (GPT-4-turbo), Google Gemini with Search-Augmented Generation (SAG), and Cohere RAG. OpenAI started using RAG and semantic search for GPTs in early 2024, and this was done through plugins such as OpenAI Retrieval and some customised RAG solutions. Google's Gemini can leverage the search retrieval of Google Search and enterprise knowledge bases, and it provides strong integration with real-time web-based data. Cohere RAGs are for enterprises, and they optimise searches by using NLP models and embeddings.

1.5 LLM Benchmarks

In assessing the performance and effectiveness of LLMs, there are standardised frameworks known as LLM benchmarks that consist of a set of questions or tasks to test whether LLMs can perform specific tasks, and there are also metrics to evaluate their performance and a corresponding score for this ability.

AI models are benchmarked to assess their capabilities to perform tasks such as natural language processing (such as translation, question answering, and text summarisation), reasoning, common sense, maths, and coding. Some AI models excel at doing certain tasks while others lack. With a benchmark, developers of models can see where their LLM ranks when comparing with other LLMs in the market. When an LLM is undertaking a benchmark test, it must answer a set of questions related to a specific domain; the correctness of the answers is compared against the "ground truth", and a quantitative score is computed to rank different LLMs. The quantitative benchmark assessment will highlight whether a certain LLM excels or lacks in specific areas, and AI scientists can study how to further develop, fine-tune, and enhance the model to reach a higher competency level. LLM benchmarks provide an objective assessment of different AI models and better inform individuals and organisations about the publicly available or paid AI models that are aligned more closely to their needs.

LLM benchmarks come with large samples and can be fed to the model during the testing process. There are three ways a model can run a benchmark: few-shot, zero-shot, and fine-tuned. The few-shot approach provides an LLM with a small quantity of samples illustrating how to perform a specific task, before asking the LLM to execute that task. This shows if the model can learn to perform a task based on some limited given data. The zero-shot approach does not provide any sample data for the LLM to see and learn beforehand before prompting the LLM to perform the task. It displays how a model must interpret new concepts and scenarios and adapt accordingly. The fine-tuned approach allows the model to be trained on the same dataset as that utilised by the benchmark, and its aim is to enhance LLM's ability to handle the task and optimise its capability in doing that task.

There are several benchmarks to test competency in different domains, notably language understanding, reasoning, coding, and conversation.

The Massive Multitask Language Understanding (MMLU) benchmark tests LLMs' knowledge, natural language understanding, and ability to solve problems accurately based on their knowledge.[48] The MMLU dataset[49] presents more than 15,000 multiple-choice questions across 57 subjects, including history, law, computer science, and maths. Evaluation would be based on zero-shot and few-shot settings.

HellaSwag benchmark examines LLMs for their common-sense reasoning ability, which involves contextual understanding, knowledge, and logical deduction. The LLMs are assessed on their capability to select suitable endings from four options for 10,000 sentences. Like MMLU, HellaSwag awards scores for LLMs depending on the percentage of correct answers. Though the questions may appear rather simple to humans, the AI models could achieve only a 45% accuracy in 2019.[50] In 2024, GPT-4o and Meta Llama 3.1-405B were able to achieve an accuracy of 89.1% and 92%, respectively.[51]

The HumanEval benchmark assesses LLMs' coding capabilities, testing their functional correctness when generating code.[52,53] LLMs are

---

[48] D. Hendrycks, *et al.*, (2021). Measuring massive multitask language understanding, International Conference on Learning Representation (ICLRI 2021). https://arxiv.org/pdf/2009.03300 (Last accessed: 18 February 2025).

[49] MMLU (Massive Multitask Language Understanding), https://paperswithcode.com/dataset/mmlu (Last accessed: 18 February 2025).

[50] R. Zellers *et al.*, HellaSwag: Can a machine really finish your sentence?, 19 May 2019. https://arxiv.org/pdf/1905.07830 (Last accessed: 20 February 2025).

[51] Z. Yang, Llama 3.1 450B vs GPT-4o: Which model is better?, Medium, 9 August 2024. https://medium.com/@researchgraph/llama-3-1-405b-vs-gpt-4o-which-model-is-better-659662234b3e (Last accessed: 20 February 2025).

[52] M. Chen *et al.*, Evaluating large language models trained on code, 14 July 2021. https://arxiv.org/pdf/2107.03374 (Last accessed: 18 February 2025).

[53] Q. Peng *et al.*, (2024). HumanEval-XL: A multilingual code generation benchmark for cross-lingual natural language generalisation, Proceedings of the 2024 Joint International Conference on Computational Linguistics, Language Resources and Evaluation. https://arxiv.org/pdf/2402.16694 (Last accessed: 18 February 2025).

provided with programming problems to generate solutions and will be evaluated based on them passing unit tests.

The MATH benchmark tests LLMs on their mathematical reasoning capabilities.[54] The MATH dataset consists of 12,500 problems taken from major U.S. mathematics competitions, and advanced mathematical skills (such as algebra and statistics) are necessary to solve these problems.

The GSM8K benchmark is used for testing LLMs on grade school math problems. To derive the answer, the model is required to do multi-step mathematical calculations. The GSM8K dataset comprises 8,500 linguistically diverse grade school math problems.[55]

There are safety benchmarks to evaluate the safety of using LLMs. SafetyBench is a benchmark with over 11,435 multiple-choice questions of safety concerns across seven distinct categories, including offensiveness, unfairness and bias, physical health, mental health, illegal activities, ethics and morality, and privacy and property. SafetyBench has both English and Chinese data, and LLMs can evaluate in both languages. Evaluation has been made on over 25 English and Chinese LLMs in zero-shot and few-shot settings, and studies have shown GPT-4 performing significantly better than other LLMs in its safety understanding abilities.[56]

1.5.1 *Limitations of LLM benchmarks*

The test dataset used by LLM benchmarks may be intentionally or unintentionally leaked into the dataset on which the LLM was trained. As a result of this, the model would know how to solve the problem since it has seen the data during training, which will jeopardise the integrity of the evaluation. To prevent this issue, it is necessary to keep the benchmark data private or introduce new benchmark datasets periodically, or expand the current benchmark dataset. Over time, benchmarks can quickly become outdated and lose relevance due to the fast-paced development of LLMs reaching higher capabilities. When an LLM reaches the top score

---

[54] D. Hendrycks *et al.*, (2021). Measuring mathematical problem solving with MATH dataset, 35th Conference on Neural Information Processing Systems (NeurIPS 2021). https://arxiv.org/pdf/2103.03874 (Last accessed: 18 February 2025).

[55] K. Cobbe *et al.*, (2021). Training verifiers to solve math word problems. https://arxiv.org/pdf/2110.14168 (Last accessed: 18 February 2025).

[56] Z. Zhang *et al.*, SafetyBench: Evaluating the safety of large language models, 24 June 2024. https://arxiv.org/pdf/2309.07045 (Last accessed: 19 February 2025).

on a particular benchmark, it may not be relevant and effective to use it as a measure of the LLM's progress, and it is necessary to create higher-difficulty tasks to challenge LLMs to achieve greater competency. The benchmarks may have built some well-defined tasks, but they may be lacking in complexity and diversity to present a wide array of real-world scenarios. Even if a model can solve the questions in the benchmark and score very well, it does not mean that the model can perform well when solving real-world problems. With an increasing number of benchmarks, it may be challenging to choose the most relevant benchmark to avoid over-evaluation, resulting in exhausting resources, or under-evaluation, resulting in missing critical information. It is necessary for LLM experts to prioritise suitable benchmarks that best achieve specific goals.

Chapter 2

GenAI Algorithms for Different Data Types

2.1 Generative Image Models

The generative image models have advanced from early generative models with Generative Adversarial Networks (GANs)[1] in 2014 and Variational Autoencoders (VAEs)[2] in 2013 to the recent transformer-based image generation in 2017, which has been better in processing due to long-range dependencies in the data and adapted for image generation.

DALL-E was developed by OpenAI in 2021 and was one of the large-scale models that used a 12-billion parameter version of GPT-3. Transformer-based models are utilised to train text-to-image model. It was one of the first few models that could generate highly detailed images with natural language prompts. DALL-E 2, with four times greater resolution and capable of producing more realistic images compared to DALL-E, uses the Contrastive Language-Image Pre-Training (CLIP) model, which is not exactly a direct Transformer model on its own. DALL-E 2 and DALL-E 3 use transformer-based components for image generation. Stability AI's Stable Diffusion 3 uses transformers as the backbone network, instead of traditional convolutional neural networks, for its multimodal diffusion model.

---

[1] I. Goodfellow, J. Pouget-Abadie, M. Mirza, B. Xu, D. Warde-Farley, S. Ozair, A. Courville, and Y. Bengio, (2020). Generative adversarial networks. *Commun. ACM*, 63(11). https://dl.acm.org/doi/pdf/10.1145/3422622 (Last accessed: 17 May 2025).

[2] D. Kingma and M. Welling, Auto-encoder variational Bayes, 10 December 2022. https://doi.org/10.48550/arXiv.1312.6114 (Last accessed: 17 May 2025).

In the U.S., most generative image models, such as OpenAI's DALL-E 2 and DALL-E 3,[3] Google's Imagen,[4] Midjourney,[5] and Stability AI's Stable Diffusion 3.5[6] (with European roots), leverage diffusion models to generate an image. Diffusion models are employed in the generation of images, videos, and sounds. The concept of diffusion is similar to how diffusion process works in physics, where particles move from areas of higher concentration to areas of lower concentration. Diffusion models are pre-trained with large datasets of images, and they can generate high-quality data (such as images) by iteratively adding noise to the images with the objective of distorting them until they become unrecognisable, and then learning to reverse the process by denoising back step-by-step until a coherent image is obtained. The essence of the Diffusion Transformer model adopted by Stable Diffusion 3 combines a denoising diffusion probabilistic model (DDPM) with the Transformer architecture, encompassing data preprocessing, noise introduction, model training, and the final data (image or video) generation. Data processing allows the input image or video to be converted into a format that can be processed by the model, and it may involve dividing the image into fixed-size patches and transforming these patches to be represented by feature vectors. The feature vectors with added noise are used to train the Diffusion Transformer model. This model learns how to reverse a noise addition process and to get back the original data (image or video) from noisy data. Following model training, new images or videos can be generated by providing noisy data or random noise to the model. A mapping relationship can be established to align noise to original data, and this is used by the generation process.

Generative AI models do not rely on labelled data to create a generative model, and this is an advantage because it is hard to have a balanced dataset with an equal number of images in various categories. Generative models undergo pre-training and derive knowledge from large datasets. These generative models are termed "foundation models" if they undergo

[3] OpenAI, DALL-E, (2021). https://openai.com/index/dall-e/ (Last assessed: 26 January 2025)

[4] C. Saharia, *et al.*, (2022). Photorealistic text-to-image diffusion models with deep language understanding, 36th Conference on Neural Information Processing Systems (NeurIPS 2022). https://proceedings.neurips.cc/paper_files/paper/2022/file/ec795aeadae0b7d230fa35cbaf04c041-Paper-Conference.pdf (Last accessed: 26 January 2025).

[5] Midjourney platform. https://www.midjourney.com/home (Last accessed: 17 May 2025).

[6] Stability AI's Stable Diffusion platform. https://stability.ai/ (Last accessed: 17 May 2025).

a pre-training process. Foundation models have several key characteristics, including pretraining on large datasets so that they can be used without further training, a generalised model which can perform many tasks, large model size and data size, no data labelling being required, and adaptability depending on prompting input.[7]

There is a diverse range of applications of diffusion models, including graphic design, film and animation, music generation, sound design, interactive media, and gaming environments. In digital creation, diffusion models help to speed up the design process significantly from conceptual designs to polished final products. These diffusion models serve as a tool to generate visual content for graphic design and illustration. In the field of film and digital animation, we can foresee more AI animation and films emerging. Stable diffusion models can generate realistic visuals for storytelling, including characters, backgrounds, and dynamic objects within a scene. Seasons, the first full AI anime-style film,[8] is less than two minutes long, and various software tools (including Daz3D, Photoshop, After Effects, Premiere, and Unreal Engine) were used to produce it. The short anime film narrates a story of ageing through the seasons. Stable diffusion is not perfect and has issues with noise and distortion in animation, and these artefacts can be reduced with software manipulation. Future models may have an improved architecture to eliminate noise.

In China, there is strong government backing for AI projects and initiatives, and there is a big push for open-source models to make them more accessible. With such a huge domestic market, there are plentiful opportunities for tech giants to integrate generative AI into different applications (such as e-commerce, social media, advertising, and gaming) to promote scalability.

The key players in the generative image space include Alibaba, Baidu, Tencent, ByteDance, and younger tech companies such as DeepSeek and start-ups. In 2023, Alibaba introduced Tongyi Wanxiang, an image generation software tool that can generate images, and this can advance

[7]B. Bhatti, Essential guide to foundation models and large language models, Medium, 6 February 2023. https://thebabar.medium.com/essential-guide-to-foundation-models-and-large-language-models-27dab58f7404 (Last accessed: 25 January 2025).

[8]D. Yalalov, The artist uses Stable Diffusion to produce the first full AI animation movie, 17 November 2022. https://mpost.io/the-artist-uses-stable-diffusion-to-produce-the-first-full-ai-animation-movie/ (Last accessed: 27 January 2025).

innovative AI art and enhance business creativity with different expressions.[9] In 2024, Baidu launched the iRAG technology with Ernie Bot, which can mitigate hallucination for text-to-image generation and produce hyper-realistic visuals across different mediums, including storyboards, posters, and comics.[10] Tencent Cloud launched a large image creation model as a service, and it can create images with different styles (such as anime, 3D, watercolour, and festive events) from input images and prompts.[11] Released in March 2025, ByteDance's InfiniteYou is able to generate high-quality and realistic images from uploading a single photo and text prompts. ByteDance provides two models, with one optimised for artistic aesthetics while the other for identity preservation. It is important for companies to pay attention to potential ethical risks and privacy violations. The demo version made available on Hugging Face does not enforce strict content moderation against misuses such as deepfakes, misleading content, or non-consensual explicit imagery.[12] DeepSeek introduced a multimodal large language model (LLM), Janus-Pro, in January 2025 after releasing DeepSeek-R1 and DeepSeek-v3.[13] Janus-Pro's image generation capability has beaten that of DALL-E 3 and Stable Diffusion. Although Janus-Pro-7B has achieved average performance compared to other known models across multiple benchmarks, it has managed to score the highest at 84.2% on the GenEval benchmark (which

[9] Alibaba Cloud Blog, Alibaba cloud unveils AI image generation model Tongyi Wanxiang to help businesses to unleash creativity and productivity, 7 July 2023. https://www.alibabacloud.com/blog/alibaba-cloud-unveils-ai-image-generation-model-tongyi-wanxiang-to-help-businesses-to-unleash-creativity-and-productivity_600170 (Last accessed: 2 May 2025).

[10] L. Mo and G. Goh, Baidu bolsters AI lineup with enhanced text-to-image tech, no-code app builder, Reuters, 12 November 2024. https://www.reuters.com/technology/artificial-intelligence/baidu-bolsters-ai-lineup-with-text-to-image-generator-no-code-app-builder-2024-11-12/ (Last accessed: 2 May 2025).

[11] Tencent Cloud, Image Creation Large Model platform. https://www.tencentcloud.com/products/aiart (Last accessed: 3 May 2025).

[12] B. Jacklin, ByteDance Launches "InfiniteYou": Next-Level AI Image Generation, Movavi, 28 March 2025. https://www.movavi.com/news/bytedance-launches-infiniteyou-next-level-ai-image-generation/ (Last accessed: 3 May 2025).

[13] M. Gupta, DeepSeek Janus-Pro: Multimodal LLM with image generation beats DALLE-3, Stable Diffusion, Medium, 28 January 2025. https://medium.com/data-science-in-your-pocket/deepseek-janus-pro-multimodal-llm-with-image-generation-beats-dalle-3-stable-diffusion-94297b946835 (Last accessed: 1 May 2025).

evaluates text-to-image generation) and achieved significantly higher performance at 84.1% for DPG-Bench accuracy (which measures the capability of the model to deal with complex text-to-image generation).

In Japan, the key players are NTT and Fujitsu, working with universities to produce culturally aware AI art. Sakana AI has worked on Swallow, which is a multimodal Japanese model that can be used for text-to-image generation. In March 2025, OpenAI released a new image generator, leveraging GPT-4o to generate Studio Ghibli-style images. However, it went against the philosophy of Studio Ghibli co-founder Hayao Miyazaki.[14] The regulatory landscape in Japan is trending towards encouraging responsible use while not stifling innovation and ensuring voice and artist rights. Their strategic goals seem to gear towards building domain-specific AI tools catering to creative industries such as anime, manga, and gaming illustration. The stylised human–AI co-creation is encouraged rather than viewing AI as a replacement. There is strong support for language-specific multimodal research.

2.2 Generative Video

After a year of text-to-image models appearing in the market in late 2022 and 2023, we saw an increasing number of text-to-video projects in 2024. The progress of generative video seems slower than text-to-image because of the sheer amount of computing resources required for training. The generative video models use various machine learning algorithms and are trained on large datasets of text, images, and videos to learn how the videos look and transition.

The development of generative video has gained traction across different regions of the world. In the U.S., there is an enormous push for technological boundaries towards sophisticated models to produce highly realistic videos. Major technology giants such as Google (DeepMind), OpenAI (Sora), and Meta (MovieGen) are at the forefront of developing large models, and they share a strong research and innovative culture.

OpenAI's Sora was released publicly in December 2024 for ChatGPT Plus and ChatGPT Pro users. The technology behind Sora is based on

[14]D. Placido, The AI-generated studio Ghibli trend explained, Forbes, 27 March 2025. https://www.forbes.com/sites/danidiplacido/2025/03/27/the-ai-generated-studio-ghibli-trend-explained/ (Last accessed: 14 May 25).

DALL-E 3, which is a diffusion transformer, and it generates a video in latent space by denoising 3D patches, and a video decompressor can then transform it.

Google's Veo2, released in December 2024, was able to generate high-quality videos that have improved realism and detail. Veo2 was able to deliver videos spanning a few minutes at resolutions of up to 4K. In the text-to-video prompt, the user can specify a genre, a specific lens, or different effects for Veo2 to generate the video. If you indicate using an 18 mm lens, it will be able to interpret that it is a wide-angle shot and provide a video accordingly. Videos produced by various models often suffer from hallucination with unwanted details (such as an extra finger or object). In addition, it is difficult for videos to maintain temporal incoherence, where the visuals and motion elements are not coherent across multiple frames. Google believes that Veo2 can produce fewer of such unwanted details. Like Sora, Veo2 is likely based on a diffusion transformer architecture, which leverages a transformer network, a diffusion model, and a latent space representation. Transformer models are very effective in dealing with sequential data, including video. According to the benchmark test MovieGenBench,[15] with participants viewing 1,003 prompts and respective videos, Veo 2 performed best on overall preference and its ability to follow prompts accurately.

In China, major technology companies in this GenVideo space include Alibaba (Wan 2.1[16]), Tencent (Hunyuan[17]), ByteDance (VideoWorld[18], OmniHuman[19], MagicVideo-V2[20], and UniDoc[21]),

[15] Google DeepMind, Veo 2, December 2024. https://deepmind.google/technologies/veo/veo-2/ (Last accessed: 4 February 2025).

[16] Wan AI. https://www.wan-ai.org/ (Last accessed: 25 April 2025).

[17] Hunyuan Video platform. https://hunyuanvideoai.com/ (Last accessed: 25 April 2025).

[18] Aibase, Doubao: The video generation model 'VideoWorld' has been open-sourced, achieving pure visual learning, 10 February 2025. https://www.aibase.com/news/15207 (Last accessed: 25 April 2025).

[19] OmniHuman-1 platform. https://www.omnihuman1.org/ (Last accessed: 25 April 2025).

[20] MagicVideo-V2 platform. https://omnihuman-1.com/bytedance/magicvideo-v2#google_vignette (Last accessed: 25 April 2025).

[21] Yicai Global, China's ByteDance reveals world's first video generation tool trained on raw visual data, 11 February 2025. https://www.yicaiglobal.com/news/chinas-bytedance-reveals-worlds-first-video-generation-tool-trained-on-raw-visual-data (Last assessed: 25 April 2025).

Kuaishou (Kling[22]), Shengshu Technology (Vidu[23,24]), and Zhipu AI (Ying[25]). These companies have strong government backing, especially when it comes to AI development, and they push towards open-source models to allow access to these models outside China. There is a large domestic market and steady adoption of unique video creation (such as micro-dramas and short videos) for social media and entertainment. There is a need to be compliant with national security regulations, which may involve censorship and labelling of AI-generated content.

In Europe, there are several strong AI startups but fewer large AI companies of the scale seen in the U.S. and China. These startups include Hugging Face[26], Mistral AI, and Synthesia. Hugging Face is both a platform and a library of open-source pre-trained models and datasets used across various domains, including natural language processing (NLP), audio processing, and computer vision. Hugging Face has provided a good summary of the state of open video generation models in diffusers and has highlighted high resource requirements, limited generalisation capabilities, and high generation latency as the key limitations.[27] Mistral AI is a French AI start-up with its headquarters in Paris, and it works on open-weight LLMs. Synthesia, based in London, develops software to produce AI-generated video content; the software algorithm allows users to create digital representations of themselves, and these avatars can be made to narrate text in multiple languages. The Synthesia software is used by companies for their communication, campaigns, training videos, and product demonstrations, to name but a few. European companies must

[22] Kuaishou news release, Kuaishou unveils proprietary video generation model 'Kling;' testing now available, 10 June 2025. https://ir.kuaishou.com/news-releases/news-release-details/kuaishou-unveils-proprietary-video-generation-model-kling (Last accessed: 25 April 2025).

[23] Shengshu Technology. https://www.shengshu.com/en (Last accessed: 25 April 2025).

[24] Vidu platform. https://www.vidu.com (Last accessed: 25 April 2025).

[25] SCMP, Zhipu AI launches video model in a sign more Chinese tech firms are taking on OpenAI's Sora, 27 July 2024. https://www.scmp.com/tech/tech-trends/article/3272135/zhipu-ai-launches-video-model-sign-more-chinese-tech-firms-are-taking-openais-sora (Last accessed: 26 April 2025).

[26] Hugging Face platform. https://huggingface.co/ (Last accessed: 19 May 2025).

[27] S. Paul, V. Aryan, and D. Nair, State of open video generation models in Diffusers, Hugging Face, 27 January 2025. https://huggingface.co/blog/video_gen (Last accessed: 19 May 2025).

strike a balance between innovation and compliance with regulatory frameworks on ethical AI and user rights.

In Japan, there is an emphasis on national needs when strengthening generative AI capabilities. There are collaborative efforts between universities, industry, and government to optimise the foundational models for the Japanese context. The key players are Fujitsu, Preferred Networks, NTT, and start-ups. The development of the generative AI market is still in earlier stages in comparison with the markets in the U.S. and China. Fujitsu introduced a video analytics AI agent in December 2024, which is focused on using work-related videos to improve efficiency and create a safer working environment for on-site work.[28]

2.3 Generative Audio

There is an enormous interest that fuels the growth of generative AI music because it can be applied to numerous domains such as films and videos, video games, advertisements, marketing, social media, interactive media, and entertainment. According to Grand View Research, the global generative music market size stood around US$440 million in 2023, and the revenue forecast for 2030 was forecasted to be US$678.2 million.[29] The growth rate was projected to be 30.4% from 2024 to 2030. Generative AI in music has enhanced technological capabilities to compose high-quality musical compositions, generate harmonies, and produce lyrics. Numerous new tools help to democratise music generation and provide an opportunity for non-musicians to create music that can sound like professional soundtracks. These AI-driven music platforms support a more efficient workflow and reduce time and costs associated with traditional music production.

Generative music has evolved significantly with the advent of AI. In the early days, between the 1950s and 1970s, the automated creation of music compositions used mathematical and stochastic methods. Professor

[28] Fujitsu, A research vision to enhance video understanding and knowledge conversion – breakthrough in long-term video analysis to support the video analytics AI agent, 28 February 25. (Last assessed: 25 April 25 https://www.fujitsu.com/global/about/research/article/202502-video-analytics-ai-agent.html).

[29] Grand View Research, Generative AI in Music Market Size, Industry Report, (2023). https://www.grandviewresearch.com/industry-analysis/generative-ai-in-music-market-report (Last accessed: 27 April 2025).

Lejaren Hiller from the University of Illinois had programmed the computer to compose *Illiac Suite* using a rule-based approach, where the score was composed by the computer and musical material was modified in accordance with various functions. He premiered a concert recital to debut *Illiac Suite* on 9 August 1956.[30] Iannis Xenakis created a composition using a stochastic approach, explained in his book *Formalized Music*,[31] where computations are made to compose a score from note densities and probabilistic weights set by the programmer. Other ways of generating music in the 1980s include using algorithmic composition systems such as fractals, Markov chains, and L-systems.

From the early 2000s to 2015, there was an interest in using machine learning to compose music and in music analysis. Recurrent neural networks (RNNs) were one of the numerous machine learning algorithms used to analyse musical structures and create new sequences. In the 2010s, there was an emergence of deep learning models and neural networks used for generative music. Magenta was a project launched by Google in 2016 to use machine learning for generating music.[32] Magenta used Long Short-Term Memory (LSTM) networks, a type of RNN, to create melodies and harmonies.

From 2016 onwards, there were advancements in music AI models with breakthroughs in transformer-based and diffusion models, significantly improving music generation capabilities. Google introduced Music Transformer in 2018, which used the transformer model's self-attention mechanisms to create music, maintaining long-range coherence.[33] This transformer model can maintain musical structure and outperform RNNs.

[30] J. Gage, 'He touched a nerve': How the first piece of AI music was born in 1956, The Guardian, 7 December 2021. https://www.theguardian.com/music/2021/dec/07/he-touched-a-nerve-how-the-first-piece-of-ai-music-was-born-in-1956 (Last accessed: 6 February 25).

[31] I. Xenakis, *Formalized Music: Thought and Mathematics in Composition*, Bloomington and London: Indiana University Press, pp. 387, 1971.

[32] A. Mishra, Understanding Google Magenta: An Overview of Google's Open-Source Music and Art Project, Medium, 12 March 2023. https://medium.com/@abhishek-mishra13k/understanding-google-magenta-an-overview-of-googles-open-source-music-and-art-project-48ea9ee80024 (Last accessed: 8 February 2025).

[33] C. Huang, *et al*, Music Transformer: Generating Music with Long-Term Structure, Google Brain, 2018. https://arxiv.org/pdf/1809.04281 (Last accessed: 8 February 2025)

OpenAI's Jukebox is a neural network-based model for generating raw audio in the format of music with vocals using text prompts, launched in 2020.[34] The model can generate coherent musical structures with verses, choruses, and bridges. Genre consistency can be managed relatively well while maintaining the stylistic elements of the track. For a longer track, it is harder to handle because they may become repetitive or lose coherence over time. Lyrical sense is hard to control beyond short phrases. It uses Vector Quantised Variational Autoencoder (VQ-VAE) and transformers to directly create raw instrumental and vocal music instead of MIDI. The user can request the model to produce stylistically consistent music based on specified parameters (genres, artists, and lyrics). Users can request "a jazz song in the style of Nat King Cole" with specific lyrics. The VQ-VAE architecture can compress audio into discrete tokens, and an autoregressive transformer model can create sequences of these tokens, which can be decoded back to audio. The vocal performance produces realistic intonation and vibrato with emotional expression; however, the lyrics can be hard to grasp due to poor articulation at times. Sometimes, the audio can sound distorted and blurry in complex musical arrangements. Jukebox's lyrical generation strengths include its ability to compose original lyrics, or users can provide lyrics for the model to sing with a realistic melody, and usually the lyrics are able to match the music's emotional tone. The limitations include the possibility of nonsensical or repetitive lyrics in longer songs and pronunciation clarity in fast-paced vocals.

Google introduced MusicLM in 2023, which can generate high-fidelity music from text descriptions.[35] It can outperform Google's earlier models in terms of audio quality and adherence to text description by combining hierarchical sequence-to-sequence with latent audio tokens.[36] MusicLM is more focused on music, able to achieve varied genres and coherent styles, but it is limited in vocal and lyrical coherence. MusicLM leads in creating long, coherent instrumental compositions.

---

[34] P. Dhariwal, *et al.*, (2020). Jukebox: A Generative Model for Music, OpenAI. https://arxiv.org/pdf/2005.00341 (Last accessed: 8 February 2025).

[35] K. Yim, and H. Manickavasagam, Turn ideas into Music with MusicLM, Google Blog, 10 May 2023. https://blog.google/technology/ai/musiclm-google-ai-test-kitchen/ (Last accessed: 8 February 2025).

[36] A. Agostinelli, *et al.*, MusicLM: Generating Music from Text, Google Research, 26 January 2023. https://arxiv.org/pdf/2301.11325 (Last accessed: 8 February 2025).

Meta launched the Audiocraft[37] framework in August 2023, to produce high-quality, realistic music and audio based on text inputs, and it comprises three different models: MusicGen, AudioGen, and EnCodec. MusicGen[38] can generate high-quality music (both mono and stereo) based on text prompts, and it is trained on Meta's licensed or owned music. MusicGen is a single-stage transformer LM operating with token interleaving patterns, and it eliminates cascading several models using hierarchical or upsampling.[39]

AudioGen focused on generating audio outputs (i.e., sound effects) based on text prompts of an acoustic scene, and 10 datasets containing different types of audio and text annotations were curated to train this model.[40,41] EnCodec can enhance music generation quality, generating music with fewer audio artefacts. EnCodec[42,43] is trained to compress audio and reconstruct the original signal with high fidelity by using an autoencoder to produce several parallel streams of audio tokens, and these different streams can capture different levels of information from the audio waveform and eventually reconstruct the audio using all the streams.

JASCO, a model developed based on the capabilities of AudioCraft, was introduced by Meta's Fundamental AI Research (FAIR) team in June 2024.[44] The model uses multimodal input integration and can generate

---

[37] MetaAI, Open Sourcing AudioCraft: Generative AI for audio made simple and available to all, Meta Blog, 2 August 2023. https://ai.meta.com/blog/audiocraft-musicgen-audiogen-encodec-generative-ai-audio/ (Last accessed: 2 August 2023).

[38] Meta AI, MusicGen Demo, (2023). https://audiocraft.metademolab.com/musicgen.html (Last accessed: 8 February 2025).

[39] J. Copet *et al.*, (2023). Simple and controllable music generation, 37th Conference on Neural Information Processing Systems (NeurIPS). https://arxiv.org/pdf/2306.05284 (Last accessed: 8 February 2025).

[40] Meta AI, AudioGen Demo, (2023). https://audiocraft.metademolab.com/audiogen.html (Last accessed: 8 February 2025).

[41] F. Kreuk *et al.*, (2023). AudioGen: Textually guided audio generation, ICLR. https://arxiv.org/pdf/2209.15352 (Last accessed: 8 February 2025).

[42] Meta AI, Encodec Demo, (2023). https://audiocraft.metademolab.com/encodec.html (Last accessed: 8 February 2025).

[43] A. Defossez, *et al.*, (2022). High fidelity neural audio compression, Meta AI. https://arxiv.org/pdf/2210.13438 (Last accessed: 8 February 2025).

[44] O. Tal *et al.*, Joint audio and symbolic conditioning for temporally controlled text-to-music generation, Hebrew University of Jerusalem & Meta FAIR Team, June 2024. https://arxiv.org/pdf/2406.10970 (Last accessed: 9 February 2025).

music with both text descriptions and musical input elements (such as chords or beats), which allows for greater control and structured music creation. By providing musical element inputs, users can guide the model to create music that aligns with certain desired rhythmic patterns or harmonic progressions. JASCO can produce high-quality output that can maintain coherence and musicality.

Riffusion, an open-source AI model, was launched in 2023, with its fundamental technology being Stable Diffusion, used for image generation.[45] Instead of generating sounds directly like the above-discussed models, Riffusion provides a unique method to generate sound by first generating images of sounds, particularly spectrograms, which are visual representations of audio frequencies over time. The spectrogram visuals produced can be converted back into audio, which facilitates the generation of music using text prompts.

In 2024, Stability AI released Stable Audio 2.0, which is able to generate high-quality full tracks up to 3 minutes at 44.1 kHz stereo. This model has a text-to-audio and audio-to-audio feature that permits users to upload audio samples and transform them using natural language prompts. The approach taken by Stable Audio 2.0 is ethical because it was trained solely on a licensed dataset obtained from the AudioSparx music library, rather than failing to declare where the corpus of music for training had been obtained. It supports opt-out requests by creators and ensures fair compensation if their works are used.

Soundraw[46] is a platform that can generate tracks with AI; it allows users to make background music and songs, and it supports distributing and selling songs. Soundraw allows users to create music depending on their preferences, mood, genre, and length. Users can make granular adjustments to the tracks, which include tempo, instruments, and intensity. Editing music can be quite restrictive. Soundraw is more suitable for content creators, such as marketers and vloggers, rather than musicians. AIVA[47] is another AI-driven platform that allows users to generate music in more than 250 different styles.

---

[45] D. Coldewey, Try 'Riffusion,' an AI model that composes music by visualizing it, Tech Crunch, 15 December 2022. https://techcrunch.com/2022/12/15/try-riffusion-an-ai-model-that-composes-music-by-visualizing-it/ (Last accessed: 9 February 2025).

[46] Soundraw platform. https://soundraw.io/ (Last accessed: 28 April 2025).

[47] AIVA. https://www.aiva.ai/ (Last accessed: 28 April 2025).

The U.S. has spearheaded innovative ideas in creating audio with tech companies (such as Google, Meta, and OpenAI) and music specialist companies (Soundraw and AVIVA) making advancements in this field. In the U.S., there are several lawsuits filed by copyright holders against AI developers because their copyrighted material was used in the training of the AI models without expressed permission. Major record companies, namely Universal Music Group NV, Warner Music Group Corp., and Sony Music Entertainment, sued Suno AI and Uncharted Labs Inc., as well as the developer of Udio AI, for copyright infringements.[48] They alleged these companies have used a large volume of their copyrighted sound recordings unlawfully for AI model training. This lawsuit is the first of its kind because it is the first time it has been brought against a music/audio-driven generative AI program. Previous lawsuits related to generative AI have been focused on text and image generation. Copyright and ethical use are concerns companies need to address. Moving forward, tech companies can only use uncopyrighted material or seek prior permission from copyright holders before training them.

China has made swift progress in advancing generative audio technology, and notable companies such as Baidu and Alibaba have introduced AI models for audio. Futureverse, an AI, metaverse, and content creation company, had partnered with Alibaba to train their text-to-music generation model JEN-1, leveraging Alibaba Cloud's Platform for Artificial Intelligence (PAI). As claimed by the start-up, JEN-1 demonstrates higher fidelity and state-of-the-art performance compared to Meta's MusicLM and Google's MusicGen.[49] Baidu showed that ERNIE-Music performed well in text-to-waveform tasks. Baidu researchers collected data from Chinese music platforms and were able to assemble 3,890 text–music pairs.[50] The texts are popular comments on platforms and have useful music-related information, including genres, musical

[48] A. Carman and R. Metz, Major Record Labels Sue AI Music Generators, The Times, 24 June 2024. https://time.com/6991466/record-labels-sue-ai-music-generator-startups/ (Last accessed: 28 April 2025).

[49] Alibaba Blog, Startup Futureverse's CEO on Making Music with AI and Alibaba Cloud, 10 January 2024. https://www.alibabacloud.com/blog/startup-futureverse%E2%80%99s-ceo-on-making-music-with-ai-and-alibaba-cloud_600749 (Last accessed: 28 April 2025).

[50] The decoder, Baidu shows ERNIE-Music – a breakthrough for text-to-waveform?, 22 February 2023. https://the-decoder.com/baidu-shows-ernie-music-a-breakthrough-for-text-to-waveform/ (Last accessed: 29 April 2025).

instruments, and human emotions, about the 20-second tracks. ERNIE-Music was able to generate a wide range of instruments, melodies, and emotions from text descriptions.

In Europe, there is a strong academic direction and greater emphasis on human-centred AI, cultural heritage, and ethical considerations. Research institutes (such as France's IRCAM) and start-ups such as Hugging Face are key players in Europe. IRCAM is a French institute specialising in music and sound research, with a focus on avant-garde and electro-acoustic art music. IRCAM has developed generative music tools such as Somax2[51] for musical improvisation and composition with AI, and RAVE[52] for audio processing using deep learning. Based in London, ElevenLabs,[53] an AI audio start-up, was established in 2022 by a pair of Polish founders, and its AI-driven platform supports text-to-speech conversion and can dub audio in more than 25 languages.

In Japan, the focus is on building generative audio that can resonate with Japanese musical aesthetics and preserve Japanese culture. Instead of replicating the LLM approach established by other big tech firms, NTT had expressed that they would want to differentiate themselves in creating generative AI capable of developing a cooperative society with numerous smaller AI systems, each having its own purpose, such as for the well-being of people and society.[54] NTT has developed a real-time low-latency voice conversion technology that produces high-quality sound using deep learning.[55] Possible applications include converting texts to a voice that suits your avatar to better reflect the persona and converting customer voice into a standard voice to protect customer privacy. Kotoba Technologies worked on Japanese-centric LLMs and employed Fugaku, a supercomputer which at one time was ranked the second fastest.[56]

[51] SOMAX2 project with source code. https://forum.ircam.fr/projects/detail/somax-2/ (Last accessed: 29 April 2025).

[52] RAVE project. https://forum.ircam.fr/collections/detail/rave/ (Last accessed: 29 April 2025).

[53] ElevenLabs platform. https://elevenlabs.io (Last accessed: 1 May 2025).

[54] NTT blog, NTT: Generative AI with a Purpose, 19 July 2023. https://group.ntt/en/magazine/blog/generative_ai/ (Last accessed: 29 April 2025).

[55] NTT newsroom, A generative AI that can instantly change your voice and speaking style – High quality and low-latency real-time voice conversion, 17 June 2024. https://group.ntt/en/newsrelease/2024/06/17/240617a.html (Last accessed: 29 April 2025).

[56] Kotoba Technologies. https://www.kotoba.tech/en/home (Last accessed: 1 May 2025).

Kotoba was able to improve the capabilities of generative audio, particularly speech, and to use it in different applications. On 28 October 2024, Kotoba Technologies released the Japanese speech generation model playground known as Kotoba SpeechGen, and it has the following features: using preset voices to create natural Japanese speech with fluency, voice cloning permitted by allowing users to upload their own voice files for cloning, and Providing multilingual capability in real time.[57]

2.4 Potential, Issues, and Future of Generative Image, Video, and Music

Generative music enables the generation of original compositions without direct human intervention. The leading generative music models, such as Google's MusicLM, Meta's AudioCraft, OpenAI's Jukebox, and other AI-based platforms, are revolutionising how music making is done. The potential of generative music is immense. It provides democratisation of music production, meaning anyone can create professional-quality music without formal training in instruments, music theory, or production tools. It allows new forms of interactive and adaptive music to be created. In mixed reality and gaming environments, AI can generate dynamic soundscapes based on user interaction or gameplay.

Rapid prototyping and ideation are significantly supported by generative AI. Businesses can iterate faster, with generative AI coming up with mock-ups and prototypes of new product designs. Furniture companies can use generative models to visualise futuristic furniture designs using input prompts. Personalisation can be offered at scale since generative AI can produce hyper-customised content for marketing, social media, and education. Healthcare enhancements and medical research advances can be made, with AI assisting in generating high-resolution medical images for diagnostic purposes and making a more accurate prediction of patients' conditions.

[57]Kotaba Technologies news, Selected for second phase of the domestic generative AI development project "GENIAC" and Beta release of the advanced Japanese speech generation model playground "Kotoba SpeechGen", 28 October 2024. https://www.kotoba.tech/en/news-all/selected-for-the-second-phase-of-the-domestic-generative-ai-development-project-geniac-amp-beta-release-of-the-advanced-japanese-speech-generation-model-playground-kotoba-speechgen (Last accessed: 1 May 2025).

The future of generative AI is promising, with potential for improved realism and control. Future music generation models can generate studio-quality music with high-fidelity audio, and users can exercise fine-tuning controls over key, tempo, instrumentation, and mood. We can envisage AI-generated music that can be created in real time based on live performance dynamics. DJs can use AI to remix tracks live and create a unique playlist for every event. There will be greater multimodal integration with AI, seamlessly integrating video, music, and text to create a full multimedia experience based on a single prompt.

There are several issues in generative AI. Ethical concerns include deepfake risks because AI can generate hyper-realistic images, videos, and audio which may be used for identity theft, misinformation, or manipulation. As seen circulating on social media, these are fake images and videos of political figures and celebrities, as well as misleading images and videos of events. AI generative elements can make fake news seem more credible and are blurring the line between fiction and reality. These AI-generated images and videos of fake events (such as disasters and government announcements) can spread misinformation and disinformation, causing widespread panic online. There may be questions of intellectual property rights over AI-generated images, videos, and audio. Who is the owner of the AI elements – the owner of the AI platform, the model's developer, the data source, or the user? There are copyright concerns regarding trained datasets for generative AI models because some copyrighted texts, images, videos, and audios are used without explicit consent from creators. Models may be biased if they are trained on biased datasets, and this will result in producing stereotypes, excluding minority representations, or producing culturally insensitive content. Artefacts produced may be inaccurate, distorted, unrealistic, or inconsistent in detail. For example, there is a lack of diversity in AI-generated characters or scenes. Quality control is a challenge because certain technical limitations may cause videos to suffer from inconsistent lighting, blurred details, and jittery motion. AI-generated human faces and movements may appear unnatural.

Open-source models will promote democratised access further, allowing even individuals without formal art training to create and come up with images and designs. Individuals, hobbyists, and small businesses can all jump into innovation. To differentiate original or AI-generated content, we can incorporate built-in digital watermarks to detect AI-generated content. To prevent unauthorised reproduction of original works, protection and authentication of digital art can be carried out using blockchain. Strong AI governance is necessary on AI-generated content to ensure ethical development and use. By addressing issues related to ethical concerns, intellectual property, bias, and authenticity, we can enrich creativity, culture, and the human experience by harnessing the potential of generative image, video, and audio. Increasingly, there are more opportunities for using generative images as a tool for collaboration, fuelling human–AI co-creation. Generative image tools can be used as creative assistants, generating new ideas, drafting storyboards, and producing numerous iterations to assist individual artists or teams of artists in their project development. The artists can explore different styles and abstract ideas with the help of the AI tool and further refine their work to better meet their end goals. The future of generative AI will be a fusion of human artistry and AI advancements, generating images, videos, and audios that are beyond our imagination.

Chapter 3

LLM Development in Japan, China, the EU, and the U.S.A.

3.1 Language and Cultural Focus

According to Statista, as of January 2024, the language most used for web content is English at 52.1%, and Japanese is at 4.3%.[1] One of the key knowledge sources for LLMs for training is the vast amount of data collected from the Internet, and if there is less Japanese data on the Internet, the system may not generate an accurate response. Japanese researchers believe in building their own LLMs because AI systems built on a foreign language did not seem to fully understand the intricacies of their language and culture.[2] The current form of ChatGPT may generate extremely rare characters not commonly used in Japanese responses, and it sometimes fails to apply cultural sensitivities when producing responses in Japanese. This can be attributed to limited data trained; moreover, the 26-character Western alphabet system is very different from the Japanese system of 2 groups of 48 characters (known as hiragana and katakana) as well as 2000 commonly used Kanji characters (though there are more than 50,000 characters). In May 2023, four organisations, namely, Tokyo

[1] Statista, Languages most frequently used for web content as of January 2024, by share of websites, 2024. https://www.statista.com/statistics/262946/most-common-languages-on-the-internet/ (Last accessed: 9 November 2024).

[2] T. Hornyak, Why Japan is building its own version of ChatGPT, *Nature*, 14 September 2023. https://www.nature.com/articles/d41586-023-02868-z (Last accessed: 28 October 2024).

Institute of Technology (Tokyo Tech), Tohoku University, Fujitsu Limited, and RIKEN, collaborated on the development of an LLM that could be widely adopted by companies and academia, using the supercomputer Fugaku which can support large-scale distributed deep learning features.[3] There has been an outpouring of investment by the Japanese government and companies into training LLMs that can better interpret Japanese cultural and linguistic nuances as compared with recent ChatGPT-like models. Japanese researchers have invented the Rakuda ranking to evaluate if LLMs can answer Japanese-specific questions and check the sensitivity of LLMs to Japanese culture. The current best Japanese LLM is ranked below GPT-4 and GPT-3.5.[4] Japanese models seek to maintain the nuances of Japanese communication, which may not be adequately sufficient in LLMs trained on English language data. Japanese LLMs may serve domestic needs well, but will likely require adaptation for international applications catering to a broader audience.

EU LLMs focus on multilingual specialisations and support multiple European languages, such as French, German, and Italian. Their emphasis is to ensure that the trained models take into consideration European cultural and ethical sensitivity and are compliant with European values and regulations. Aleph Alpha's Luminous model is a European-based AI model.[5] BLOOM (BigScience Large Open-science Open-access Multilingual Language Model) is an open-source model, with 1200 contributors from 39 countries. With support from French research agencies such as CNRS and GENCI, the training of the model was conducted on the Jean Zay supercomputer based in Paris.[6] By focusing on linguistic

---

[3] Press Release, Tokyo Tech, Tohoku University, Fujitsu, and RIKEN start collaboration to develop distributed training of large language models, 22 May 2023. https://www.fujitsu.com/global/about/resources/news/press-releases/2023/0522-01.html (Last accessed: 29 October 2024).

[4] M. Bastian, Japan develops its own cultural sensitive language model, The Decoder, 15 September 2023. https://the-decoder.com/japan-develops-its-own-culturally-sensitive-language-model/ (Last accessed: 29 October 2024).

[5] M. Mezger, Quickstart with a European-based large language model: Aleph Alpha's 'Luminous', Adesso Blog, 10 July 23. https://www.adesso.de/en/news/blog/quickstart-with-a-european-based-large-language-model-aleph-alphas-luminous.jsp (Last accessed: 3 November 2024).

[6] Novita AI, BLOOM : An in-depth guide for the multilingual large language model, 19 April 2024. https://medium.com/@marketing_novita.ai/bloom-an-in-depth-guide-for-the-multilingual-large-language-model-a9aaa7cd08a4 (Last accessed: 3 November 2024).

diversity and cultural inclusivity in a diverse population, European LLMs may not have sufficient resources to meet the scale of the U.S.-developed LLMs, which are more focused on the English language.

Chinese LLMs are designed to work with high-precision accuracy with Mandarin and Chinese dialects, Chinese language nuances, and align to Chinese cultural and government sensitivity. *China Science Daily* has reported that Baidu's Ernie 3.5 has surpassed ChatGPT3.5, GPT-4, and LLaMa models (such as LLaMa-7B and LLaMa-65B) in Chinese language capabilities.[7,8] Alibaba's Tongyi Qianwen model (Qwen2.5) performed better than GPT-4 in language and creation capabilities but lacked in other categories such as knowledge and math, according to the evaluation platform OpenCompass.[9,10] Chinese models serve domestic needs, but their strict adherence to socialist values and state policies may not be so adaptable to other cultural contexts.

U.S.-developed LLMs like Meta's Llama, OpenAI's GPT, and Google's Gemini are English-centric models, aligned to Western cultural perspectives, practices, and values. These U.S. LLMs can have global reach, but may require localisation efforts for more diverse cultural settings.

3.2 Architecture

Most of the notable LLMs (such as OpenAI's ChatGPT, Meta's LLaMA, and Google's Bard and Gemini) in the U.S. have been developed based on the Transformer architecture because of its scalability, parallelisation capability, and self-attention mechanism.

[7]Baidu Research, Introducing ERNIE 3.5: Baidu's knowledge-enhanced foundation model takes a giant leap forward, 27 June 23. https://research.baidu.com/Blog/index-view?id=185 (Last accessed: 7 November 2024).

[8]China Science Daily, 独家：百度文心大模型3.5已内测应用，实测得分超 ChatGPT, 20 June 2023. https://mp.weixin.qq.com/s/QVdkmofRSTgjQ7UOFX7s1g (Last accessed: 7 November 2024).

[9]S. Chiang, Alibaba rolls out latest version of its large language model to meet robust AI demand, *CNBC News*, 10 May 24. https://www.cnbc.com/2024/05/09/alibaba-rolls-out-latest-version-of-its-large-language-model.html (Last accessed: 7 November 2024).

[10]OpenCompass, CompassBench large language model leaderboard. https://rank.opencompass.org.cn/leaderboard-llm/?m=24-03 (Last accessed: 7 November 2024).

Increasingly, Mixture of Experts (MoE), which divides an AI model into separate parts ("experts") and allows selective activation of specific parts of the model for a task, can enhance efficiency and greatly reduce computation costs. This approach was rumoured to be used in OpenAI's GPT-4.[11] Multimodal integration was supported, it encompasses training of text, images, audio, videos, and code for a model. This allowed utilising transformer-based multimodal embeddings to represent these real-world data. This allows Google Gemini to perform semantic searches with text and other multimodal inputs.[12] LLMs from top tech firms are deeply integrated within their hyperscale cloud network, namely, Azure, AWS, and Google Cloud. As models may not be able to understand the context and human preferences fully and may produce biased output, they are fined-tuned with Reinforcement Learning from Human Feedback (RLHF), a technique that builds in human preferences, values, and expectations into the training process.[13]

A knowledge graph is a representation of entities and the relationships between them. Entities can include objects, situations, and events. Knowledge graphs are used in healthcare, recommender systems, fraud detection, and as virtual assistants. Netflix uses a knowledge graph to recommend content by linking user preferences with similar content. Chinese LLMs like Baidu's Ernie integrate knowledge graphs into their LLM to counter the limitations of LLMs such as "hallucination" and to enhance factual accuracy that is critical in domains such as medicine or law.

In December 2024, a Hangzhou-based start-up in China launched DeepSeek V3 LLM, which had a significant breakthrough in terms of performance based on benchmark tests, outperforming reputed models such as Meta and OpenAI in various benchmark categories. DeepSeek

[11] S. Betts, Peering inside GPT-4: Understanding its Mixture of Experts (MoE) architecture, *Medium*, 29 July 2023. https://medium.com/@seanbetts/peering-inside-gpt-4-understanding-its-mixture-of-experts-moe-architecture-2a42eb8bdcb3 (Last accessed: 14 May 2025).

[12] C. Shelar, Gemini in BigQuery: Unlocking multimodal search with vector embeddings, *Medium*, 5 December 2024. https://medium.com/google-cloud/gemini-in-bigquery-unlocking-multimodal-search-with-vector-embeddings-part-2-69e26c36fee5 (Last accessed: 14 May 2025).

[13] N. Lambert, L. Casticato, L. Werra and A. Havrilla, Illustrating Reinforcement Learning from Human Feedback (RLHF), HuggingFace, 9 February 2022. https://huggingface.co/blog/rlhf (Last accessed: 14 May 2025).

was a spin-off in July 2023 from its parent company High-Flyer Quant (a major Chinese Quantitative Hedge Fund), which uses AI to manage quantitative hedge funds. DeepSeek V3, with 671 billion parameters and 14 billion Multi-Token Prediction (MTP) Module weights, was trained in 55 days at a cost of US$5.58 million, utilising 2.8 million GPU hours, and this has significantly outperformed the other leading AI models on cost efficiency. OpenAI has reported that GPT-4's training cost was over US$100 million, and it took 100 days to train it, utilising 25,000 Nvidia A100 GPUs. The training cost of Llama 3 was at least $600 million in terms of GPU cost alone, clocking 6.4M GPU hours, utilising 24,576 Nvidia T100 Tensor Core GPUs.[14] Meta had announced plans to scale its infrastructure to 350,000 H100 GPUs. Despite DeepSeek V3 being trained on the Nvidia H800 GPU, a less superior GPU compared to Nvidia A100 and Nvidia H100, it was able to perform to the same level as OpenAI's GPT-4.0 and Anthropic's Claude 3.5.

Due to U.S. sanctions in 2022, Nvidia's two most advanced chips, A100 and newer H100 AI chips, were not made available to Chinese companies with the intent to slow down China's AI development, citing national security concerns. These chips are important to develop generative AI models, like OpenAI's ChatGPT and Meta's Llama LLM. For export to China, Nvidia had to release lesser superior versions (with reduced capabilities) known as A800 and H800 of the two chips A100 and H100, respectively. Moreover, it was reported that H800 has half the chip-to-chip transfer rate of the flagship H100.[15] Low transfer rates will require more training time, given that AI models are to be trained on a large corpus of data. The U.S.'s AI chips rule focused on two restrictions: (1) how fast chips can communicate with one another since thousands of chips had to be linked up and (2) how much computing power the AI chip can have.[16]

---

[14]Nvidia Blog, Wide open: Nvidia accelerates inference on Meta Llama 3, 18 April 2024. https://blogs.nvidia.com/blog/meta-llama3-inference-acceleration/#:~:text=Meta%20engineers%20trained%20Llama%203,NVIDIA%20Quantum-2%20InfiniBand%20networks.

[15]Reuters, Nvidia tweaks flagship H100 chip for export to China as H800, 22 March 2023. https://www.reuters.com/technology/nvidia-tweaks-flagship-h100-chip-export-china-h800-2023-03-21/ (Last accessed: 4 January 2025).

[16]S. Nellis and K. Freifeld, US mulls new export restriction on computing power in AI chips, *Reuters*, 29 June 2023. https://www.reuters.com/technology/us-mulls-new-export-restriction-computing-power-ai-chips-2023-06-28/ (Last accessed: 15 January 2025).

As DeepSeek does not have the most powerful chips compared to other leading AI companies in the U.S., its success is attributed to its architecture that reduces computational cost, hence increasing the efficiency of the model. The DeepSeek V3 adopted a Mixture-of-Experts (MoE) architecture, where it was able to engage only a subset of expert neurons for a given input instead of activating the entire network simultaneously, reducing computational cost, resulting in higher throughput and faster inference time. DeepSeek has another architectural feature known as Multi-head Latent Attention (MLA), which improves the model's ability to work with longer-range dependencies in text and is more effective in text summarisation, logical reasoning, answering questions, and conversational AI. Besides DeepSeek, ByteDance's Doubao also adopts a lightweight MoE and implements parameter tuning to scale on limited compute resources. To handle longer contexts and a lower memory requirement, some LLMs have used a mixture of dense and sparse attention models.

Alibaba launched a new revamped version of the AI app Quark, an AI assistant with a Qwen-based reasoning model powered by Alibaba's custom AI models on 13 March 2025, and this version of the application already has over 200 million users from the China market.[17] Alibaba claimed that their newly unveiled AI model Qwen QwQ-32B can rival DeepSeek RI and has met expectations in official benchmark tests.[18] Alibaba announced its strategic partnership with Apple for its AI model to feature on iPhones, and it had struck up another partnership with Monica, the company that launched Manus AI.

Although Baidu was the first Chinese company to launch LLM in China sometime in March 2023, it was not able to significantly increase its prominence in the AI race with so many domestic players such as Alibaba, Tencent, and Bytedance integrating their models into their respective businesses and gaining user traction. On 16 March 2025, Baidu launched 2 AI models: multimodal foundation model Ernie 4.5 and reasoning model Ernie X1. Baidu claimed that its reasoning model Ernie X1 could perform as well as DeepSeek R1 and at half its price; however,

[17]Huaxia, Alibaba revamps flagship AI app Quark for enhanced user experience, *Xinhua News*, 14 March 2025. https://english.news.cn/20250314/37ea14f84d984cc7aa76b6914efae0e7/c.html (Last accessed: 17 March 2025).

[18]A. Bao, Alibaba launches new version of AI assistant tool as competition heats up, *CNBC*, 13 March 2025. https://www.cnbc.com/2025/03/13/alibaba-launches-new-version-of-ai-assistant-tool-as-competition-heats-up.html (Last accessed: 17 March 2025).

it did not produce benchmark results. The price of business access to the application programming interface API of Ernie X1 is US$0.28 per million token inputs and US$1.12 per million token outputs, and that is about half of what Deep Seek is charging for its reasoning model R1.[19] Baidu's Ernie 4.5 with multimodal capabilities, which support images, audio, and video, indicated that it managed to surpass OpenAI's GPT-4o for a number of benchmark platforms, such as CCBench and OCRBench. The text capabilities of Ernie 4.5 are on par with OpenAI's GPT-4.5 and outperformed DeepSeek v3 on numerous benchmarks. Robin Li, Baidu's CEO, said Ernie 4.5 would be made open source from 30 June 2025, a deviation from its past practice of closed-source AI development. Many Chinese companies have shifted to this mindset as they believe open source will drive broader adoption, as the barrier of entry is lower.

In Europe, there is architecture focus by European initiatives like OpenEuroLLM and Pythia. Both are non-Llama based models. EU companies and residents are excluded from Llama 4 multimodal models due to strict restriction and compliance imposed on AI systems because of EU's AI Act enacted in 2024. These initiatives are open and transparent about their data. The architecture, datasets, training scripts, and evaluation criteria are open for audit. The LLMs are designed to enhance explainability, fair audit, and mitigate biasness.

In Japan, the Research and Development Centre for Large Language Models at National Institute of Informatics has developed llm-jp-3-7.2b and llm-jp-3-172b-instruct3[20] using culturally aware LLaMa variants that use Rotary Positional Encoding (RoPE) with a Japanese tokeniser vocab to achieve better performance working on kanji, kana, and syntax. The LLMs are subjected to instruction and role tuning so that there is greater emphasis on politeness, role adaptation, and nuances in various contexts in native communication. NTT has a multimodal LLM that is still a work in progress. There is also a focus on extending the context window for the

[19] X. Shen, Baidu launches new AI models, touts superiority to DeepSeek, OpenAI on benchmarks, *SCMP*, 16 March 2025. https://www.scmp.com/tech/big-tech/article/3302563/baidu-launches-new-ai-models-touts-superiority-deepseek-openai-benchmarks?module=perpetual_scroll_0&pgtype=article (Last accessed: 17 March 2025).

[20] NII News, A fully open large language model with approximately 172 billion parameters (GPT3-Level): "llm-jp-3-172b-instruct3" now publicly available – Achieving performance beyond GPT-3.5, 24 December 24. https://www.nii.ac.jp/en/news/release/2024/1224.html (Last accessed: 14 May 25).

number of allowable tokens to achieve long-context capability when doing research work.

3.3 Proprietary, Open Source, and Commercialisation

Open-source LLMs can foster greater collaboration and advance innovation in the AI space. Proprietary LLMs can offer competitive advantages for technology companies since they have intellectual property rights and there is a higher potential to derive greater revenue. LLMs across different regions have adopted distinct approaches regarding proprietary or open-source models.

In the U.S., Meta's LLaMA is considered an open-source, free-of-charge model, with downloadable AI models, and it helps to facilitate research and development. However, it does come with restrictions on commercial usage and that means it is not fully open source. Most of the other U.S. technology companies like OpenAI, Google DeepMind, Microsoft, and Anthropic offer primarily proprietary LLMs that have limited transparency regarding their architecture, full training dataset, and code. These LLMs are accessible via API or integration into their products or services, and are not downloadable. OpenAI's GPT-4 models are accessible via API if you are on a paid subscription. Microsoft's offers integration of GPT into its Microsoft Office software and browsers. Google's Gemini and Anthropic's Claude are accessible via a web browser. U.S. companies focused on a closed model to ensure they have a competitive advantage over others and can achieve enterprise monetisation through enterprise licensing and subscription-based services. These LLM models can be integrated into applications within the tech firm's ecosystem, and some of these applications may be in the form of tools for productivity, customer service, code generation, and content creation.

In China, LLMs have officially sanctioned accessibility. Many Chinese companies developed proprietary LLMs, and they are required to seek approval from the Chinese government for their LLMs to be released to the public. Beijing has stringent requirements for AI models. The first batch of LLMs approved by a Chinese regulatory body was in August 2023, and they were mostly general AI models. In January 2024, China approved another batch of LLMs for commercial use, which are several specific LLMs. Established in 2023, the China Electronic Standardisation Institute, which is under the Ministry of Industry and Information Technology (MITT), enacted a local standard for LLMs to support AI development initiatives in China.[21] Chinese companies are interested in developing open-source AI models because they are likely to embed them in their commercial applications, which may go global. These Chinese companies would also like their AI models to be used overseas so that they can circumvent tech restrictions and be an important player in the AI arena.[22] As reported by SCMP, Robin Li, founder of Baidu, believed that releasing Ernie Bot to hundreds of millions of users could help in improving the model because the feedback could encompass a broad set of use cases.[23] ErnieBot is embedded into Baidu's search engine and is accessible using a dialogue button at the top of search results, similar to how ChatGPT is integrated into the Bing search engine. Alibaba's AI model Tongyi Qianwen (often shortened to Qwen) was the most popular on Hugging Face, a repository of LLMs, which was attributed to its performance on competitive benchmarks and the highly favourable licensing terms that Qwen offers, making it easier for it to be adopted by companies without extensive legal issues.[24] Qwen is available in different sizes and parameters. Users can download their preferred size. Larger parameter models will require greater computing resources and higher costs. Smaller

---

[21] B. Jiang and A. Cao, China to create and implement national standard for large language models in move to regulate AI, while using its power to transform industries, *SCMP*, 7 July 2023. https://www.scmp.com/tech/policy/article/3226942/china-create-and-implement-national-standard-large-language-models-move-regulate-ai-while-using-its?module=inline&pgtype=article (Last accessed: 15 January 25)

[22] J. Yoon, Why China is suddenly flooding the market with powerful AI models, *Financial Times*, 19 March 25. https://www.ft.com/content/13df6250-dffb-40fc-bb79-309764fa3905?utm_source=chatgpt.com (Last accessed: 13 May 25).

[23] B. Jiang, Baidu, SenseTime open AI chatbots to the public after China grants first approvals for such services, *SCMP*, 31 August 2023. https://www.scmp.com/tech/tech-trends/article/3232982/baidu-sensetime-open-ai-chatbots-public-after-china-grants-first-approvals-such-services?module=inline&pgtype=article (Last accessed: 15 January 2025).

[24] A. Kharpal, China wants to dominate in AI – And some of its models are already beating their U.S. rivals, *CNBC*, 16 December 2024. https://www.cnbc.com/2024/12/17/chinese-ai-models-are-popular-globally-and-are-beating-us-rivals-in-some-areas.html (Last accessed; 15 January 2025).

parameter models are more economical to run. Many Chinese LLMs (such as Tencent's Hunyuan Turbo S[25] and Huawei's Pangu[26]) are offered as cloud-based services for domestic enterprises, which businesses can utilise in accordance with Chinese data laws. The Chinese government is supportive of AI integration and has given permission to numerous LLMs for commercial applications.

In Europe, the commitment is towards open-source development for digital sovereignty. OpenEuroLLM is a European initiative with a consortium of 20 institutions, aiming to develop an open-source LLM model that can encompass 24 EU languages and achieve ethical AI usage. OpenEuroLLM wants the models to be implemented for various sectors, such as healthcare and public administration. At the forefront of LLM development in Europe, we have Mistral AI, LightOn, Nyonic OpenGPT-X, and Aleph Alpha.[27] These models are aligned with the EU AI Act that supports accountability, transparency, and various EU languages. There are guidelines being established for the use of LLMs in regulatory science and for medicines regulatory activities.[28]

Japan's LLM scene is more research-oriented and companies develop LLMs with academia. For commercialisation, LLMs are focused on specific industries, such as automotive and consumer electronics. Rakuten's AI team developed an LLM with exceptional performance in Japanese,

---

[25] M. Gupta, Tencent Hun Yuan Turbo S: The fastest reasoning LLM, *Medium*, 28 February 25. https://medium.com/data-science-in-your-pocket/tencent-hunyuan-turbo-s-the-fastest-reasoning-llm-d64a02bed5c8 (Last accessed: 13 May 25).

[26] Huawei Cloud, Reshaping industries with AI: Huawei Cloud launches Pangu Models 3.0 and Ascend AI Cloud Services, 7 July 23. https://www.huaweicloud.com/intl/en-us/news/20230707180809498.html (Last accessed: 13 May 25).

[27] M. Amersfoorth, Europe's Open-Source AI pioneers: 10 groups shaping LLMS under the EU AI act, Tech Blog, 10 March 25. https://techblog.finalist.nl/blog/europes-open-source-ai-pioneers-10-groups-shaping-llms-under-eu-ai-act?utm_source=chatgpt.com (Last accessed: 13 May 25).

[28] European Medicine Agency, Guiding principles on the use of large language models in regulatory science and for medicines regulatory activities, 29 August 24. https://www.ema.europa.eu/en/documents/other/guiding-principles-use-large-language-models-regulatory-science-medicines-regulatory-activities_en.pdf?utm_source=chatgpt.com (Last accessed: 13 May 25).

training on top of Mistral-7B (another open-source model).[29] Rakuten researchers attempted to break Japanese words into fewer tokens, thereby achieving lower computing costs. Rakuten was confident that its model was one of the highest-performing Japanese models and encouraged people to take its foundation model and make a new one. Japanese companies, such as NEC, are developing proprietary LLMs catered to government and Japanese enterprises.[30] Japanese models are targeted towards the domestic market, with less focus on broad global reach or open-source distribution compared to U.S. models. For commercial strategies, Japanese firms such as NTT and Fujitsu, cater to local business needs and have targeted applications, like healthcare and customer service.

3.4 Use Cases and Applications

Leading Chinese LLMs have been integrated into different use cases and applications serving Chinese companies' business needs. Tencent's Hunyuan LLM is centred on conversational AI and gaming, and it is also integrated into social media platforms such as QQ and WeChat. Huawei's PanGu LLM seeks to provide enterprise solutions for various industries, namely, finance, manufacturing, healthcare, mining, railway, and R&D. A coding assistant developed by Tencent used the Hunyuan foundation model; it was reported that coders use it to enhance productivity.[31] Apart from applying Huawei's PanGu model in different industries, Huawei has developed another version called the PanGu Government model that was integrated into an intelligent government service assistant called Xiaofu, which can map users' intent to a pre-defined service. The PanGu Government Model was trained with

[29] Rakuten Today, Rakuten's open LLM tops performance charts in Japanese, 20 April 2024. https://rakuten.today/blog/rakutens-open-llm-tops-performance-charts-in-japanese.html (Last accessed: 16 January 25).

[30] NEC, NEC joins the race to develop Japan's own Large Language Model (LLM), 28 September 23. https://www.nec.com/en/global/insights/article/ChatGPT-for-Japanese-governments/index.html?utm_source=chatgpt.com (Last accessed: 13 May 25).

[31] Tencent, Tencent unveils new AI upgrades, proprietary innovations, and global solutions, 5 September 2024. https://www.tencent.com/en-us/articles/2201930.html (Last accessed: 8 November 24).

government data records including government policy information, hotline data, government knowledge bases, and common knowledge.[32] To improve e-commerce searches, personalised recommendations, and customer support, Alibaba integrated LLM Tongyi Qianwen into Taobao, its e-commerce platform.[33]

---

[32]Huawei Cloud (2023), *Op. cit.*

[33]Alibaba Cloud Community, Alibaba integrates LLM Tongyi Qianwen into Taobao to refine E-commerce searches for users, 18 September 2023. https://www.alibabacloud.com/blog/alibaba-integrates-llm-tongyi-qianwen-into-taobao-to-refine-e-commerce-searches-for-users_600401 (Last accessed: 9 November 2024).

Chapter 4

Future of LLMs and Generative AI

In 2023, we saw an explosion of generative text and generative images using LLMs. In 2024, we experienced a wave of generative videos such as OpenAI's Sora,[1] released on 15 February 2024, and Google DeepMind's Veo,[2] released on 16 December 2024. What can we look forward in 2026 and beyond?

4.1 Progressing to higher levels of artificial general intelligence

As reported by Bloomberg,[3] OpenAI has defined five levels of artificial general intelligence (AGI) and is progressing nearer to level 2. These five levels include: level 1 – conversational AI, level 2 – reasoning AI, level 3 – autonomous AI, level 4 – innovating AI, and level 5 – organisational AI. In level 1, an example of conversational AI is employing chatbots to help in drafting a presentation. In level 2, we have reasoning AI, which provides reasoning to solve problems at doctoral-level education. In level 3, autonomous AI allows the AI agents to operate autonomously on behalf of the user, for example, to plan and book a company function venue. At level 4, innovating AI is used to improve processes, not merely run them.

[1] Sora, https://openai.com/index/sora/.

[2] Veo, https://deepmind.google/technologies/veo/veo-2/.

[3] Bloomberg, OpenAI Scale Ranks Progress Toward 'Human-level' Problem Solving, 11 July 2024. https://www.bloomberg.com/news/articles/2024-07-11/openai-sets-levels-to-track-progress-toward-superintelligent-ai (Last accessed: 11 January 2025).

In level 5, an organisational AI involves an AI that can perform the work of the entire organisation without human intervention. According to Forbes, Sam Altman, CEO of OpenAI, has predicted that it will reach this super AI level 5 within 10 years.

4.2 AI agents

AI agents are the next frontier of generative AI, with virtual coworkers assisting to complete complex multistep workflows, enhancing productivity, and boosting innovation.[4] AI agents go beyond generating text and answering questions like what earlier-generation LLMs can achieve; they are able to interact with other agents and humans to complete end-to-end tasks. There are use cases we can envisage. The AI agent can help users research different travel itineraries, plan a holiday based on budget and preferences, handle logistics across various online platforms (such as airlines, hotels, and restaurant and event/activity reservations), even taking into consideration reward points and discounts, and eventually book the complete itinerary most suitable for the user. A customer service AI agent can sift through customers' feedback emails, draft a suitable response, and email it back to the customer directly. AI agents can be employed to assist consumers in doing shopping, more so for commodities such as batteries and cooking oil, rather than fashion, which has an aesthetic element that users may want greater control over. A programming agent can code, test, iterate, refactor, and deploy new software features it assists to develop based on a programmer's description of the requirement in layman's terms. In the past, it was rather complex and very costly to automate such end-to-end processes because of the large variation of inputs and outputs, as well as the difficulties in interacting with so many different platforms.

Let us clarify the key differences between AI assistants and AI agents. AI assistants rely on user input prompts to get started and there is a need for continuous user prompts. AI assistants are developed on foundation models (such as OpenAI's ChatGPT models or Meta's Llama). An AI assistant will try to understand user queries and provide relevant information or suggest the next course of action. The users are required to review the recommendations for relevance and decide what to do next. AI assistants

[4] L. Yee, M. Chui, R. Roberts, and S. Xu, Why agents are the next frontier of generative AI, McKinsey Quarterly, 24 July 2024. https://www.mckinsey.com/capabilities/mckinsey-digital/our-insights/why-agents-are-the-next-frontier-of-generative-ai#/ (Last accessed: 10 January 2025).

can be fine-tuned to do more specific tasks; however, most AI assistants do not retain information from prior user interactions because they may not have persistent memory. This results in them not being able to continuously learn and evolve from previous conversations. AI assistants rely on a new update from a developer to have improved capabilities.

AI agents help users (individuals or businesses) to maximise outcomes, which may include opportunities, success rates, efficiency, effectiveness, lowest costs, and income. AI agents can work independently once given the initial prompt by users, which states the specific goals. AI agents can work autonomously and more proactively in helping users achieve their goals. Unlike AI assistants that require users to approve their suggested actions, AI agents have greater autonomy and can independently solve problems and make decisions, even using external data sources, applications, and tools. With persistent memory, AI agents can recall prior sessions and are able to learn and adapt to the user's needs accordingly to enhance their performance. AI agents can break down complex workflows into smaller steps and ensure effective execution across multiple steps to achieve a result. These AI agents can work together with other AI agents and tools which specialise in different domains to complete a multi-step complex job together.

There are different types of AI agents, including simple reflex agents, model-based reflex agents, goal-based agents, utility-based agents, and learning agents, and they differ in terms of technical complexity, cost, and specific use case requirements. A simple reflex agent is a basic type of agent which uses current sensory input and follows a set of predefined condition–action rules to make decisions. They do not take into consideration past experiences and future issues. For example, in a heavy industry manufacturing factory, the detection of unknown obstacles in the work zone can trigger a shutdown of machinery. A simple reflex agent has limitations because it requires conditions to be predefined and cannot deal with complex and dynamic problems since it does not retain information from past sessions and cannot learn or adapt. A model-based reflex agent is like a simple reflex model with memory; it can retain memories of experiences and have a model of the environment. For example, robots working on factory floors use their memory to recognise and store the map of the factory floor and possible obstacles to avoid. Goal-based agents are fixated on having a clear objective regarding what the agent wants to achieve. While reflex models are based on a set of predefined rules or world models, goal-based agents work through a series of actions to reach their desired goal. For example, in manufacturing plant task scheduling, the sequence of work can be scheduled accordingly to ensure deadlines are met. Learning agents are capable of learning from their interaction with the environment and learning through it. The learning agent can modify its behaviour based on the responses and its experience and feedback. In smart building energy management, a learning agent can learn energy usage patterns to optimise energy resource consumption. Instead of aiming to achieve a specific state like a goal-based agent, a utility-based agent can assess the outcomes of competing goals and choose one that gives maximum overall utility. For example, for resource allocation in manufacturing production, the utility-based agent seeks to balance machine usage with energy and water consumption, as well as production targets. Apart from these five types of AI agents, which may work individually or with other AI agents, there are hierarchical agents and multi-agent systems (MASs) that must collaborate with other AI agents to achieve goals. Hierarchical agents are organised in a tiered structure with higher-tier agents coordinating and delegating work to lower tiers. Complex tasks can be broken down into manageable sub-tasks. For example, in robotic task planning, various robot tasks can be split into basic movements. MASs have multiple agents working together individually or collaboratively in a shared environment. They may exist as cooperative systems or competitive systems. In a cooperative MAS, the agents share resources and data to fulfil common objectives, such as in a manufacturing plant where numerous robots work together to complete jobs. In a competitive MAS, the agents compete for resources under a set of rules. For example, in communication networks, environmental resources can be bid and reserved by different agents.

Big Tech giants in the U.S. have invested heavily in AI agents for their LLM-powered applications, shifting from providing knowledge to a more action-based approach. This includes Microsoft Copilot, Amazon's Q, and Google's Project Astra. Increasingly, companies are integrating AI agents into their systems. The U.S. Department of Government Efficiency (DOGE) under the Trump administration is reportedly designing benchmarks for over 300 job roles and deploying AI agents to automate the jobs of 70,000 people across different federal agencies.[5]

---

[5]C. Haskins and V. Elliott, A DOGE Recruiter is Staffing a Project Deploy AI Agents Across the US Government, Wired, 2 May 2025. https://www.wired.com/story/doge-recruiter-ai-agents-palantir-clown-emoji/ (Last accessed: 3 May 2025).

Apart from government operations, there is a big drive for corporate adoption of AI agents, and there are numerous examples in the finance and healthcare sectors. Agentic AI for healthcare ranges from administrative task automation and patient management and engagement to healthcare research, aiming to establish a more intelligent and responsive system. Ascertain, a start-up, has managed to raise US$10 million to scale its agentic AI platform. It aims to build a management solution that reimagines healthcare workflows and improves efficiency and quality within the healthcare system by handling arduous administrative tasks, including documentation and compliance.[6] Another agentic AI start-up, named VoiceCare AI, a healthcare artificial general intelligence (HAGI) company, raised US$3.85 million to automate back-office tasks to ease administrative burdens and improve operational efficiency.[7] Numerous patient-facing AI agents can provide preliminary medical assessments and provide the findings to a human clinician for validations. In this way, patients can receive real-time consultations with healthcare professionals with AI agents in the back-end providing a comprehensive diagnosis based on the symptoms and medical records presented. Doctronic, a New York-based start-up, received $5m, to develop an AI-powered medical consultation platform.[8] The Doctronic platform can provide personalised possible diagnoses and action plans based on symptoms, compared to an online Google search. AION Labs, a venture studio formed by global pharmaceutical firms, including Pfizer, Merck, and AstraZeneca, and technology leaders, including AWS, has leveraged AI agents for research and diagnostics in numerous areas, such as antibody and drug discovery.[9]

[6]VKTR, Ascertain Raises $10 Million in Series A Funding to Scale Agentic AI Platform, Press Release, 22 April 2025. https://www.vktr.com/the-wire/ascertain-raises-10-million-in-series-a-funding-to-scale-agentic-ai-platform/ (Last accessed: 3 May 2025).

[7]VoiceCare AI, Agentic AI Startup, VoiceCare AI Launches to Automate Healthcare Back Office and Super-Staff Workforce, PR Newswire, 14 Feb 2025. https://www.prnewswire.com/news-releases/agentic-ai-startup-voicecare-ai-launches-to-automate-healthcare-back-office-and-super-staff-workforce-302376944.html (Last accessed: 4 May 2025).

[8]Apoio.ai, AI meets medicine: How doctronic is transforming health access across the Globe, 18 April 2025. https://apoio.ai/ai-meets-medicine-how-doctronic-is-transforming-health-access-across-the-globe/ (Last accessed: 4 May 2025).

[9]B. Buntz, Inside AION Labs, the AI-focused venture studio with the backing of AstraZeneca, Pfizer, AWS and other power players, R&D World, 25 December 2024. https://www.rdworldonline.com/inside-aion-labs-the-ai-focused-venture-studio-with-the-backing-of-astrazeneca-pfizer-aws-and-other-power-players/ (Last accessed: 4 May 2025).

Visa has partnered with leading LLM companies such as U.S. companies Anthropic, Microsoft, Perplexity, and OpenAI and France's Mistral to pilot a project that allows consumers to outsource spending to AI agents.[10] AI agents can take over some of the shopping, particularly those errands that are considered boring (e.g., for items like groceries and DIY items) or too tedious (e.g., for flight travel and accommodation bookings). With a set of clear conditions and spending limits, the AI agents can make payments and complete purchases. To work with Visa represents a win-win situation for these LLM companies who wish to compete in the digital commerce space with big tech companies like Amazon and Google. With the ease of digital payment using Apple Pay, which offers a digital wallet and uses Mastercard as Apple Card's network, Visa is working hard to integrate its payment into more platforms to ensure it can maintain a strong foothold on credit card payments.

In China, there are many start-ups working on AI agents for different applications. Manus AI, a new AI agent by Chinese start-up Monica, made a grand entry onto the AI scene on 6 March 2025, receiving significant attention, much like DeepSeek had done in January 2025. How is Manus AI different from other AI agents discussed so far? It is the first AI agent company that demonstrated real end-to-end completion of tasks given to them by operating autonomously to execute all the tasks across various platforms. Many of the other end-to-end AI agents were still in research and work-in-progress development phases. Manus AI's team claimed that the general AI agent has the capability to outperform OpenAI models on three difficulty levels represented in the GAIA benchmark test, which tests general AI agents on real-world solving skills.[11] Manus AI has demonstrated its capability to complete multi-step real-world tasks without requiring human guidance through a series of use cases, including deep analysis of stocks, comparative analysis of insurance policies, and website construction. Manus AI product partner Zhang Tao had to come forward to apologise and clarify that their server resources were not able to cope with the surge in public interest, and its

[10] M. O'Brien, Visa wants to give artificial intelligence 'agents' your credit card, AP, 1 May 2025. https://apnews.com/article/ai-artificial-intelligence-5dfa1da145689e7951a181e2253ab349 (Last accessed: 4 May 2025).

[11] A. Ojha, China releases new AI agent Manus; claims to outperform OpenAI models, Investing.com, 6 Mar 2025. https://www.investing.com/news/stock-market-news/china-releases-new-ai-agent-manus-outperforms-openai-models-3910899 (Last accessed: 13 Mar 25).

service remained limited a day after launch.[12] The creator of Manus has announced that it will collaborate with Alibaba to develop a Chinese version of the application that meets domestic Chinese needs.[13] Alibaba has an AI assistant, Quark, which leverages the Qwen model and can perform many tasks, ranging from answering user questions that require deep thinking to generating meeting minutes and travel planning.[14] China's Zhipu, an AI start-up, unveiled a free AI agent called AutoGLM Rumination, which can perform deep research, including web searches, research report writing, and travel planning.[15] Zhipu claimed that its AI agent is powered by its own proprietary models which match DeepSeek's R1 in terms of performance while using much less computing resources and being up to eight times faster.

With a comprehensive regulatory framework in the EU, the approach for companies in Europe is to ensure AI agents can strike a balance between achieving enterprise solutions goals and aligning with European values (strong ethics, transparency, data privacy, and fairness). French start-up H Company was founded by Google DeepMind alumni and researchers from Stanford University, with backing from Europe's wealthiest man, LVMH CEO Bernard Arnault, and Google ex-CEO Eric Schmidt, alongside other prominent companies such as Amazon and Samsung. H is an AI agent meant for businesses and can perform tasks such as business process outsourcing, robotic process automation, and quality assurance. H is a little less expensive to train because it has 2 billion parameters compared to 175 billion parameters for ChatGPT 3.[16] This company was able

---

[12] W. Chen, Was Manus another DeepSeek moment? Chinese AI agent faces doubts after rapid rise to fame, SCMP, 7 March 2025. https://www.scmp.com/tech/big-tech/article/3301547/was-manus-another-deepseek-moment-chinese-ai-agent-faces-doubts-after-rapid-rise-fame?module=perpetual_scroll_0&pgtype=article (Last accessed: 14 March 2025).

[13] A. Cao, AI agent Manus partners with Alibaba's Qwen to develop Chinese version, SCMP News, 11 March 2025. https://www.scmp.com/tech/big-tech/article/3301986/ai-agent-manus-partners-alibabas-qwen-develop-chinese-version (Last accessed: 4 May 2025).

[14] The Business Times, Alibaba unveils AI agent app in race to keep up with rivals, 13 March 2025. https://www.businesstimes.com.sg/companies-markets/telcos-media-tech/alibaba-unveils-ai-agent-app-race-keep-rivals (Last accessed: 4 May 2025).

[15] Reuters, China's Zhipu AI launches free AI agent, intensifying domestic tech race, 31 March 2025. https://www.reuters.com/technology/artificial-intelligence/chinas-zhipu-ai-launches-free-ai-agent-intensifying-domestic-tech-race-2025-03-31/ (Last accessed: 4 May 2025).

[16] P. Davies, What is H? Here's everything we know about the French AI start-up backed by Europe's richest person, Euro News, 23 November 2024. https://www.euronews.com/

to raise US$220 million even before selling a product. Germany-based Cognigy's AI agents can provide personalised and scalable customer service for support contact centres. It has partnered with 1,000 brands worldwide, including notable ones such as Bosch, Mercedes-Benz, Toyota, DHL, Lufthansa Group, Nestlé, and Frontier Airlines.[17]

In Japan, the strategy towards the adoption of AI agents is geared towards meeting societal and industry needs of an ageing population, healthcare, automation, and improving business efficiency. Chugai, Softbank, and SB Intuition have announced their collaboration to work on AI agents that can support clinical researchers to develop new drugs and deploy innovative treatments faster.[18] NTT Data announced the launch of Smart AI Agent, which has already impacted key sectors: It has improved regulatory reporting processes in banking, enhanced data analysis and operational efficiency in the automotive industry, and optimised marketing processes for a gas company.[19] In 2025, Softbank collaborated with OpenAI to develop an AI data centre to help companies train models on clients' data and provide customised AI agent services.[20]

While AI agents can provide automation and make decisions, they do carry significant technical risks and limitations that must be mitigated carefully to avoid costly blunders when integrated into critical workflows. AI agents may generate incorrect information and make wrong decisions

---

next/2024/11/23/what-is-h-and-why-is-the-french-start-up-creating-a-buzz-in-ai (Last accessed: 5 May 2025).

[17] D. Seeley, Global AI agent leader cognigy relocates U.S. HQ from San Francisco to North Texas, Dallas Innovates, 16 April 2025. https://dallasinnovates.com/global-ai-agent-leader-relocates-u-s-hq-from-san-francisco-to-north-texas/ (Last accessed: 5 May 2025).

[18] Chugai Pharmaceutical, Chugai, SoftBank Corp., and SB Intuitions Sign Memorandum of Understanding for Joint Research aimed at Innovating Clinical Development Processes and Accelerating New Drug Development through Generative AI – Aiming to Create Advanced Services in the Pharmaceutical and Healthcare Industry, 30 January 2025. https://www.chugai-pharm.co.jp/english/news/detail/20250130153000_1131.html (Last accessed: 6 May 2025).

[19] NTT Data, NTT Data Launches Smart AI Agent to Accelerate Generative AI Adoption and Drive $2 Billion in Revenue By 2027, 28 January 25. https://services.global.ntt/en-us/newsroom/ntt-data-launches-ai-agent-to-boost-ai-adoption-and-drive-2-billion-dollar-revenue-by-2027 (Last accessed: 6 May 2025).

[20] CNA news, Softbank, OpenAI to build AI data centre in Japan, Nikkei reports, 14 March 2025. https://www.channelnewsasia.com/business/softbank-openai-build-ai-data-centre-japan-nikkei-reports-4999406 (Last accessed: 6 May 2025).

on behalf of the user due to the hallucinations of LLMs. There may be significant consequences such as financial losses if an AI agent is trading in the market and makes a wrong decision to transact at a loss during market volatility. If the objectives and constraints are not specified correctly, it may lead to autonomous AI agents taking wrong actions. Computational resources are expensive and may be limited, which may impede scalability and performance when a high volume of users request agents to execute tasks for them, leading to possible slowdowns and crashes. There are security vulnerabilities such as prompt injection and unauthorised access for AI agents interacting with APIs, and they can be subjected to cyberattacks. It is necessary to ensure third-party integrations will not have data exposure risks because AI agents may accidentally leak confidential data if they are not programmed properly. Ethical risks may result from AI agents trained using flawed and biased data, causing unfair and discriminatory outcomes for various domains such as loan approvals, hiring, university admissions, and other automated selection schemes using AI agents. AI agents may misuse data or leak private data, resulting in data privacy issues. They may generate false information, whether intentionally due to manipulative purposes or unintentionally due to flaws in design and algorithms.

Societal risks include excessive reliance on AI agents, leading to humans losing essential skills, and job displacement, with AI agents replacing some human job roles. It may be challenging to establish and implement ethical AI guidelines for different communities and cultures. Regulatory frameworks may not be able to keep up with the rapid progress in AI agents, so they will not be able to assign responsibility and liability adequately.

4.3 Generative Virtual Playgrounds

Researchers in the academic world and top research labs are embarking on building generative virtual environments. We can anticipate generative virtual worlds appearing in video games, and a sketch can be converted into a playable environment with just a few clicks.

AI pioneer Fei-Fei Li, together with Justin Johnson, Christoph Lassner, and Ben Mildenhall – all world-renowned technologists in computer vision and graphics – launched their new start-up, World Labs, with a US$230 million investment from prominent investors, including

Andreessen Horowitz, NEA, Radical Ventures, Marc Benioff, and Nvidia's NVentures in 2024.[21] This start-up is already valued at over US$1 billion, and it is expected to ship the world's first products that can be used in robotics and games in 2025[22]. World Labs aims to create AI systems that can perceive and interact with 3D environments, and this is progressing beyond traditional 2D visuals. World Labs wants to create "large world models" (LWMs) that can visualise, understand, generate, and interact within 3D worlds at a human spatial intelligence level. LWMs can understand about 3D worlds from images, videos, and other modalities. In the initial stage, they hope to generate 3D worlds with physics, semantics, and control. This will allow any user to imagine and generate their own worlds. Over time, the trained LWMs will be more powerful, with capabilities that can be effectively applied across different domains.

Google DeepMind revealed a generative model known as Genie 2 in December 2024, with the capability of using a starter image or text to transform into an entire 3D virtual world. It can be a character exploring a dense forest, mountain meadow, or other scenes, created using this new tool. The initial stage of this project would likely impact the gaming and design industry in the VR space. Genie 2 stands out from other similar AI models (such as Decart's Minecraft simulator Oasis) because it can remember off-screen characters better and can render them accurately as they appear at good resolution. As the project is very new and there are limitations in the current version, the generated environment is only in first-person and isometric views, lasting less than one minute, and for most simulations, it ends within 10–20 seconds.[23] There are IP implications because Genie 2 is trained on video data.[24] DeepMind, a subsidiary

[21] World Labs, https://www.worldlabs.ai/about (Last accessed: 12 January 2025).

[22] C. Fink, Fei-Fei Li's World Labs AI Out of Stealth With $230 Million, New Snap Specs, Neurallink Targets Blindness, Forbes, 23 September 2024. https://www.forbes.com/sites/charliefink/2024/09/19/fei-fei-lis-world-labs-ai-out-of-stealth-with-230-million-new-snap-specs-neuralink-targets-blindness/ (Last accessed 12 January 2025).

[23] Google DeepMind Genie 2: A large-scale foundation world model, 4 December 2024. https://deepmind.google/discover/blog/genie-2-a-large-scale-foundation-world-model/ (Last accessed: 12 January 2025).

[24] Kyle Wiggers, DeepMind's Genie 2 can generate interactive worlds that look like video games, Tech Crunch, 4 December 2024. https://techcrunch.com/2024/12/04/deepminds-genie-2-can-generate-interactive-worlds-that-look-like-video-games/ (Last accessed: 12 January 2025).

of Google, has access to YouTube for model training. The question now is whether Genie 2 has the permission to create copies of video games based on YouTube videos. There is controversy surrounding Genie 2 democratising access to tools, and at the same time, it could lead to job displacement as companies may adopt AI, causing some human artists and developers to lose their jobs.[25]

4.4 Generative AI in Sciences

Generative AI can revolutionise transformation in life sciences with scientific discovery and developments across many fields. One notable field is in the biopharma industry, undertaking drug development, personalised healthcare, and protein engineering. Accenture highlighted several challenges[26] in this industry. It is extremely lengthy and costly to develop a drug, with costs exceeding billions and the average time to market being 12 years.[27] The cost of capital to invest in drug development is high, drug manufacturing is complex, and some biopharma companies are experiencing a low average revenue CAGR of 4.5%[28] due to patent expirations, market forces, and government pricing pressure. With desired attributes such as the ability to analyse large corpora of data and identify patterns and links that experienced researchers may not have spotted. As discussed in the Cognizant Benelux Blog,[29] we can envisage drugs getting to the

---

[25] S. Pandey, DeepMind's Genie 2 explained: The AI tools that aims at redefining interactive 3D worlds, digit.in, 10 December 2024. https://www.digit.in/features/general/deepminds-genie-2-explained-the-ai-tool-that-aims-at-redefining-interactive-3d-worlds.html (Last accessed: 12 January 2025).

[26] Accenture, Reinventing life sciences in the age of generative AI, 30 August 24. https://www.accenture.com/us-en/insights/life-sciences/reinventing-life-sciences-age-generative-ai (Last accessed: 12 January 2025).

[27] Bio Stock, Drug Development – The Four Phases, 2 January 2023. https://biostock.se/en/2023/01/drug-development-the-four-phases/ (Last accessed: 1 June 2025).

[28] M. Mikulic, Projected pharmaceutical spending CAGR worldwide between 2023 and 2027, by market and product type, Statista, 13 August 24. https://www.statista.com/statistics/491199/cagr-pharmaceutical-markets-by-product-type/.

[29] G. Kuruppath, The Power of GenAI in Life Sciences: From Accelerating Drug Development to Decoding the Complexity of the Human Body, Cognizant Benelux Blog, 2 April 2024. https://www.cognizant.com/nl/en/insights/blog/articles/power-of-gen-ai-in-life-sciences (Last accessed: 12 January 2025).

market faster; more targeted and effective treatment can be tailored based on an individual's genetic make-up, and innovative protein structures can be created with desired features. Innovative protein structure designs allow for the development of therapeutic protein drugs, including monoclonal antibodies, enzymes, and hormones. In biopharmaceutical development, a deep knowledge of protein structure is of paramount importance because by using precise structural configurations, they can achieve their intended biological functions, and any structural alterations in proteins can significantly impact treatment efficacy and safety.[30] GenAI can assist in protein structure analysis and allow scientists to design proteins with optimal characteristics for their specific application.

LLMs are leveraged for predictive chemistry, such as predicting the properties of different molecules and materials. Researchers are trying to create a model that produces molecules with a set of desired properties, and they have tested GPT-3 to correlate chemical information text fragments, deriving promising results, though some of the correlations are not always meaningful cause–effect relationships.[31] Though some of the LLM predictions may not be true, they may serve as a guide, and LLMs can throw up some plausible ideas and possible correlations for researchers to take further and carry out experiments to validate the predictions. In the field of chemistry, there are numerous chemistry-related LLMs and autonomous agents. In a recent paper, specific AI agents have been explored for literature review in chemistry, chemical innovation, experiment planning, automating cheminformatics tasks, and hypothesis creation; it was noted that there are vast opportunities to fundamentally change how chemical research can be conducted, alongside challenges to be addressed to realise the full potential of LLMs.[32]

---

[30] CfPIE, The Role of Protein Structure Analysis in the Success of Biopharmaceuticals, 3 September 2024. https://www.cfpie.com/the-role-of-protein-structure-analysis-in-the-success-of-biopharmaceuticals (Last accessed: 12 January 2025).

[31] K. M. Jablonka, P. Schwaller, A. Ortega-Guerrero, and B. Smith, (2024). Leverage large models for predictive chemistry. *Nat. Mach. Intell.*, 6, 161–169. https://www.nature.com/articles/s42256-023-00788-1 (Last accessed: 16 March 2025).

[32] M. C. Ramos, C. J. Collison, and A. D. White, (2025). A review of large language models and autonomous agents in chemistry, *Chem. Sci.*, 16, 2514–2572. https://pubs.rsc.org/en/content/articlepdf/2025/sc/d4sc03921a (Last accessed: 17 March 2025).

4.5 AI in National Security

Due to increasing geopolitical tensions and its ambition to remain a superpower in both the military and economic spheres, the U.S. military has significantly increased spending on GenAI and is partnering with data analytics firm Palantir Technologies and defence tech company Anduril Industries to use defence data for AI training.[33] The work is focused on solving two issues that limit adoption of AI for national security purposes: data readiness and processing data at scale.[34] Currently, government data collected by sensors, weapons, vehicles, and robots are not retained for AI training. There is a need to implement next-generation encryption for tactical data collected. It is challenging to deploy developed models at scale with government partners using defence products. Anduril partnered with OpenAI to boost the nation's defence system by protecting army personnel from unmanned drone attacks and other aerial devices.[35]

In 2024, the U.S. Army extended Palantir's contract with a US$400.7 million contract to provide an AI-enabled data platform.[36] This contract is for four years and can amount to nearly US$620 million if additional options are undertaken. With the U.S. Army Vantage system having more than 180 unique data sources, the Palantir software can be leveraged to optimise operational efficiencies and processes across the army enterprise.[37]

---

[33] Reuters, Palantir, Anduril sign partnership for AI training in defense, 7 December 2024. https://www.reuters.com/technology/artificial-intelligence/palantir-anduril-sign-partnership-ai-training-defense-2024-12-06/ (Last accessed: 13 January 2025).

[34] Anduril, Anduril and Palantir to Accelerate AI Capabilities for National Security, 12 June 2024. https://www.anduril.com/article/anduril-and-palantir-to-accelerate-ai-capabilities-for-national-security/ (Last accessed: 13 January 2024).

[35] Anduril Industries, Anduril Partners with OpenAI to Advance U.S. Artificial Intelligence Leadership and Protect U.S. and Allied Forces, 4 December 2024. https://www.anduril.com/article/anduril-partners-with-openai-to-advance-u-s-artificial-intelligence-leadership-and-protect-u-s/ (Last accessed: 13 January 2025).

[36] J. Judson, US Army extends Palantir's contract for its data-harnessing platform, Defense News, 19 December 2024. https://www.defensenews.com/land/2024/12/18/us-army-extends-palantirs-contract-for-its-data-harnessing-platform/ (Last accessed: 13 January 2025).

[37] Palantir, Palantir Expands Army Vantage Partnership with $618.9M Contract, 18 December 2024. https://investors.palantir.com/news-details/2024/Palantir-Expands-Army-Vantage-Partnership-with-618.9M-Contract/ (Last accessed: 13 January 2025).

According to *Reuters*, Chinese researchers linked to the People's Liberation Army (PLA) have developed an AI model called ChatBIT for military use, leveraging publicly available Meta's Llama, according to three academic papers.[38] ChatBIT was fine-tuned to optimise question-answering for the military sector. According to Meta, Llama models' terms of use prohibit their use for "military, warfare, nuclear industries or applications, espionage" and other activities subject to U.S. defence export controls, as well as for the development of weapons and content intended to "incite and promote violence". However, Meta's models are open-source and made public, so there is a limit to how the policies can be enforced.

PLA scientists use LLMs like Baidu's Ernie and iFlyTek's Spark to predict the behaviour of human conflicts. According to a peer-reviewed paper published in the Chinese academic journal *Command Control & Simulation*, the researchers stated that humans and machines could benefit from the simulation results, assisting in human decision-making and improving the machines' combat cognition level.[39] Sun Yifeng's team in PLA research shared details of a simulation of a U.S. military invasion of Libya in 2011, in which Ernie was provided with information about weapons and the deployment of both armies. Sun confirmed that Ernie could successfully predict the U.S. military's next move after numerous rounds of dialogue.

There is a global race for military AI drones, with China and the U.S. pushing towards military AI applications.[40] As reported by the *South China Morning Post (SCMP)*, Chinese scientists in China's defence industry have developed generative AI to enhance the performance of military drones, and their research teams have reported their experimental results

---

[38] J. Pomfret and J. Pang, Exclusive: Chinese researchers develop AI model for military use on back of Meta's Llama, Reuters, 1 November 2024. https://www.reuters.com/technology/artificial-intelligence/chinese-researchers-develop-ai-model-military-use-back-metas-llama-2024-11-01/ (Last accessed: 13 January 2025).

[39] C. McFadden, China train A!-general to predict 'enemy humans' on the battlefield, Interesting Engineering, 14 January 2024. https://interestingengineering.com/military/china-training-ai-predict-humans (Last accessed: 14 January 2025).

[40] M. Bastian, Chinese researchers experiment with LLMs to control military drones, the decoder, 2 November 2024. https://the-decoder.com/chinese-researchers-experiment-with-llms-to-control-military-drones/ (Last accessed: 13 January 2025).

in the *Journal of Detection and Control.*[41] The LLM can command a military drone with weapons to attack enemy radar systems. This research project, considered to be in its testing stage, is a collaboration between the Chengdu Aircraft Design Institute (under the Aviation Industry Corporation of China) and Northwestern Polytechnical University in Xian. Chengdu Aircraft Design Institute is reputable and has designed China's heavy stealth fighter, the J-20. The LLM is fed with a large amount of information, including book series on radar, electronic warfare material, electronic warfare operation manuals, weapons inventory records, and air combat data. In electronic warfare, the attacker will try to attack the target by emitting specific electromagnetic waves, while the defender will try to evade attacks by constantly altering signals so that the attacker is required to change its strategy based on surveillance signals. The LLM can process and analyse the numerical data; then, a translator can be used to convert the LLM's responses to instructions for controlling the electronic warfare jammer. The LLM system is capable of adjusting the strategy up to 10 times per second, outperforming human experts and traditional AI systems.[42] Interestingly, the LLM was proven to be superior in creating false targets on enemy radar screens, disrupting the attacker's strategies.

Despite the U.S.'s earlier ban on powerful semiconductors, Chinese companies were able to train their AI models using lower-end chips, and Nvidia has also created dedicated chips for the Chinese market to overcome these restrictions.[43] In August 2023, an executive order was implemented in the U.S. to prevent American investments from aiding countries of concern in developing military capabilities, and these restrictions apply to AI systems, quantum technologies, semiconductors, and microelectronics. Some workarounds to access AI chips include smuggling, transhipment via third

---

[41] S. Chen, J-20 designer arms electronic warfare drones with generative AI, SCMP, 1 November 2024. https://www.scmp.com/news/china/science/article/3284588/words-can-kill-j-20-designer-arms-electronic-warfare-drones-generative-ai (Last accessed: 1 November 2024)

[42] S. Palve, China's J-20 Mighty Dragon's Designer Unveils "ChatGPT Military" That Can Attack Enemy Radars with EW Drones, The EurAsian Times, 5 November 2024. https://www.eurasiantimes.com/chinas-j-20-mighty-dragons-designer/ (Last accessed: 1 June 2025).

[43] Oxford Analytica, China will continue to advance its military AI, 11 November 2024. https://www.oxan.com/insights/china-will-continue-to-advance-its-military-ai/ (Last accessed: 14 January 2025).

markets, and utilising cloud services. The *SCMP* reported that China has managed to access restricted advanced chips and that Southeast Asian countries such as Singapore and Malaysia were allegedly key hubs for GPU smuggling.[44]

According to *Reuters*, the U.S. further tightened its grip on AI chip flows across the globe in January 2025.[45] The new U.S. controls on AI chips set export quotas for about 120 countries, but exports to 18 allies, including the U.K., the Netherlands, and Japan, will be exempted from these rules. This move is to ensure that the U.S. can continue to lead AI in both chip design and AI development.

[44] SCMP, Exclusive - With China in sights, US plans curb on countries' advanced semiconductor access: sources, 12 December 2024. https://www.scmp.com/tech/tech-war/article/3290435/chip-war-us-plans-cap-countries-semiconductor-access-targeting-chinese-smuggling (Last accessed: 14 January 2025).

[45] Reuters, US tightens its grip on AI chip flows across the globe, 14 January 2025. https://www.reuters.com/technology/artificial-intelligence/us-tightens-its-grip-ai-chip-flows-across-globe-2025-01-13/ (Last accessed: 14 January 2025).

Chapter 5

Development of GPUs and Software Toolkit for AI Compute

Due to geopolitical tensions and U.S. sanctions on most high-performance AI chips since 2022, Chinese companies have been eagerly trying to reduce AI hardware dependence. Nvidia's dominance in the GPU industry was questioned when DeepSeek unveiled its V3 in December 2024, followed by R1 in January 2025 since it was claimed that DeepSeek was able to achieve LLM performance using Nvidia GPUs with much lower capabilities.

To compete in this AI "arms race", how dependent are Chinese companies on Nvidia chips? Are there any alternatives for Chinese AI companies? Several Chinese companies are working on semiconductors, including Huawei, Baidu, and Alibaba, as well as start-ups such as Biren Technology and Enflame. According to an article, Huawei's Ascend 910D chip does not currently pose a challenge to Nvidia. Although Ascend910D has used packaging technology to improve performance through the integration of more silicon dies, its performance still pales in comparison to Nvidia's H100.[1] Baidu had self-developed a cluster of 30,000 third-generation P800 Kunlun chips, and the CEO stated that it could support the

[1] B. Nguyen, Why Nvidia investors shouldn't worry about Huawei's new AI chip, Market Watch, 28 April 2025. https://www.marketwatch.com/story/why-nvidia-investors-shouldnt-worry-about-huaweis-new-ai-chip-69f33b81 (Last accessed: 18 May 2025).

training of models like DeepSeek.[2] In 2025, Alibaba launched C930, a server-grade XuanTie RISC-V processor to support high-performance computing, and it is positioned to rival Intel Xeon and AMD EPYC.[3] However, they are deemed to be lagging behind Nvidia for now, and it would be highly unlikely for them to close the technological gaps in general-purpose GPUs in the short term. Tencent-backed and Shanghai-based Enflame was founded by former Advanced Micro Devices (AMD) employees who wanted to sell their chips to domestic firms sourcing alternatives to Nvidia chips.[4] Enflame and Biren design chips that developers utilise to train datasets and manage AI services.[5]

To produce the GPU chips, Chinese GPU players need to tap on semiconductor companies to manufacture them, as they primarily handle the designing part. Taiwan Semiconductor Manufacturing Company (TSMC) had been helping Chinese companies to manufacture the chips until U.S. restrictions, which prohibited semiconductor companies from doing so.

In the field of semiconductor chip manufacturing, chip manufacturers will strive to achieve a lower nanometre (nm) chip, with a "nanometre" referring to the width of circuit lines on a semiconductor chip. A smaller nanometre on a chip means more transistors can be fitted in the same area, achieving higher transistor density and leading to better performance since more calculations can be performed simultaneously.

In November 2024, TSMC could not continue shipping chips to companies in China due to the U.S. government's request. Prior to this request, a TSMC chip was discovered in a Huawei-made AI processor, the Ascend

[2] C. Pan and B. Goh, China's Baidu says its Kunlun chip cluster can train DeepSeek-like models, Reuters, 25 April 2025. https://www.reuters.com/world/china/chinas-baidu-says-its-kunlun-chip-cluster-can-train-deepseek-like-models-2025-04-25/ (Last accessed: 19 May 2025).

[3] W. Williams, Alibaba doubles down on RISC-V architecture with a new secretive 'server-grade' chip will put AMD and Intel on alert, Techradar, 9 March 2025. https://www.techradar.com/pro/alibaba-doubles-down-on-risc-v-architecture-with-a-new-secretive-server-grade-chip-that-will-put-amd-and-intel-on-alert (Last accessed: 19 May 2025).

[4] C. Pan, China's Nvidia wannabe, Tencent-backed AI chip start-up Enflame, flags IPO intention, SCMP, 28 August 2024. https://www.scmp.com/tech/tech-war/article/3276213/chinas-nvidia-wannabe-tencent-backed-ai-chip-start-enflame-flags-ipo-intention (Last accessed: 18 May 2025).

[5] A. Kharpal, China seeks a homegrown alternative to Nvidia – these are some of the companies to watch, CNBC, 17 September 2024. https://www.cnbc.com/2024/09/17/chinese-companies-aiming-to-compete-with-nvidia-on-ai-chips.html (Last accessed: 18 May 2025).

910B, released in 2022. On 11 November, TSMC had informed Chinese chip design companies that it would not be able to supply 7 nm or below chips targeted for AI and GPU customers in China.[6] In 2022, the U.S. Commerce Department restricted Nvidia and AMD from shipping AI chips to China, and this restriction was extended to chip equipment makers, such as Applied Materials, Lam Research, and KLA, from exporting tools used for making advanced chips to China.

Additional new rules were implemented in January 2025 that prevented the export of chips consisting of more than 30 billion transistors created with a 16 nm process node or lower to China unless a licence was issued to them by the U.S. Department of Commerce.[7] Nvidia H800 is a GPU manufactured by TSMC with a 4 nm process node and featuring 80 billion transistors and 16896 CUDA cores. DeepSeek's AI model was trained on more than 2,000 Nvidia H800 chips.[8] In accordance with U.S. regulations on preventing exports to China, exceeding 30 billion transistors produced using a 16 nm process node or lower, DeepSeek's use of Nvidia H800 GPUs had exceeded the limit by almost three times, and it utilised a 4 nm process node for which DeepSeek did not hold a licence. To avoid U.S. tariffs, leading semiconductor companies are locating factories in the U.S. to mitigate national security risks, as cited by the U.S. administration. On 3 March 2025, TSMC's CEO, U.S. President Donald Trump, announced that the company would invest US$100 billion in the U.S. to build five additional chip facilities, including fabrication and advanced packaging facilities, and Trump even described it as the "most powerful company" in the world.[9] In January 2025, former Commerce Secretary Gina Raimondo proudly told *Reuters* during the interview that

[6] K. Freifeld, & F. Potkin, Reuters, Exclusive: US ordered TSMC to halt shipments to China of chips used in AI applications, 10 November 2024. https://www.reuters.com/technology/us-ordered-tsmc-halt-shipments-china-chips-used-ai-applications-source-says-2024-11-10/ (Last accessed: 3 March 2025).

[7] A. Friedman, TSMC stops shipping powerful GPU chips to China used to train AI models, Phone Arena, 9 February 2025. https://www.phonearena.com/news/tsmc-stops-shipping-more-cutting-edge-chips-to-china_id167434 (Last accessed: 3 March 2025).

[8] DeepSeek, DeepSeek-V3 Technical Report, 27 December 2024. https://arxiv.org/html/2412.19437v1 (Last accessed: 3 March 2025).

[9] S. Subin, Trump announces $100 billion investment in U.S. from TSMC, calls it 'most powerful company' in world, CNBC, 3 March 2025. https://www.cnbc.com/2025/03/03/tsmc-to-announce-100-billion-investment-in-us-chip-plants.html (Last accessed: 3 March 2025).

TSMC was making 4 nm chips on American soil and the American workers are of similar level with Taiwan in terms of yield and quality.[10] With the U.S.'s Department of Commerce convincing TSMC to expand in the U.S., the company is scheduled to produce the most advanced 2 nm technology in an Arizona lab in 2028, using its cutting-edge manufacturing technology, known as "A16" at that site. This move will propel the U.S. to produce 20% of the world's leading chips by 2030, emerging from 0% before TSMC's production efforts in Arizona.[11] TSMC is prohibited from producing 2 nm chips overseas currently and must wait until 2028 at the earliest to do so in the US due to Taiwan's technology protection rules.[12] Taiwanese law limits local chipmakers to only producing one-generation less advanced chips abroad. TSMC will commence mass production of 2 nm chips in Taiwan in 2025. Taiwan's National Science and Technology Council (NTSC) and the Ministry of Economic Affairs allowed TSMC to produce advanced chips in a foreign country after three years of producing in Taiwan.[13] TSMC has begun building a facility in Tainan to use for its 1 nm process fabrication, and it is ahead of Intel and Samsung Electronics.[14]

Is there any possibility for China to find an alternative chipmaker within China? Unfortunately, SMIC, China's biggest chipmaker, lagged behind TSMC in terms of technology capabilities in the shorter term. One key reason can be attributed to its inability to gain access to an important piece of machinery from Dutch ASML required for manufacturing

---

[10] D. Shepardson, TSMC begins producing 4-nanometer chips in Arizona, Raimondo says, Reuters, 11 January 2025. https://www.reuters.com/technology/tsmc-begins-producing-4-nanometer-chips-arizona-raimondo-says-2025-01-10/ (Last accessed: 4 March 2025).

[11] Business Wire, U.S. to Hold Over 20% of Advanced Semiconductor Capacity by 2030, TSMC Expands Investment to US$165 Billion, Says TrendForce, 5 March 2025. https://www.businesswire.com/news/home/20250305063041/en/U.S.-to-Hold-Over-20-of-Advanced-Semiconductor-Capacity-by-2030-TSMC-Expands-Investment-to-US%24165-Billion-Says-TrendForce (Last accessed: 1 June 2025).

[12] L. Wang, TSMC cannot make 2nm chips abroad now: MOEA, Taipei Times, 8 November 2024. https://www.taipeitimes.com/News/biz/archives/2024/11/08/2003826545 (Last accessed: 4 March 2025).

[13] C. AI, & F. Huang, TSMC to launch 2nm in U.S. in 'more or less' 2028: NSTC head, Focus Taiwan CAN English News, 29 November 2024. https://focustaiwan.tw/business/202411290005 (Last accessed: 4 March 2025).

[14] H. Jang & J. Lee, TSMC to build 1nm process giga-fab in Taiwan, The Chosun Daily, 4 February 2025. https://www.chosun.com/english/industry-en/2025/02/04/EDZONQBBUJBJTGRZZTA32Z4CJI/ (Last accessed: 4 March 2025).

advanced chips.[15] Besides, TSMC's manufacturing capacity is taken up by developing more advanced chips for Huawei's smartphones and AI chips, leaving very limited resources for GPU design startups and other Chinese design companies. ASML's ultraviolet lithography machines formed a critical part of the chip supply chain, and they are used by chipmakers such as Nvidia and TSMC.

One of the key reasons for Nvidia's ecosystem lock-in is the Compute Unified Device Architecture (CUDA). CUDA is Nvidia's proprietary parallel computing platform that supports developers to write code that can be optimised for Nvidia's GPUs, accelerating complex computing tasks using parallelism – handling thousands of tasks simultaneously, giving Nvidia an edge in the high-performance computing (HPC), gaming, and AI sectors. In the traditional approach, a CPU can process one task at a time, which is known as serial processing. Using GPUs with CUDA, we can do parallel processing and perform tasks significantly faster than using CPUs. Typically, it may take a CPU hours to train a small AI model, but with a CUDA-optimised GPU, training time can be reduced to minutes since thousands of computations can be run in parallel. An enormous amount of computational power is required for training AI models. CUDA allows GPUs to speed up AI workloads, and this makes deep learning much more efficient and faster. CUDA-optimised Nvidia GPUs are used by OpenAI, Meta, and Google for training their LLMs ChatGPT, Llama, and Gemini, respectively. Numerous key libraries use CUDA, including: TensorFlow and PyTorch for providing AI training and assisting in inference acceleration; cuDNN for optimising GPUs to perform deep learning computations; and TensorRT, which provides AI optimisation to achieve fast inference. Due to ecosystem lock-in, AI scientists and engineers prefer Nvidia's CUDA to AMD's ROCm and Intel's oneAPI, and they do not want to recode AI models for GPUs from AMD and Intel. Both CUDA's equivalents provided by competitors AMD and Intel pale in comparison. AMD's ROCm lacks widespread adoption, while Intel's oneAPI does not have a strong developer base and is not fully developed for deep learning. AMD is lagging behind Nvidia in strong AI and cloud adoption. Similarly, Intel performs quite poorly when competing with Nvidia on GPUs and AI accelerators.

[15] A. Kharpal, China would love a domestic Nvidia rival – but that's proving quite the challenge, CNBC, 19 September 2024. https://www.cnbc.com/2024/09/19/china-looks-for-domestic-nvidia-rival-but-thats-proving-challenging.html (Last accessed: 3 March 2025).

CUDA can assist in making video rendering and playback faster by allowing programs like Adobe Premiere Pro and After Effects to enable CUDA in their project settings. When undertaking 3D rendering and animation, CUDA can be enabled for GPU acceleration for software such as Blender and Maya. Autodesk AutoCAD is a piece of software used for 2D drafting and 3D modelling. GPU acceleration can be enabled to speed up graphics rendering and perform basic operations such as panning, zooming, and rotating models. Real-time ray tracing, a method of graphics rendering that simulates the physical lighting of a scene and its objects (which includes realistic reflections, lighting effects, and shadows), is commonly used in gaming and 3D animation; this is supported by Nvidia RTX.[16] CUDA gives Nvidia its wide moat and market dominance due to its ability to lock in companies, AI firms, and researchers. Without CUDA, Nvidia's GPUs are only hardware, and Nvidia's reputed AI hardware (H100, A100, and RTX GPUs) is fully optimised because of it.

China is eagerly seeking alternatives to circumvent reliance on Nvidia's CUDA ecosystem due to the need for AI hardware independence and due to U.S. export restrictions. DeepSeek had managed to achieve 10 times the efficiency when training LLMs compared with other leading tech companies such as Meta and OpenAI.[17] This significant breakthrough was due to the implementation of many finely grained optimisations and the use of low-level assembly-language Parallel Thread Execution (PTX) coding, which sits below Nvidia's CUDA level. CUDA programs, which are in a high-level language, are required to be compiled into the low-level language PTX code before being compiled into specific GPU architectures and eventually executed on Nvidia GPUs. PTX can be optimised for parallelisation.

There are numerous ways Chinese companies can bypass Nvidia's CUDA to get to the PTX level. A PTX-compatible compiler can allow CUDA code to run on non-Nvidia GPUs, such as a PTX-to-Huawei compiler used on Huawei Ascend AI chips to execute CUDA-based AI code. Chinese companies can create runtime environments to interpret PTX and

[16] A. Walia, Nvidia RTX: Top 29 Games that Utilise Ray Tracing the Best, Game Rant, 16 February 2025. https://gamerant.com/nvidia-rtx-top-games-utilize-rtx-best/ (Last accessed: 9 March 2025).

[17] B. Wang, China DeepSeek AI is Over Ten Times More Efficient in AI Training, nextBig Future, 28 December 2024. https://www.nextbigfuture.com/2024/12/china-deepseek-ai-is-over-ten-times-more-efficient-in-ai-training.html (Last accessed: 1 June 2025).

run them on domestically produced hardware (GPUs and FPGA accelerators). PTX emulation layers can trick CUDA applications into thinking they are run on Nvidia hardware. Chinese companies can translate PTX to Open Computing Language (OpenCL), AMD's ROCm, or other Nvidia CUDA-equivalent layers so that AI workloads can execute on AMD and other Chinese GPU architectures. In addition, Chinese AI firms are exploring open-source alternatives to replace CUDA and PTX, including Heterogeneous Interface for Portability (HIP), SYCL (Intel's CUDA alternative) and OpenCL. China is pouring resources into developing its own AI accelerators and frameworks, and here are a few promising ones. Huawei has developed its own AI processor, Huawei Ascend, to combine with Huawei's MindSpore, an open-source deep learning framework. The Biren BR100 AI chip is a powerful 7 nm GPU and is supposed to rival the Nvidia A100. The Biren BR100 claimed to outperform the A100.[18] Cambricon Technologies from Beijing designed specialised 7 nm chips for data centres and AI projects. Cambricon-1A is one of the processors Cambricon has launched, which is used in Huawei Technologies' products. Cambricon is deemed the most valuable AI company, with some investors hoping that this firm may replace Nvidia chips to achieve Beijing's self-sufficiency.[19] Moore Threads produces China's next-generation GPUs to support graphics and AI compute chips. Moore Thread MTT S80 is built on TSMC's 7 nm process and designed to give high performance for gaming and AI workloads at a significantly cheaper price compared to Nvidia's RTX, although it has lower performance compared to older Nvidia's GPUs such as GTX 1050 Ti. However, for now, Moore Threads GPUs seem to lag the market leaders such as Nvidia, but with its continued refinement of technology over time, Moore Threads can possibly close the gap.[20]

---

[18] L. Anisimoff, China Develops Chip to Rival Nvidia's Powerful A100, ChannelNews, 12 January2023. https://www.channelnews.com.au/china-develops-chip-to-rival-nvidias-powerful-a100/ (Last accessed: 9 March 2025).

[19] Z. Xin, Cambricon, China's AI chip leader and answer to Nvidia, predicts first quarterly profit, SCMP, 15 January 2025. https://www.scmp.com/tech/tech-trends/article/3294878/cambricon-chinas-ai-chip-leader-and-answer-nvidia-predicts-first-quarterly-profit (Last accessed: 9 March 2025).

[20] M. Gupta, After DeepSeek, China launches GPU: Moore Threads, target Nvidia, Medium, 10 February 2025. https://medium.com/data-science-in-your-pocket/after-deep-seek-china-launches-gpu-moore-threads-mtt-s80-target-nvidia-472a5fee941e (Last accessed: 9 March 2025).

Chapter 6

Conclusion

The speed of development in the generative AI space is phenomenal, with the U.S. and China taking the lead. Since the release of OpenAI's ChatGPT for public use near the end of 2022, we have seen how fast and far we have progressed. Almost every month, we have seen several tech giants and start-ups in the U.S. and China releasing a newer and better version of their LLMs or generative AI tools. The later-released LLMs continue to push the limits of LLM benchmarks, resulting in newer and more sophisticated capabilities being added to them. It is difficult for smaller players such as start-ups to enter the market to develop a fully native LLM because it will require a massive amount of computing resources. Even research labs at universities which significantly contributed to tech companies in the past may not be able to achieve that much compared to research conducted within the research labs of tech giants in recent years due to a lack of sufficient computing resources to undertake high-volume machine learning work. Researchers and scientists from tech giants' own in-house research labs are encouraged to conduct research and publish in top-tier publications. From our observation, there is a shift to a "winner takes all" syndrome. Big tech firms in the U.S. and China have this advantage because they already have a large following for their existing tech products and service offerings, allowing them to integrate LLMs and generative AI tools into their ecosystem and extend their reach globally, scale, and monetise. Due to geopolitics, Chinese firms have difficulties obtaining the latest chipsets from Nvidia to train their data. Since Chinese firms are looking for alternatives and building their own in-house chip development capabilities, it may take a while for them to catch up with Nvidia. The development of algorithms and architectures behind LLMs and generative AI will continue to evolve over time from the transformer architecture designs. Optimisation of existing algorithms or inventing more efficient ones to reduce compute resource usage and cost will be key. This is even more so for Chinese firms, which cannot get hold of the latest chips from Nvidia.

The future of LLMs and generative AI is certainly entering exciting times. With agentic AI shifting from experimental to foundational and fully operational mode, it will allow work to be delegated to digital colleagues seamlessly, and organisational goals can be achieved by a human team working with digital colleagues. To enhance agentic AI offerings, there are a few key aspects to focus on: establishing a framework that is trusted, explainable, and safe; strengthening human–AI collaboration models; and optimising interoperability between digital agents and real-world systems. Though there are limitations in the current generative virtual playground, the future is bright, with so much interest and investment pouring into this research area. We will be able to witness very realistic and relevant digital assets in the virtual environment generated. Science and national Security will break new ground with new innovations inspired and brought about by this technology. Apart from the increasing number of applications that LLMs and generative AI can contribute to, these applications will be more integrated into the ecosystem, enabling more seamless access for users.

Section 2

Legal and Ethical Frameworks

by Lee Cheng Tan

Chapter 7

Regulatory "Arms Race"

The release of OpenAI's ChatGPT in November 2022 triggered two parallel artificial intelligence (AI) "arms races".

The following year saw major tech players and aspirants compete with one another as they poured in millions and billions of dollars to develop and release their own advanced AI models and tools in a rush to be first to market. Every industry fashioned its own self-talk about the limitless potential of AI to drive this state of frenzy. Initially, various prominent tech figures tried to rein in the exuberance. Hundreds of the biggest names in the industry signed an open letter in March 2023 to "Pause AI" – urging leading labs to halt training of new systems for six months.[1] The main warning in the letter is against creations that even their creators cannot understand or predict, let alone control. Dramatically, the "Godfather of AI", Geoffrey Hinton, resigned from Google so that he could freely speak out about the risks of "scary AI chatbots".[2] A part of him, he said, now regrets his life's work.[3] Hinton, together with two graduate students, pioneered research into neural networks and deep learning, which paved the way for generative AI systems such as

[1] Future of Life Institute. Pause giant AI experiments: An open letter - future of life institute, July 1, 2024. https://futureoflife.org/open-letter/pause-giant-ai-experiments/.

[2] Z. Kleinman, and C. Vallance, AI 'godfather' Geoffrey Hinton warns of dangers as he quits Google. *BBC*, May 2, 2023. https://www.bbc.com/news/world-us-canada-65452940.

[3] C. Metz, 'The Godfather of AI' Quits Google and Warns of Danger Ahead. *The New York Times*, 4 May 2023. www.nytimes.com/2023/05/01/technology/ai-google-chatbot-engineer-quits-hinton.html.

ChatGPT. One of these graduate students was Ilya Sutskever, who went on to become a co-founder of OpenAI and its chief scientist. Another of Hinton's illustrious students is Yann LeCun, who became Meta's chief scientist of AI. Hinton's stature in the industry certainly makes his warnings extra ominous. However, rather than scaling back, the race to develop cutting-edge AI algorithms gathered momentum and, in January 2025, experienced its modern-day "Sputnik Moment" when a Chinese-made model called DeepSeek (深度求索) released its latest version.[4] Its release prompted the then newly inaugurated U.S. President, Donald Trump, to tell American tech companies to heed this wake-up call and to be laser-focused on competing to win.[5]

Unsurprisingly, therefore, a regulatory "arms race" developed in tandem. National and supranational regulators compete with one another to churn out laws and guidelines to govern the development and use of AI within their jurisdictions.

In her book, *Digital Empires: The Global Battle to Regulate Technologies*, Anu Bradford depicts China, the European Union (EU) and the U.S. as the three dominant powers that are competing to shape the global digital world order.[6] There's an intense race amongst them to draft legislation to rein in the power of AI, in alignment with their own interests and values. The governments in all three jurisdictions share a deep regulatory concern about AI but take different paths. The label "empire" reflects their ambition to expand their respective spheres of influence via their own models of governance, seeking to pull other countries into the "orbits of the American, Chinese, or European digital empires".[7] Of course, beyond the rules, these digital empires are also expanding and exporting their tech companies and offerings, as well as promoting their own brand of digital capitalism.

This section of the book discusses and broadly compares the three governance frameworks in China, the EU and the U.S. as they relate to

---

[4]Ng, B. Drenon, T. Gerken, and M. Cieslak, What Is DeepSeek - and Why Is Everyone Talking About It?, *BBC,* 28 January 28, 2025. https://www.bbc.com/news/articles/c5yv5976z9po.

[5]*Ibid*

[6]A. Bradford, (2023). *Digital Empires: The Global Battle to Regulate Technologies*. 1st ed. US: Oxford University Press, 2023. https://doi.org/10.1093/oso/9780197649268.001.0001.

[7]A. Bradford, (2023), *Op. cit.*

generative AI and, in particular, large language models (LLMs). The comparison will be underpinned by the following selected topics:

- **Data Protection:** Governments cannot regulate AI without regulating access to and use of data. The concept of AI has been around for decades. However, the exponential growth in both computational power and global data in recent years combined to give LLMs such as ChatGPT a lethal edge. This explains why there is now a battle for semiconductor chips and a surge in the number of data centres being built.[8] Chatbots and LLMs require access to massive amounts of data to train their algorithms and to produce outputs. Datasets scraped from the internet may range from personal data or private information obtained without consent or which are no longer accurate. Many countries have their own data protection frameworks. The explosive growth in the number of LLMs and the use of generative AI naturally give rise to several legal concerns regarding data privacy and the enforcement of data subjects' rights.
- **AI Laws:** Various pieces of legislations, big and small, were mooted, and some of them were passed in almost lightning speed to tackle the risks associated with AI. Mainly, these AI laws aim to set up guardrails to engender trust in the use of the advanced technology. This is achieved by imposing obligations of accountability, explainability, and human oversight. The discussion of AI legislation – proposed or passed – in China, the EU, and the U.S. focuses on these three key governance mechanisms regarding the development and use of generative AI. A brief look at how each jurisdiction tackles "deepfakes" (i.e., computer-created artificial videos in which images are combined to create new footage depicting events, statements, or actions which did not actually happen) will serve as a useful comparison.
- **Copyright:** Both the outputs and inputs of generative AI models raise important intellectual property rights issues. The first is whether AI-generated contents are copyrightable, since human authorship remains the cornerstone of copyright protection. The next question is whether these contents themselves infringe copyright. The training behind most of the stunning and mesmerising generative output requires the collection and compilation of enormous databases. These

[8] B. Conerly, Chip fabs, data centers propping up construction. *Forbes*, June 21, 2024. https://www.forbes.com/sites/billconerly/2024/06/19/chip-fabs-data-centers-propping-up-construction/.

"training sets" include millions of audios, images, texts, and videos; some, if not most, are copyrighted. Several leading media companies and content producers have already filed lawsuits against companies such as ChatGPT's OpenAI, Anthropic, Midjourney, Stability AI, and DeviantArt for copyright infringement.[9] Perhaps, a deeper question is whether existing copyright laws are adequate or should be recast to deal with generative AI.

- **Regulators:** Law is but one component of a general regulatory system in society, and its effectiveness does not rely solely on the wording adopted. The gap between law on paper and law in action is informed by and depends on actions taken by regulators. For comparison, the key regulators tasked with monitoring and implementing rules on generative AI will be profiled in each jurisdiction.
- **Ethics:** While laws and regulations establish enforceable rights and obligations regarding the development and deployment of generative AI, ethics address the gaps and nuances that legislation cannot or is not yet ready to address. Ethics can also motivate and guide businesses to go above and beyond what is legally required in order to engender trust and responsible actions. The Alan Turing Institute defines AI ethics as "a set of values, principles and techniques that employ widely accepted standards of right and wrong to guide moral conduct in the development and use of AI technologies".[10] Potential harms such as bias, discrimination, abuse, or negative unintended consequences of AI systems can thus be avoided or tackled. Many tech companies have undertaken voluntary ethical practices as a form of self-regulation to commit to the safe development and deployment of this advanced technology. The following chapters will review the ethical frameworks adopted, if any, in each of the three jurisdictions and offer a glimpse of the self-regulation undertaken by the tech companies in them.

---

[9] Generative AI Lawsuits Timeline: Legal Cases vs. OpenAI, Microsoft, Anthropic, Nvidia and More. Sustainable Tech Partner for Green IT Service Providers, July 21, 2024. https://sustainabletechpartner.com/topics/ai/generative-ai-lawsuit-timeline/.

[10] D. Leslie, Understanding artificial intelligence ethics and safety: A guide for the responsible design and implementation of AI systems in the public sector. *The Alan Turing Institute*, 2019. Accessed September 10, 2024. https://doi.org/10.5281/zenodo.3240529.

Chapter 8

China

8.1 AI with Chinese Social Characteristics

China is not shy about its bold ambitions to be a leading AI superpower. It has even set a deadline to achieve this goal. The State Council (the Chinese government's main administrative organ or cabinet) presented the country's AI development strategy in 2017 and boldly declared its aspiration to be a leading AI superpower by 2030.[1] The end of the Covid-19 pandemic and the mortgage crisis faced by the country afterwards provided impetus for the country to do whatever it takes to harness AI and reap all its economic benefits. At the start of President Xi Jinping's third term, the CCP set up a body known as the Central Science and Technology Commission (CSTC) as part of a far-reaching overhaul and streamlining of government and party organs to oversee the nation's drive towards self-reliance in science and technology. Vice-Premier Ding Xuexiang heads the Commission, reflecting a strong political will to focus on technological advancements since it is led by a member from the Politburo Standing Committee – the highest, innermost decision-making circle.[2] DeepSeek's

[1] DigiChina. Full Translation: China's 'New Generation Artificial Intelligence Development Plan' (2017), dated 1 October 2021. Available at https://digichina.stanford.edu/work/full-translation-chinas-new-generation-artificial-intelligence-development-plan-2017/.

[2] W. Zheng, China reveals Ding Xuexiang as head of Communist Party science and technology body. *South China Morning Post*, June 27, 2024. https://www.scmp.com/news/china/politics/article/3268226/chinas-ding-xuexiang-revealed-head-party-science-and-technology-body.

meteoric rise, which sounded a real possibility that China might overtake the U.S. in the AI arms race, caused the Nasdaq to plummet 3% in a single day.[3] Without a doubt, this impact is seen as a testament to the country's technological prowess and, more importantly, its self-reliance.

With global AI governance still in a nascent stage with yet-to-be-established norms, China is also keen to lead in the setting of global AI standards.[4] Bradford describes China's AI regulatory model as state-driven. As will be seen in the following, both the state's and the CCP's role in many aspects of AI development is deep and multifaceted. China has been proactively developing its own governance principles and regulations for AI systems. After all, the country is home to major big tech players such as Alibaba, Baidu, ByteDance, and Tencent – probably the only companies that can rival the U.S. tech giants.

Some may gloss over these governance efforts due to the country's track record of deploying AI for mass surveillance.[5] Chinese cities are under the heaviest closed-circuit television (CCTV) surveillance in the world.[6] It is estimated that half of around 1 billion of such cameras installed in the world are in China.[7] Public cameras are monitored by the police who use automated facial recognition algorithms to tackle crime. Such technological surveillance is part of the "Golden Shield Project" created in the late 1990s as a tool for public security. The project integrates online government population databases to enable monitoring and control of citizens to maintain stability of society and the regime. The country also uses mass data and surveillance information to support its

---

[3] S. Carew, A. Cooper, and A. Banaerjee. DeepSeek sparks AI stock selloff; Nvidia posts record market-cap loss. *Reuters*, 28 January, 2025. https://www.reuters.com/technology/chinas-deepseek-sets-off-ai-market-rout-2025-01-27/.

[4] J. Cheng, and J. Zeng, (2023). Shaping AI's future? China in global AI governance, *32 J. Contemp. China* 794, 797.

[5] Carnegie Endowment for International Peace. China's new AI governance initiatives shouldn't be ignored. n.d. https://carnegieendowment.org/posts/2022/01/chinas-new-ai-governance-initiatives-shouldnt-be-ignored?lang=en.

[6] P. Bischoff, Surveillance camera statistics: which are the most surveilled cities? *Comparitech*, May 23, 2023. https://www.comparitech.com/vpn-privacy/the-worlds-most-surveilled-cities/.

[7] L. Burbano, Surveillance camera statistics: which cities have the most CCTV cameras? *TOMORROW CITY,* July 28, 2023. https://www.tomorrow.city/surveillance-camera-statistics-which-cities-have-the-most-cctv-cameras/.

Social Credit System introduced in 2014.[8] This comprises a diverse network of measures aimed at promoting levels of trust and positive social behaviour, both on the part of corporations and individuals. Without question, the Chinese government's surveillance prowess has been vastly enhanced by big data processing and facial recognition AI. The country no doubt sees AI as a powerful tool to maintain social stability and the CCP's grip over information flow. However, China is also keenly aware of AI's potential for its economy. It has been tipped as the country that will benefit most from this advanced technology – projected to achieve a staggering 26% boost to its GDP in 2030.[9] The country thus needs to put in place a governance framework that can reap stellar economic dividends while maintaining its political system's core tenets. Angela Zhang Huyue described this complicated balancing act of achieving growth and maintaining control as a high-wire acrobatic manoeuvre in her book, *High Wire: How China Regulates Big Tech and Governs its Economy.*[10]

8.2 Data Protection

The "Cybersecurity Law (网络安全法)"[11] (CSL), which came into effect in June 2017, is the country's first legislation to regulate its cyberspace.[12] CSL's focus is cybersecurity, but it also established basic principles for data protection, including requirements for data localisation, security assessments, and personal information protection. Companies which qualify as "critical information infrastructure" must store personal

[8] M. Pei, Xi Jinping's high-tech surveillance state. *Australian Financial Review*, February 29, 2024. https://www.afr.com/world/asia/in-china-a-poor-social-score-affects-where-you-can-sleep-dine-or-live-20240222-p5f6y9.; Z. Yang, China just announced a new social credit law. Here's what it means. *MIT Technology Review*, August 21, 2023. https://www.technologyreview.com/2022/11/22/1063605/china-announced-a-new-social-credit-law-what-does-it-mean/.

[9] PwC estimated that the greatest economic gains from AI will be in China economy (26% boost to GDP in 2030 compared with North America's 14.5% boost). PwC. PwC's Global Artificial Intelligence Study: Sizing the prize. n.d. https://www.pwc.com/gx/en/issues/data-and-analytics/publications/artificial-intelligence-study.html.

[10] A. H. Zhang, (2024). *High Wire How China Regulates Big Tech and Governs Its Economy.* 1st ed. US: Oxford University Press. https://doi.org/10.1093/oso/9780197682258.001.0001.

[11] Cybersecurity Law of the People's Republic of China "网络安全法". China Law Translate, November 27, 2019. https://www.chinalawtranslate.com/en/2016-cybersecurity-law/.

[12] Cybersecurity Law of the People's Republic of China, (2019), *Op. cit.*

information collected within China.[13] Until this law, Chinese data privacy requirements were scattered across various laws and regulations, both at national and regional levels.[14] Apple immediately responded to CSL by opening its first data centre in China and granting ownership of its Chinese customers' data to a Chinese state-owned company, Guizhou-Cloud Big Data.[15] CSL's data privacy provisions are repeated in a subsequent comprehensive data law, which is discussed later in this chapter. One important point about the CSL is that it codified the authority of the agency known as the Cyberspace Administration of China (CAC) – an agency that wields immense power and influence.

The next piece of legislation, the "Data Security Law (数据安全法)"[16] (DSL), which came into effect in September 2021, set up a framework that classifies data collected and stored in China based on its potential impact on Chinese national security and regulates its storage and transfer depending on the data's classification level. DSL is generally seen as a response to the U.S. Clarifying Lawful Overseas Use of Data Act (CLOUD Act), which gives U.S. law enforcement agencies the authority to compel companies falling under U.S. jurisdiction to produce requested data regardless of where the data are stored. The important data and core data covered relate to the country's national security and are non-personal. DSL tasked CAC with the overall coordination powers over online data security.

The third piece of legislation is the "Personal Information Protection Law (个人信息保护法)"[17] (PIPL), which came into effect in November 2021. PIPL is a comprehensive framework that specifically regulates the protection of personal information. As it is largely modelled after the EU's 2018 General Data Protection Regulation (GDPR), there are broad

---

[13] *Ibid* Note 11, Article 37.

[14] Linklaters LLP. China: Key pointers on the Cybersecurity Law | DigiLinks | Blogs | Insights | Linklaters. n.d. https://www.linklaters.com/en/insights/blogs/digilinks/2021/may/china---key-pointers-on-the-cybersecurity-law.

[15] J. Nicas, R. Zhong, and D. Wakabayashi, Censorship, Surveillance and Profits: A Hard Bargain for Apple in China. *The New York Times*, May 17, 2021. https://www.nytimes.com/2021/05/17/technology/apple-china-censorship-data.html.

[16] Data Security Law of the People's Republic of China "数据安全法". China Law Translate, June 25, 2021. https://www.chinalawtranslate.com/en/datasecuritylaw/.

[17] Personal Information Protection Law of the Republic of China "个人信息保护法". China Law Translate. available at https://www.chinalawtranslate.com/en/Personal-Information-Protection-Law/.

similarities between the two. PIPL applies to all types of data activities (e.g., collection, storage, usage, reorganisation, transmission, provision, disclosure, and deletion) involving the personal information of data subjects in China. It also applies to activities outside China that are aimed at providing products or services to individuals in China or analysing their behaviour. PIPL also follows a principle-based approach which must be complied with when processing personal information. These principles largely overlap with those under GDPR and are as follows: lawfulness, legitimacy, necessity, and good faith; purpose limitation; transparency; quality of handling; data security; and accountability.[18] An LLM provider must be able to demonstrate PIPL compliance of these principles through audits, training, and comprehensive data handling policies.

Many key provisions relating to data protection are present in all three laws. Chinese law uses a definition similar to GDPR's for personal data – namely information relating to an individual which, by itself or in combination with other information, will disclose an individual's identity.[19] Like GDPR, Chinese law emphasises the requirement of informed consent in the collection, use, and processing of personal information. Informed consent requires informing a person about what data will be collected, how they will be used, who will use them, and for what purposes they will be used before consent is given.[20] China issued a set of national standards (effective 1 December 2023), outlining some best industry practices to guide organisations in implementing notice and consent requirements in personal data processing activities.[21] In principle, any company wishing to train their LLM on Chinese data must obtain explicit and voluntary consent from data subjects before collecting or processing their personal information. Under the PIPL, the collection of "sensitive personal information"[22] requires separate and standalone consent. This category includes the data subject's biometrics, religious beliefs, health,

[18] Articles 5–9 of the PIPL.

[19] Article 76 of Cybersecurity Law, supra, Note 11.

[20] Cybersecurity Law Article 22; PIPL Article 13.

[21] TC260 the "Notice and Consent Standards").

[22] Article 28. https://www.fieldfisher.com/en/insights/china%E2%80%99s-personal-information-protection-law-what-d.

finances, and geographical locations, as well as data on children under the age of 14.[23]

Important data and personal information of Chinese citizens must be processed and stored within China. To transfer any personal data outside of China, an LLM must either pass a security assessment by CAC, sign and file a standard contract with CAC, or obtain certification from a CAC-accredited institution.[24] In March 2024, China implemented the "Provisions on Promoting and Regulating Cross-border Data Flows".[25] With the new provisions, the earlier statutory requirements will be waived if the LLM processes personal information (excluding sensitive data) of fewer than 100,000 individuals in China.[26] However, security assessments by CAC remain mandatory if the LLM is transferring sensitive personal information of over 10,000 individuals.

PIPL provides for the highest penalties in terms of fines, which are no more than RMB 50 million or 5% of the offending company's previous annual revenue.[27] The Chinese law does not establish any centralised authority to enforce its provisions. Like GDPR, PIPL also has extraterritorial application.[28] Its provisions apply to personal data processing outside China if the purpose is to provide products or services to individuals in China or to analyse their behaviour.

As with GDPR, PIPL provides data subjects with several rights, such as the right to access their data, correct inaccuracies, delete data, and data portability.[29] Prior to PIPL, Chinese law did not recognise the right to be forgotten. In 2015, Ren sued the search engine company, Baidu, to request the deletion of search results that associated him with a biotech company he no longer worked for. Both the Haidian District Court of Beijing and the appellate Beijing No. 1 Intermediate People's Court dismissed the

---

[23] Briefing, China. PIPL vs GDPR - Key Differences and Implications for Compliance in China. China Briefing News, July 21, 2022. https://www.china-briefing.com/news/pipl-vs-gdpr-key-differences-and-implications-for-compliance-in-china/.

[24] Article 38 PIPL.

[25] Provisions on Promoting and Regulating the Cross-Border Flow of Data "促进和规范数据跨境流动规定". China Law Translate, June 12, 2024. https://www.chinalawtranslate.com/en/Provisions-on-Promoting-and-Regulating-the-Cross--Border-Flow-of-Data/.

[26] Ibid, Article 8.

[27] PIPL Article 66.

[28] PIPL Article 3.

[29] PIPL Article 44–49.

case.[30] This is different from the situation in the EU, where the European Court of Justice (ECJ) in fact upheld such a right even before GDPR was implemented.

DiDi Chuxing's dire data breaches

The importance of data privacy and the PIPL was dramatically illustrated shortly after the law was passed. The Chinese ride-hailing company, DiDi Chuxing, was listed on the New York Stock Exchange in late June 2021 and raised US$4.4 billion, making this the largest IPO since Alibaba at the time. The company had apparently received but ignored a warning from CAC a few months earlier to postpone its listing until a thorough self-examination of cybersecurity risks associated with its services.[31] Within days after the IPO listing, CAC initiated a regulatory review, and soon after, 25 of DiDi's apps were removed from its app store for "grave issues of collecting and using personal information in violation of laws and regulations".[32] The company was also banned from recruiting new drivers.[33] Inspection teams from at least seven cybersecurity-related agencies visited the company's offices for on-site reviews.[34] The publicised review took its toll, and less than six months after its IPO, DiDi shockingly announced it would delist from the

[30] G. Du, China's first right to be forgotten case. *China Justice Observer*, February 21, 2021. https://www.chinajusticeobserver.com/a/china-s-first-the-right-to-be-forgotten-case.

[31] A. H. Zhang, The Didi Case and the Party's Influence over Data Enforcement. *U.S.-Asia Law Institute*, September 20, 2022. https://usali.org/usali-perspectives-blog/the-didi-case-and-the-partys-influence-over-data-enforcement.; Y. Jing, K. Zhai, and C. Driebusch, Didi Tried Balancing Pressure From China and Investors. It Satisfied Neither. *The Wall Street Journal*, July 9, 2021. https://www.wsj.com/articles/didi-ipo-china-regulators-investors-trouble-11625873909?mod=article_inline.

[32] Cyberspace Administration of China: Remove 25 Apps Including "Didi Enterprise Edition". *Sina*, July. 9, 2021. https://finance.sina.com.cn/tech/2021-07-09/doc-ikqcf-nca5945007.shtml.

[33] Didi's China Rivals Go Full Speed for Customers After App Ban. *Nikkei Asia,* July 28, 2021. https://asia.nikkei.com/Business/China-tech/Didi-s-China-rivals-go-full-speed-for-customers-after-app-ban.

[34] Chinese Regulators Send Teams to Didi for Cybersecurity Review. *Reuters,* July 16, 2021. https://www.reuters.com/technology/chinese-regulators-send-on-site-teams-conduct-cybersecurity-review-didi-2021-07-16/.

NYSE.[35] By February 2022, the company saw its listed share price fall 70% since its IPO and planned to lay off 20% of its staff.[36] The regulatory review eventually ended in July 2022, and DiDi was slapped with a staggering RMB 8 billion fine on the grounds of excessive data collection and privacy infringement going back seven years.[37] No formal decision was published to explain or break down the fine, but the astronomical quantum must have been based on the 2021-enacted PIPL, which provides for a fine of up to 5% of a firm's revenue in the previous year.[38] If so, this would mean that DiDi was being retroactively punished for conduct prior to the adoption of the personal data protection regulation. In June 2022, DiDi delisted from the NYSE.[39]

Any LLMs that want to train Chinese data will need to understand the three key pieces of legislation that make up China's personal data protection framework. And as DiDi's case amply demonstrated, any data privacy violation can lead to dire consequences. From August 2023, Beijing started requiring tech companies to seek CAC's approval before making their LLMs available to the public.[40] Within six months, more than 40 AI models, including those from Alibaba, Baidu, and ByteDance, were so approved. Such approvals are prima facie evidence that these Chinese LLMs would have complied with privacy protection requirements.

---

[35] W. Tan, Less than 6 months after its IPO, China's Didi says it will delist from the New York Stock Exchange. *CNBC*, December 3, 2021. https://www.cnbc.com/2021/12/03/didi-on-delisting-from-us-and-list-in-hong-kong.html.

[36] Y. Wang, Chinese ride-sharing firm Didi global reportedly laying off thousands of employees. *Forbes*, February 16, 2022. https://www.forbes.com/sites/ywang/2022/02/15/chinese-ride-sharing-firm-didi-global-reportedly-laying-off-thousands-of-employees/.

[37] Graham Webster, Translation: Chinese Authorities Announce $1.2B Fine in Didi Case, Describe "Despicable" Data Abuses, DigiChina.stanford.edu (Jul. 21, 2022). https://digichina.stanford.edu/work/translation-chinese-authorities-announce-2b-fine-in-didi-case-describe-despicable-data-abuses/.

[38] PIPL Article 66.

[39] J. Shen, A timeline of Didi and its year-long cybersecurity investigation. *TechNode*, July 22, 2022. https://technode.com/2022/07/22/a-timeline-of-didi-and-its-year-long-cybersecurity-investigation/.

[40] J. Ye, China Approves over 40 AI Models for Public Use in Past Six Months. *Reuters*, January 29, 2024. https://www.reuters.com/technology/china-approves-over-40-ai-models-public-use-past-six-months-2024-01-29/.

Despite the presence of three national laws and regulatory endorsement, Chinese consumers understand the inherent challenges in enforcing privacy protection. With its elaborate surveillance network and mechanisms, the Chinese government is the largest data controller in the country.[41] The country's tech giants have for years collected massive amounts of personal data and shared them with their affiliates and business partners. These firms also cooperate and work with the authorities to ensure censorship. One of the most powerful tools used by the Chinese government is Tencent's online messaging app, WeChat, which has more than 1 billion users in China.[42] The bottom line for China is whether there will be sufficient political will to uphold data privacy while pursuing the national ambition to trump the U.S. in this AI race.

8.3 AI Laws

In this hot race, China can lay claim to being the first country to introduce specific laws to regulate AI. In late 2021, the "Provisions on the Management of Algorithmic Recommendations in Internet Information Services (互联网信息务算法推荐管理规定)" (Algorithmic Recommendation Rules) was promulgated.[43] These regulations apply to the use of algorithms in the provision of online information services within the mainland territory of the People's Republic of China.[44] Service providers are held accountable and must ensure their algorithms are "oriented towards mainstream values", "actively transmit positive energy", and not "disrupt economic and social order".[45] The law mandates human oversight, as it requires algorithmic recommendation service providers to establish technical measures to check published information and to

[41] A. H. Zhang, (2024), *Op. cit.*

[42] J. Yang, WeChat Becomes a Powerful Surveillance Tool Everywhere in China. *The Wall Street Journal*, December 22, 2020. https://www.wsj.com/articles/wechat-becomes-a-powerful-surveillance-tool-everywhere-in-china-11608633003.

[43] China Law Translate. Provisions on the Management of Algorithmic Recommendations in Internet Information Services, (January 4, 2022). Accessed August 19, 2024. https://www.chinalawtranslate.com/en/Provisions-on-Promoting-and-Regulating-the-Cross--Border-Flow-of-Data/. These laws came into effect on 1 March 2022 per Article 35.

[44] Article 2 Algorithmic Recommendation Rules.

[45] Article 6 Algorithmic Recommendation Rules.

periodically check, assess, and verify algorithm mechanisms, models, data, and outcomes to ensure compliance with the law, ethics, and morals, and even prevention of addiction among users.[46] The law also specifically requires providers to "establish and improve mechanisms for manual intervention and users' independent selections" on key pages such as homepages and recommendations.[47] Users are given the right to turn off algorithmic recommendations for an app or website and to select or delete specific user tags for personalising content recommendations.[48] Users also have the right to obtain an explanation if an algorithm has a major impact on their rights.[49] Service providers are required to disclose the basic operating logic, purpose, and main operating mechanisms to users.[50] Most crucially, this law created a new regulatory tool – the Algorithm Registry. Companies that use algorithms to provide online content which have "public opinion properties or … social mobilization capabilities" must file details about their algorithms with regulators within 10 days of launching.[51] Such service providers must disclose key basic information about their algorithm, list all open-source and "self-built" datasets that the algorithm was trained on, and conduct algorithm security self-assessments. They must put in place mechanisms for manual intervention in "top searches" and "hot topics" to ensure conformity to "mainstream value orientations".[52] The law gives regulators express powers to carry out security assessments and oversight inspections, and service providers are required to retain network logs and cooperate.[53]

According to Matt Sheehan, who researched and traced the roots of China's AI regulations,[54] it is entirely within expectation that China would be quick to set up legal guardrails when it comes to content. The term "algorithm recommendation" started to appear rather frequently in state- and party-run media from late 2016. Eventually, one popular app by

---

[46] Article 7 & 8 Algorithmic Recommendation Rules.

[47] Article 11 Algorithmic Recommendation Rules.

[48] Article 17 Algorithmic Recommendation Rules.

[49] Article 17 Algorithmic Recommendation Rules.

[50] Article 16. Algorithmic Recommendation Rules.

[51] Article 24 Algorithmic Recommendation Rules.

[52] Article 6 & 11 Algorithmic Recommendation Rules.

[53] Article 28 Algorithmic Recommendation Rules.

[54] M. Sheehan, Tracing the Roots of China's AI Regulations. *Carnegie Endowment for International Peace, February 27, 2024.* https://carnegieendowment.org/research/2024/02/tracing-the-roots-of-chinas-ai-regulations?lang=en.

ByteDance called *Jinri Toutiao* (literally "Today's Headlines") was singled out for criticism by the *People's Daily*, one of the CCP's flagship newspapers (also known as *Renmin Ribao* in Chinese). Articles with titles such as "Algorithm Cannot Be Allowed to Decide Content"[55] criticised the proliferation of vulgar and undesirable content on the platform and possible copyright infringement. As Sheehan explained, since taking power in 1949, the CCP has largely been able to decide which news stories are featured prominently in the media. If algorithms were allowed to decide what content gets pushed to Chinese people, it would undermine the party's goal of a unified public narrative of events. This strand of control is also manifest in the next two pieces of AI legislation.

8.3.1 *Deepfakes*

The "Provisions on the Administration of Deep Synthesis Internet Information Services (互联网信息服务深度合成管理规定)" (Deep Synthesis Rules)[56] came into effect on 10 January 2023. These rules govern the use of algorithms to generate or alter text, images, video, audio, and other virtual renderings within China. The law and the term "deep synthesis" specifically address the party's concerns about deepfakes. Service or platform providers must superimpose a visible watermark over the synthetic content generated to clearly identify text, images, audio, video, or other content generated or edited using AI.[57] Technical logs must be retained to enable tracing of the origin of the synthetic content. Providers of deep synthesis are required to disclose the basic operating logic, purpose, and main operating mechanisms of the deep synthesis services in an appropriate manner.[58] Organisations must provide necessary notification to and obtain separate consent from individuals before providing editing functions for biometric information, such as facial features and voice prints.[59] Lastly, if the AI-powered services or products have

[55] Y. Sheng, Algorithm recommendation: Algorithms should not be allowed to determine content (评算法推荐：不能让算法决定内容). *People's Daily*, September 18, 2017. http://opinion.people.com.cn/n1/2017/0918/c1003-29540709.html.

[56] China Law Translate, Provisions on the Administration of Deep Synthesis Internet Information Services "互联网信息服务深度合成管理规定". dated 1 February 1, 2023. Available at https://www.chinalawtranslate.com/en/deep-synthesis/.

[57] Article 16 & 17 Deep Synthesis Rules.

[58] Article 8 Deep Synthesis Rules.

[59] Article 14 Deep Synthesis Rules.

"public opinion attributes or social mobilisation capabilities", service providers must submit a filing with the Algorithm Registry.[60] Several months after these rules were passed, CAC released its first list of approved suppliers of "deep fake" technology – a white list that included owners of 41 algorithms, including the usual suspects: Alibaba, Baidu, and Tencent.[61]

China's legislative response to powerful LLMs was unveiled in July 2023 in the form of the "Interim Measures for the Management of Generative Artificial Intelligence Services (生成式人工智能服务管理办法)" (GAI Interim Measures 2023).[62] These measures seek to build on existing regulations to create a horizontal piece of legislation to comprehensively regulate AI and to position the country as a key player in shaping global governance norms and standards. It foreshadows a dedicated national law on AI. These interim requirements apply to all generative AI services offered to the public in China, whether the providers are onshore or offshore. There is a carve-out for internal research or use of generative AI technology by industrial organisations, companies, educational and research institutions, and other professional organisations. Providers of generative AI services must sign service agreements with users setting out both sides' rights and obligations. For services with "public opinion properties or social mobilization capacity", companies must apply to the regulator for a security impact assessment before providing services to the public and carry out filing with the Algorithm Registry.[63] Tech companies must ensure that AI-generated contents uphold the political values of the CCP, prevent discrimination, respect intellectual property rights, and safeguard

---

[60] A. Roberts and T. Ke,. Regulating ChatGPT and the Metaverse for social good: How do China's first-ever deepfake rules affect AI governance. *Linklaters*, July 7, 2023. https://techinsights.linklaters.com/post/102iitc/regulating-chatgpt-and-the-metaverse-for-social-good-how-do-chinas-first-ever-d.

[61] J. Cai, China publishes white list of deep fake providers to preserve national security and 'core socialist values.' *South China Morning Post*, June 20, 2023. https://www.scmp.com/news/china/politics/article/3224775/china-publishes-white-list-deep-fake-providers-preserve-national-security-and-core-socialist-values.

[62] The Measures for the Management of Generative Artificial Intelligence Services (生成式人工智能服务管理办法). *Office of the Central Cyberspace Administration of China,* July 13, 2023. http://www.cac.gov.cn/2023-07/13/c_1690898327029107.htm. See also China Law Translate (2 August 2023). Available at https://www.chinalawtranslate.com/en/generative-ai-interim/.

[63] Article 17 GAI Interim Measures 2023.

user data privacy. Pushing out these measures so soon after the Deep Synthesis regulations reflects the Chinese government's objective to craft its own governance model for generative AI.

After the GAI Interim Measures 2023 were passed, many scholars noted a visible scaling back of obligations.[64] Compared with the draft put forth for public consultation three months before implementation, the final version of these interim rules markedly reduced the legal obligations imposed on service providers.[65] The earlier draft mandated that service providers must ensure that AI-generated content fulfilled the requirements of "truth, accuracy, objectivity and diversity of the data".[66] These strict liability requirements were deleted and replaced with a requirement that service providers employ effective measures to increase transparency, accuracy, and reliability of generated content.[67] A proposed three-month deadline to require service providers to report illegal content and implement content filtering measures was removed.[68] Instead, service providers are merely required to employ measures and report to their own relevant departments in charge if they discover any illegal content.[69] Even the monetary penalty provision stipulating a fine of up to 100,000 yuan was removed. Further, new provisions were added to emphasise the promotion of innovation, development, and security in generative AI. This last message was reinforced by having the GAI Interim Measures signed off by the CAC along with six other ministries and government agencies. Zhang sees this latest legislation as sending a strong pro-growth signal to the industry while exhorting various stakeholders to work together to accelerate technological progress.[70]

---

[64] A. H. Zhang, The Promise and Perils of China's Regulation of Artificial Intelligence. January 28, 2024. University of Hong Kong Faculty of Law Research Paper No. 2024/02. Available at SSRN: https://ssrn.com/abstract=4708676 or http://dx.doi.org/10.2139/ssrn.4708676.

[65] Translate, China Law. Comparison Chart of Current vs. Draft rules for Generative AI. China Law Translate, July 13, 2023. https://www.chinalawtranslate.com/en/comparison-chart-of-current-vs-draft-rules-for-generative-ai/.

[66] Article 4(4) and 7(4) GAI Interim Measures 2023.

[67] Article 4(5) and 7(4) GAI Interim Measures 2023.

[68] Article 15 GAI Interim Measures 2023.

[69] Article 14 GAI Interim Measures 2023.

[70] A. H. Zhang, (2024), *Op. cit.*

8.3.2 *Algorithm Registry: Distinctive feature of China's AI laws*

Regardless of whether China will eventually pass a law similar to the EU's AI law, a prominent and unique feature of its AI governance is the creation and use of the Algorithm Registry (算法备案系统). Under all three AI regulations, providers whose algorithms have "public opinion properties or capacity for social mobilization" are required to submit a filing of their algorithm with the registry within 10 business days of operation. To recap, the registry was created by the Algorithmic Recommendation Rules.[71] While the EU takes an expansive risk-based approach in its AI Act (discussed in the following chapter) directed at all applications of AI technology, China zeroes in on a more fundamental unit in the supply chain: the algorithm. This may require companies to undertake multiple filings for the same app if different algorithms are used for content recommendations, content filtering, and other functions. Sheehan's research into Chinese AI governance shows how, in practice, regulators treat the registration process more like a licensing regime than a simple registration process, as they withhold their official acceptance of registrations until satisfied with the safety and security of the models.[72] CAC's registry webpage provides disclosure of these filings, which include submissions from platform giants such as Alibaba and Tencent.[73] Algorithm providers are expected to list the names of each open-source and self-built dataset used to train the model, specifying the source of that data, and disclosing whether the algorithm inputs involve biometric or other personal information.[74] Companies are also required to upload PDF files of their "Algorithm Security Self-Assessment".[75]

In October 2023, a key Chinese standards body released a draft standard that laid out specific tests a generative AI model must pass before

---

[71] Article 24, Algorithm Recommendation Rules.

[72] M. Sheehan, (2024), *Op. cit.*

[73] Cyberspace Administration of China. Internet Information Service Algorithm Registration System (互联网信息服务算法备案系统). Accessed August 20, 2024. https://beian.cac.gov.cn/#/index.

[74] M. Sheehan, What China's Algorithm Registry Reveals about AI Governance. *Carnegie Endowment for International Peace*, December 12, 2022. https://carnegieendowment.org/posts/2022/12/what-chinas-algorithm-registry-reveals-about-ai-governance?lang=en.

[75] M. Sheehan, (2022), *Op. cit.*

registering (referred to as TC260).[76] This standard, if implemented, establishes a highly specific oversight process targeting algorithmic bias, data privacy, and copyright infringement, as well as guidelines on how to answer questions about China's political system and its history. It also provides specific parameters for training data, such as mandating that each dataset used must contain less than 4% objectionable content; and for sensitive prompts covering ideology, politics, race, and gender, among other topics – over 90% of the model's outputs must be acceptable.

The registry is clearly a very powerful iterative regulatory tool, as it allows Chinese regulators to build up knowledge and can be calibrated to deal with evolving technology. At the same time, the registration requirement will keep out foreign competition since it is highly unlikely that any foreign AI service provider would be comfortable with the extent of disclosure required. With this tool, Chinese AI governance achieves, at least on paper, the aims of accountability, explainability, and human oversight.

8.4 Copyright

When it comes to granting copyright protection to AI-generated works, the Chinese courts take a decidedly proactive and expansive approach. In late 2023, the Beijing Internet Court ruled in favour of a plaintiff, Li, who created an image using Stable Diffusion, a generative AI model which produces photorealistic images from text and image prompts.[77] Li generated the picture of a young woman by inputting various prompts (including negative prompts) and adjusting the parameters, subsequently posting the output image on his social media account with the hashtags #AI, #AI Illustration, and #AI Drawing. When he discovered that the same image was published by the defendant without permission, Li brought a claim

[76] National Technical Committee 260 on Cybersecurity of Standardization Administration of China (SAC/TC260; 全国网络安全标准化技术委员会) see Center for Security and Emerging Technology. Basic Safety Requirements for Generative Artificial Intelligence Services | Center for Security and Emerging Technology, May 14, 2024. https://cset.georgetown.edu/publication/china-safety-requirements-for-generative-ai-final/.

[77] L.K. Tan, J. Lau, and H. Wong, China: A landmark court ruling on copyright protection for AI-generated works. *Global Litigation News*, May 8, 2024. https://globallitigationnews.bakermckenzie.com/2024/05/08/china-a-landmark-court-ruling-on-copyright-protection-for-ai-generated-works/.

for copyright infringement. Like the EU and the US, Chinese copyright protection requires human authorship and proof of originality.[78] In a detailed analysis, the court held that an AI model cannot be a copyright owner since it has no free will and is not a natural person, an unincorporated association, or a legal person.[79] The developer of the AI model was not involved in the creation of the image and, in any case, the licence agreement does not claim any right to the output, so the AI model cannot lay any claim to ownership. The only candidate in this case who can claim copyright protection is Li. As far as originality is concerned, the court acknowledged that Li inputted detailed prompts to arrive at an image output that matched his expectations, using phrases such as "Japan idol", "cool pose", and "viewing at camera" and continually refining prompts as well as adjusting various parameters to reflect his personal choice and preference. Thus, the image output was not a mechanical production but reflected Li's intellectual input. The court held that the Stable Diffusion image output generated by Li qualifies as an original work of art and that, as its author, Li is the copyright owner. The Beijing Internet Court decision is similar to an earlier 2019 ruling by the Shenzhen Court.[80] The central issue is also whether AI-generated content with some form of human input is copyrightable. The Nanshan District People's Court in Shenzhen held that a financial report generated by an intelligent writing assistance system with creative input from a team from Tencent exhibited some degree of originality and was protected by copyright vested in the company.

Though each case should be determined on its own merits, the Chinese courts have demonstrated a keen willingness to recognise the copyrightability of AI-generated works with some human input. This openness is a stark contrast to the more tentative judicial attitudes taken by EU and U.S. courts. Also, the Chinese courts have not elaborated on the extent of copyrightability for such AI-generated outputs. As pointed

---

[78] China Law Translate, Copyright Law of the People's Republic of China 中华人民共和国著作权法 (2021年版), China Law Translate, November 27, 2020, https://www.chinalawtranslate.com/en/Copyright-Law-of-the-PRC-(2021-Version)/.

[79] Article 11 Copyright Law of the People's Republic of China.

[80] WIPO Lex, 2022 WIPO Intellectual Property Judges Forum, Session 3: Nanshan District People's Court, Shenzhen, Guangdong, China [2019]: Shenzhen Tencent v. Shanghai Yingxun, Case No. Y0305MC No. 14010. n.d. https://www.wipo.int/wipolex/en/judgments/details/1540.

out by Mark Lemley, protection should not extend to the baseline output generated by AI systems but is limited to the expression causally linked to the human user through prompts and other input – what Lemley terms "the idea–expression dichotomy".[81]

"Ultraman" beats AI

Three Internet courts located in Beijing, Hangzhou, and Guangzhou have jurisdiction over online copyright infringement matters. These courts generally take only a few months to reach their judgements. Several months after the decision by the Beijing Court, the Guangzhou Internet Court released another landmark ruling which held an AI-generated text-to-image content service provider liable for copyright infringement.[82] This decision is significant because it is the first case to discuss a service provider's duty of care under China's GAI Interim Measures 2023 (Interim Measures for the Management of Generative Artificial Intelligence Services issued in July 2023). The plaintiff in this case owned exclusive rights to the famous Japanese cartoon series, "Ultraman". The defendant operates a website with AI conversation and image generation functions provided by a third party through an application programming interface (API). The plaintiff discovered that the defendant's website would generate images that bore a close resemblance to "Ultraman" images through prompts that included the word "Ultraman". In its judgement released in February 2024, the court found the defendant service provider liable for copyright infringement and must implement technical measures such as keyword filters to prevent the generation of images substantially similar to "Ultraman".[83] The court also ruled that the defendant breached their duty of care under the GAI Interim Measures 2023, which required the establishment of complaint reporting mechanisms for intellectual property rights (IPR) infringement, adequate warnings to its users to respect IPR, and conspicuous labelling of AI-generated output.[84] Although this was a

[81] M. A. Lemley, How Generative Ai Turns Copyright Law on its Head, *Social Science Research Network*, January 1, 2023, https://doi.org/10.2139/ssrn.4517702.

[82] Bird and Bird. Liability of AI Service Providers for Copyright Infringement: Guangzhou Internet Court reaches world's first decision. n.d. https://www.twobirds.com/en/insights/2024/china/liability-of-ai-service-providers-for-copyright-infringement.

[83] Bird and Bird, *Op. cit.*

[84] Article 15, 4(3) & 4(5) and 12 GAI Interim Measures 2023 respectively, infra note??

momentous judgement, being the first of its kind to hold a generative AI service provider liable for copyright infringement and to invoke the GAI Interim Measures, the amount of damages awarded seemed disproportionately low. The plaintiff sought damages of RMB 300,000 (US$42,320) but was merely awarded RMB 10,000 (US$1,410).

The plaintiff had also asked for an order requiring the defendant to remove all "Ultraman" images from its training dataset. However, as the image generation function was provided by a third party not named in the action, the court did not make the order.[85] Overall, the Chinese courts appear willing to recognise the copyrightability of AI-generated works with human input, while at the same time requiring generative AI providers to respect IP rights. No doubt, many IP practitioners and regulators will be watching the Chinese judicial space for further developments.

8.5 Regulators

There is little doubt that Chinese regulators will prevail if and when they undertake any form of investigation or prosecution. During the regulatory storm from 2020 to 2022, the massive crackdown on major Chinese tech firms wiped out over US$1 trillion of their market capitalisation.[86] Besides DiDi Chuxing's data breach prosecution described earlier, the most shocking was the abrupt suspension of the proposed Shanghai-Hong Kong listing plan of Alibaba's Ant Group, which would have raised more than US$34 billion.[87] Shortly after, Alibaba was investigated by China's antitrust authority, the State Administration for Market Regulation, and fined a record US$2.8 billion for violating anti-monopoly regulations.[88] The fine was three times that imposed on Qualcomm a few years earlier by the

---

[85] Bird and Bird, *Op. cit.*

[86] D. Kwok, and S. Murdoch, Beijing's Regulatory Crackdown Wipes $1.1 Trillion off Chinese Big Tech. *Reuters*, July 12, 2023. https://www.reuters.com/technology/beijings-regulatory-crackdown-wipes-11-trln-offchinese-big-tech-2023-07-12/.

[87] R. Zhong, In Halting Ant's I.P.O., China Sends a Warning to Business. *The New York Times*, November 6, 2020. https://www.nytimes.com/2020/11/06/technology/china-ant-group-ipo.html.

[88] R. Zhong, China Fines Alibaba $2.8 Billion in Landmark Antitrust Case. *The New York Times*, September 1, 2021. Accessed September 9, 2024. https://www.nytimes.com/2021/04/09/technology/china-alibaba-monopoly-fine.html.

same regulator.[89] Alibaba and its founder, Jack Ma, were the epitome of China's big tech success story. Their tumble from grace shocked the world. The regulatory storm extended to education and training, gaming, and other industries. Chinese regulators have demonstrated that they can be quite effective at curbing the clout of powerful tech companies. As Sheehan explained, "[i]n China, the companies do not believe that if they challenge the CAC on the constitutionality of this provision they're gonna win in court. They have to figure out how to work with it or work around it. They don't have that same safety net of the courts and independent judges".[90]

The super regulator: CAC

The Cyberspace Administration of China (CAC) is a powerful agency, as it represents both the CCP and the government.[91] Its predecessor was part of the CCP propaganda department, and the agency now derives its authority from the Central Cybersecurity and Information Commission chaired by President Xi Jinping. Its party–state dual role and its direct link with the top leadership accord this agency influential top-notch bureaucratic status. The CAC also helped set up the China Internet Investment Fund (CIIF) to implement the 1% golden equity scheme whereby the state acquires "golden shares" in the domestic big tech companies. This stake confers special rights over business decisions, enabling the state investor to appoint a director to the board and have insider access to key corporate decisions and the power to veto them.[92] Since then, the CIIF has invested in more than 40 Chinese tech firms, including Alibaba, ByteDance (which owns Douyin and TikTok), the popular video app Kuaishou, SenseTime,

---

[89] N. Randewich and M. Miller, Qualcomm to pay $975 million to resolve China antitrust dispute, *Reuters*, February 10, 2015. https://www.reuters.com/article/technology/qualcomm-to-pay-975-million-to-resolve-china-antitrust-dispute-idUSKBN0LD2EL/.

[90] W. Henshall, How China's New AI Rules Could Affect U.S. Companies. *TIME*, September 19, 2023. https://time.com/6314790/china-ai-regulation-us/.

[91] J. Horsley, Behind the Facade of China's Cyber Super-Regulator, dated 8 August 2022 in DigiChina.stanford.edu. Available at https://digichina.stanford.edu/work/behind-the-facade-of-chinas-cyber-super-regulator/.

[92] China moves to take 'golden shares' in Alibaba and Tencent units. *The Financial Times*, January 12, 2023. https://www.ft.com/content/65e60815-c5a0-4c4a-bcec-4af0f76462de.

and Tencent.[93] All three AI legislations mentioned above were drafted and led by the CAC, even if other ministries and agencies are included as co-signatories.

In her book, *High Wire: How China Regulates Big Tech and Governs Its Economy*,[94] Angela Zhang explained that the Chinese regulatory regime is characterised by three features, namely hierarchy, volatility, and fragility. The regulatory bureaucrats must interact with state leaders above and below them, platform giants, and ordinary consumers. With this hierarchical decision-making structure, top-down policies constantly have to balance competing objectives such as growth or stability, innovation or privacy, etc. The absence of institutional checks and balances and inefficient transmission of information within the hierarchy results in volatile swings between tightening and easing. When regulatory actions overreach or result in unintended outcomes, the system starts to crumble and reveals its fragility. For instance, the seemingly capricious crackdown on Chinese tech companies not only eroded investor confidence but might have even fuelled suspicions among foreign policymakers, as demonstrated by the U.S. bill forcing ByteDance to divest TikTok or face a national ban.[95] These three features may unwittingly create a regulatory crisis for China in the field of AI, as they did in the crackdown on the property sector and the pandemic lockdowns.[96]

However, from a regulatory point of view, there is one factor that may distinguish the AI sector from others in the country: There is widespread collaboration between the government and various actors in the AI industry to realise China's vision to be an AI superpower. Both central and local governments have jointly established over 190 AI industry alliances.[97] The leading industry association is the Artificial Intelligence Industry

---

[93] A. H. Zhang, China's Golden Tech Grab. *Project Syndicate*, June 29, 2022. https://www.project-syndicate.org/commentary/china-regulatory-crackdown-tech-firms-golden-share-ownership-stake-by-angela-huyue-zhang-2022-05.

[94] A. H. Zhang, (2024). *High Wire: How China Regulates Big Tech and Governs Its Economy.* New York, NY: Oxford University Press.

[95] A. H. Zhang, Why Big Tech May Never Recover in China. *TIME*, May 7, 2024. https://time.com/6973119/china-big-tech-crackdown-backfiring/.

[96] D. Low, China's Chronic Zero COVID Trauma. *The Diplomat*, February 15, 2024. https://thediplomat.com/2024/02/chinas-chronic-zero-covid-trauma/.

[97] G. Liu (刘刚), China's AI Tech Industry Development Under New Challenges and Opportunities (新挑战和机遇下的中国人工智能科技产业发展). *CHINESE INSTITUTION*

Alliance (AIIA), which enjoys a close relationship with the government, including key agencies such as the CAC, the Ministry of Science and Technology (MOST), the Ministry of Industry and Information Technology (MIIT), and the National Development and Reform Commission (NDRC).[98] AIIA's over 500 members, including major tech firms, state-owned enterprises, and top Chinese universities, come together for conferences and key discussions. There appears to be a palpable shared sense of mission, summed up by prominent AI scholar Zhang Linghan of the China University of Political Science and Law, who said that "the failure to develop AI is the biggest threat to our national security".[99]

Given that the Chinese government has invested heavily in the industry, coupled with its declared ambition to get ahead in this race, it is more likely than not that even a super regulator like the CAC will tread carefully in the days ahead when enforcing AI regulations.

8.6 Ethics

In China's hierarchical structure, ethical concerns regarding AI have been voiced from the top. At the 2018 Political Bureau study session on AI development, President Xi Jinping (as General Secretary) stressed that it is important "to establish and improve laws and regulations, systems and institutions, and ethics and moral principles that ensure healthy development of AI".[100] According to the country's AI Development Strategy, a comprehensive system should be in place by 2030[101] – presumably, this would also include ethical codes.

OF NEW GENERATION ARTIFICIAL INTELLIGENCE DEVELOPMENT STRATEGIES, June 24, 2020. (archived at https://perma.cc/GZ5V-6SWG).

[98] A. C. Johansson, China's AI Ecosystem. *CENTER FOR ASIAN STUDIES*, November 14, 2022. https://www.hhs.se/contentassets/bc962221471a415ba8ac01fbbf160277/chinas-ai-ecosystem-nov-2022.pdf.

[99] L. Zhang, (张凌寒), Six Highlights of the New Generative AI Regulations–Failure to Develop Is the Greatest Insecurity (一文读懂生成式 AI 新规六大亮点—不发展是最大的不安全). *CAIJING (财经)*, July 14, 2023. https://www.mycaijing.com/article/detail/496986?source_id=40.

[100] DigiChina. Translation: Xi Jinping Calls for 'Healthy Development' of AI - DigiChina, April 22, 2022. https://digichina.stanford.edu/work/xi-jinping-calls-for-healthy-development-of-ai-translation/.

[101] DigiChina. (2021), *Op. cit.*

The MOST released a document called "Ethical Norms for New Generation Artificial Intelligence", which is a set of ethical codes governing AI for the entire life cycle of its development in September 2021.[102] The codes set out six basic general ethical principles, including ensuring that AI will be "controllable and trustworthy". The other principles are improving human well-being, promoting fairness and justice, protecting privacy and safety, strengthening accountability, and raising ethical literacy. This national code, however, does not specify how these norms are to be enforced and does not prescribe any punishments for those who violate them.[103] The overarching goal is to ensure that AI is always under the control of humans. The Chinese government's discourse and focus on ethics may appear hypocritical to the West, given the state's use of AI for mass surveillance and censorship. However, AI ethics are broad social standards for what is good and right, and in China, national security and stability are the highest collective goods to be prioritised over privacy, transparency, and individual rights. Ethical questions about AI will be framed around such collective interests, which will ultimately be determined by the party-state.[104]

Though the conversation on AI ethics is overseen by Beijing, it is a multi-stakeholder conversation in China involving the state, think tanks, academia, and tech companies. One highly influential think tank is the China Academy for Information and Communication Technology (CAICT). CAICT is supervised by the MIIT and is home to technical experts and policy analysts who worked closely with the super regulator, CAC, on AI governance projects.[105] The Beijing Academy of Artificial Intelligence (BAAI), a leading AI research institute backed by MOST and the Beijing municipal government, is another notable institution. In 2019, BAAI published the "Beijing AI Principles", a set of ethical standards

---

[102] CSET, Ethical Norms for New Generation Artificial Intelligence Released | Center for Security and Emerging Technology, Center for Security and Emerging Technology, October 21, 2021. https://cset.georgetown.edu/publication/ethical-norms-for-new-generation-artificial-intelligence-released/.

[103] CSET, (2021), *Op. cit.*

[104] Merics. Lofty principles, conflicting incentives: AI ethics and governance in China, June 24, 2021. https://merics.org/en/report/lofty-principles-conflicting-incentives-ai-ethics-and-governance-china.

[105] M. Sheehan, China's AI Regulations and How They Get Made. *Carnegie Endowment for International Peace*, July 10, 2023. https://carnegieendowment.org/research/2023/07/chinas-ai-regulations-and-how-they-get-made?lang=en.

which calls for AI systems to be developed in a responsible and sustainable way that benefits humanity.[106] Various scholars are also influential in AI ethics research. Duan Weiwen (段伟文) from the Chinese Academy of Social Sciences is one of the country's most prominent thinkers on philosophical, ethical, and social issues surrounding AI and Big Data.[107] Duan is a staunch advocate for targeted work to tackle ethical risks rather than abstract prescriptions.[108] Another is Zeng Yi (曾毅) from the Chinese Academy of Sciences who directed the team that wrote the Beijing AI Principles. Zeng was voted by *Time* magazine as one of the 100 Most Influential People in AI in 2023, in the same section as Geoffrey Hinton and Timnit Gebru.[109] Both Duan and Zheng publish prolifically and actively contribute to online public discourse on AI ethics in China to raise awareness.[110] Another giant figure is Xue Lan (薛澜) from Tsinghua University and also director of the university's Institute for AI International Governance, which produced sophisticated reports drawing lessons from algorithm governance from other countries and made recommendations to CAC and the Chinese government.[111] Both Zeng and Xue sit on the MOST's National New Generation AI Governance Expert Committee, which drafted the 2021 Ethical Norms. Chinese senior academics and scientists have a far stronger voice in policy discussions when compared to their American peers. They are consulted on policy development and tend to make up governmental advisory bodies. With many of its elite scientists raising ethical and safety concerns about AI, the CCP and Chinese government are also taking steps to firm up their stand.[112]

---

[106] The State Council, the People's Republic of China. Beijing publishes AI ethical standards, calls for international cooperation, May 27, 2019. https://english.www.gov.cn/news/top_news/2019/05/27/content_281476683735418.htm.

[107] Lofty principles, conflicting incentives: AI ethics and governance in China. *Merics*; June 24, 2021. https://merics.org/en/report/lofty-principles-conflicting-incentives-ai-ethics-and-governance-china.

[108] Lofty principles, conflicting incentives: AI ethics and governance in China. (2021), *Op. cit.*

[109] TIME100 AI, *Time.* September 7, 2023. https://time.com/collection/time100-ai/.

[110] Y. Mao, K. Shi-Kupfer, (2023). Online public discourse on artificial intelligence and ethics in China: Context, content, and implications. *AI & Soc* 38, 373–389. https://doi.org/10.1007/s00146-021-01309-7.

[111] M. Sheehan, (2023), *Op. cit.*

[112] M. Sheehan, China's views on AI safety are changing—Quickly. *Carnegie Endowment for International Peace*, August 27, 2024. https://carnegieendowment.org/research/2024/08/china-artificial-intelligence-ai-safety-regulation?lang=en.

In 2022, the CAICT published China's AI Industry White Paper to provide guidance on the ethics, safety, and trustworthiness of industrial AI applications, emphasising risk prevention, human oversight, and alignment with social ethics.[113] This paper identified tech companies as playing a major role in fostering trust in AI and exercising self-discipline and self-governance. Corporate self-regulation has largely taken the form of ethical codes. Tencent, for example, released its AI principles, described as "available, reliable, comprehensible and controllable", in 2018.[114] Another company, Megvii (an Alibaba-backed facial recognition software firm) created an AI ethics committee to oversee the implementation of its AI principles.[115] Although Chinese policy-making is largely a top-down exercise, when it comes to AI ethics, the private sector decidedly plays a crucial role. Some notable think tanks also include executives from tech companies in their boards and membership. The founding members of the influential BAAI, for instance, include Baidu, ByteDance, Megvii, Meituan, and Xiaomi.[116] The CEO of Megvii also sits on the MOST's National New Generation AI Governance Expert Committee.[117]

According to Zhang, despite the foregoing, it is difficult to assess or track the effectiveness of China's AI ethics framework because it is highly decentralised and relies heavily on self-regulation by academic institutions, research institutes, and the tech companies themselves.[118]

8.7 Summary

Without a doubt, the Chinese digital empire is state-driven. The state is not merely a regulator but also an advocate, sponsor, and investor in AI. Ministries championing AI development, along with state sponsors and

---

[113] Artificial Intelligence White Paper (2022). *Center for Security and Emerging Technology*, June 15, 2022, https://cset.georgetown.edu/publication/artificial-intelligence-white-paper-2022/.

[114] 'ARCC': An Ethical Framework for Artificial Intelligence. *Tencent Research Institute,* April 9, 2020. https://www.tisi.org/13747. In Chinese.

[115] S. Dai, China facial recognition unicorn Megvii pledges to guard against weaponisation of AI on road to IPO. *South China Morning Post,* August 26, 2019. https://www.scmp.com/tech/enterprises/article/3024395/china-facial-recognition-unicorn-megvii-pledges-guard-against.

[116] Lofty principles, conflicting incentives: AI ethics and governance in China, (2021), *Op. cit.*

[117] Translation: Chinese Expert Group Offers 'Governance Principles' for 'Responsible AI,' New America. n.d., https://www.newamerica.org/cybersecurity-initiative/digichina/blog/translation-chinese-expert-group-offers-governance-principles-responsible-ai/.

[118] A. H. Zhang, (2024), *Op. cit.*

investors, are poised to become a potent counterbalance against stringent AI regulation. Given these dynamics, the CAC's proposed measures may well be softened to accommodate the growth of China's AI industry. In the end, the regulations will likely remain broad and vague, allowing for considerable agency discretion. As a leading scholar on Chinese tech regulation, Angela Zhang, noted, nurturing generative AI development "is more than an economic stimulant: it is a matter of national pride".[119] In fact, months after the GAI Interim Measures 2023 were passed, strong rumours emerged that the unified national AI legislation may not even materialise.[120] One reason is that the vast majority of experts believe the timing to craft unified national AI legislation may not have arrived since the technology is evolving so rapidly.[121] Throughout 2024, China's slowing economy remained under stress from its property crisis, weak consumer confidence, and, of course, the ever-present rivalry with the U.S. In response, Beijing released a slew of stimulus measures during that year to cut interest rates, increase lending for housing development, and support its equities markets.[122] Whether these measures will achieve significant results is likely to impact the country's AI strategy. However, China has shown time and again that resilience is one resource it has in great abundance. The rise of DeepSeek is a stark reminder that the country can overcome all odds and constraints. Adverse conditions can spark greater innovation and efficient use of resources. Zhang opined that U.S. export controls and regulations targeted to rein in Chinese companies have in fact forced them to be more innovative and more efficient in utilising resources.[123]

---

[119] A. H. Zhang, China has too much invested in AI to smother its development. *Nikkei Asia*, May 17, 2023. https://asia.nikkei.com/Opinion/China-has-too-much-invested-in-AI-to-smother-its-development.

[120] S. Zhuang, China likely to ditch unified AI legislation due to 'considerable disagreement', timing. *South China Morning Post*, July 17, 2024. https://www.scmp.com/news/china/politics/article/3270544/china-likely-ditch-unified-ai-legislation-due-considerable-disagreement-timing.

[121] S. Zhuang, (2024), *Op. cit.*

[122] R. Woo, and L. Gao, China's Central Bank unveils most aggressive stimulus since pandemic. *Reuters*, September 25, 2024. https://www.reuters.com/world/china/china-unveils-broad-stimulus-measures-revive-economy-2024-09-24/.

[123] A. Zhang, US export controls have forced Chinese Tech companies to be more innovative. *Financial Times*, January 23, 2025. https://www.ft.com/content/c99d86f0-2d17-49d0-8dc6-9662ed34c831.

Chapter 9

European Union

9.1 Extending the "Brussels Effects"

In *The Brussels Effect: How the European Union Rules the World,*[1] Anu Bradford argued that the EU exerts an enormous influence over global commerce by setting standards through regulations in areas such as antitrust, data privacy, food safety, and environmental protection. The "Brussels Effect" (first coined by Bradford in 2012) occurs when multinational companies succumb to market forces and voluntarily extend EU standards to their operations worldwide. The effect is reinforced when foreign governments pass legislation and regulations modelled on European rules. The EU's General Data Protection Regulation (GDPR) is the epitome of this "Brussels Effect".

The EU has shown that it has the political will and machinery to regulate the digital economy and that it does not hesitate to take on the U.S. big tech. Over the years, U.S. tech companies have been slapped with jaw-dropping fines for breaching EU regulations. Google's highest antitrust fine was 4.12 billion euros (approximately US$4.5 billion), originally charged in July 2019 due to anti-competitive restrictions on Android devices and mobile networks to favour its search engine network.[2] Apple avoided having to pay 1.84 billion euros in fines by agreeing to open up

[1] A. Bradford, (2020). *The Brussels Effect*, 1st ed. New York, NY: Oxford University Press.
[2] Statista. EU Commission Google antitrust fines 2017-2023, February 16, 2024. https://www.statista.com/statistics/1008143/google-antitrust-fines-eu-commission/.

its mobile wallet technology to other providers free of charge for 10 years.[3] When the EU passed the Digital Markets Act (DMA) in July 2023, it targeted Apple, Amazon, Alphabet (which owns Google), Meta Platforms, and Microsoft by designating them as digital "gatekeepers", along with ByteDance.[4] The DMA imposes a series of obligations on these gatekeepers to ensure that they do not engage in anti-competitive practices.[5] This includes allowing users to decide what apps they want on their phone and to delete pre-loaded Apple or Google software. The European Commissioner for Internal Market and Services, Thierry Breton, described the DMA as "D-day" for the large players and warned they must play by European rules to operate in the market.[6] These were not empty threats, as the EU followed up with real action. In April 2025, the EU antitrust regulators handed out the first sanctions under the DMA, fining Apple 500 million euros (approximately US$570 million) and Meta 200 million euros (approximately US$230 million).[7]

In early 2024, the EU Artificial Intelligence Act[8] was unanimously endorsed by its 27 member states. The comprehensive legal framework contains 180 recitals and 113 articles and is 459 pages long. The legislation lays down a harmonised horizontal legal framework that regulates the entire lifecycle of different types of AI systems. Bradford describes the EU regulatory models as human-centric and rights-driven.[9] This contrasts with the U.S. market-driven model, which puts tech companies in charge, and the Chinese state-driven model, which regulates the tech industry

---

[3] A. White and E. Hancock, Apple's payments offer ends EU antitrust probe, *POLITICO*, July 11, 2024. https://www.politico.eu/article/apple-settles-eu-antitrust-probe-into-iphone-payments/.

[4] Digital Markets Act (DMA). Commission designates six gatekeepers under the Digital Markets Act, September 6, 2023. https://digital-markets-act.ec.europa.eu/commission-designates-six-gatekeepers-under-digital-markets-act-2023-09-06_en.

[5] Digital Markets Act (DMA). Digital Markets Act, July 1, 2024. https://digital-markets-act.ec.europa.eu/index_en.

[6] L. O'Carroll, EU unveils 'revolutionary' laws to curb big tech firms' power, *The Guardian*, September 6, 2023, https://www.theguardian.com/world/2023/sep/06/eu-unveils-package-laws-curb-power-big-tech-giants.

[7] I. Rahman-Jones, EU hits apple and meta with €700m of fines, *The BBC,* April 23, 2025. https://www.bbc.com/news/articles/cm248vzg9jwo.

[8] EU Artificial Intelligence Act | Up-to-date developments and analyses of the EU AI Act, n.d. https://artificialintelligenceact.eu/.

[9] A. Bradford, (2023). *Digital Empires: The Global Battle to Regulate Technologies*. 1st ed. US: Oxford University Press. https://doi.org/10.1093/oso/9780197649268.001.0001.

with the underlying aim of political power preservation. In this AI "arms race", there is no doubt that the EU has every hope that the "Brussels Effect" will extend its run.

9.2 Data Protection

Any developer of AI systems that wants to include European data in training the algorithms or to develop AI applications for the European market must comply with the General Data Protection Regulation (GDPR).[10] Widely regarded as the "gold standard" for data protection, the principles and framework established by the GDPR frequently serve as a blueprint and model for many other countries' data privacy laws. China's data legislation, the PIPL, is one such example.

Implemented in May 2018, the milestone regulation was adopted by both the European Parliament and the European Council after more than four years of discussion and negotiations. As an EU regulation (instead of a directive[11]), the GDPR is directly applicable and has binding legal force across the EU without the need for transposition. Prior to the GDPR, the EU's data protection regime was governed by the 1995 Data Protection Directive.[12] A directive does not apply automatically and needs to be transposed into the national laws of each member state. This resulted in national legislatures applying their own interpretation of the directive and gave rise to a patchwork of data protection compliance requirements across the EU. Moreover, there were inconsistencies in how each country's data protection authorities (DPAs) interpreted and enforced these laws. This led to organisations doing business in the EU facing inconsistent data protection compliance requirements among member states. The GDPR heralded a harmonised data protection regime and created a single digital market by allowing an unhindered flow of data within the entire common market.

The GDPR provides and protects privacy rights of all individuals physically located in the EU regardless of nationality, whether their

---

[10] Regulation (EU) 2016/679 of the European Parliament and of the Council of 27 April 2016 on the Protection of Natural Persons with Regard to the Processing of Personal Data and on the Free Movement of Such Data and Repealing Directive 95/46/EC.

[11] Prior to the GDPR, the EU's data protection regime was governed by the 1995 Data Protection Directive.

[12] Directive 95/46/EC of the European Parliament and the Council of 24 October 1995.

information is processed online or offline.[13] Personal data are defined as "any information relating to an identified or identifiable natural person".[14] It governs the processing of such personal data by organisations operating within the EU as well as by those outside the EU that offer goods or services to individuals there.[15] The GDPR distinguishes between "data controllers" and "data processors". The former are entities that control the collection of data and make decisions as to their uses. The latter carry out instructions provided by the data controllers. The GDPR imposes different obligations and responsibilities on these two groups of data handlers. The regulation adopts a principle-based approach and sets out seven principles for the lawful processing of personal data, namely lawfulness, fairness and transparency; purpose limitation; data minimisation; accuracy; storage limitation; integrity and confidentiality (security); and accountability.[16]

One of the key bases for lawful data processing is consent.[17] Individuals (data subjects) must consent to the collection and processing of their personal data, and they must be informed of the collection and the use that will be made of such data. The regulation also limits the quantity and purpose for which data can be collected, meaning only data that are adequate, relevant, and limited to what is necessary for the purposes for which they are processed may be collected.[18] All entities, whether private companies or government agencies collecting and processing the data, must ensure the accuracy, integrity, and security of the data. Data can further be stored only for a limited period.[19] Organisations must demonstrate that they have the necessary documentation such as privacy notices[20] to prove that they are

---

[13] Regulation 2016/679 of the European Parliament and of the Council on the Protection of Natural Persons with regard to the Processing of Personal Data and on the Free Movement of Such Data, and Repealing Directive 95/46/EC.

[14] Article 4(1).

[15] Article 3.

[16] Article 5 of the GDPR.

[17] Article 6 GDPR. The other legal bases include contract, legal obligation, vital interests, public task or legitimate interest.

[18] Article 15 GDPR.

[19] GDPR, art 5(1)(f).

[20] Other common examples include controller–processor contracts, data breach records, data protection impact assessment reports, relevant policies and procedures and staff training records.

meeting their compliance requirements to meet the accountability requirement. Further, data subjects are accorded very specific rights: the right to be informed, the right of access, the right to rectification, the right to object to processing, the right to restrict processing, the right to data portability, the right to be forgotten, and rights in relation to automated decision-making and profiling. Each member state has its own DPA to enforce the GDPR, together with the European Data Protection Board.[21] Noncompliance with the GDPR may result in administrative fines of up to 20 million euros or up to 4% of the company's total worldwide annual turnover for the preceding financial year, whichever is higher.[22]

Italian DPA takes on OpenAI and DeepSeek

An LLM trained or intends to train on data governed by GDPR faces several challenges. In March 2023, the Italian Data Protection Authority (Garante per la protezione dei dati personali) imposed a temporary ban on the processing of Italian users' data by OpenAI's ChatGPT on the grounds of suspected infringement of the GDPR. Amongst others, the privacy regulator pointed to the lack of consent or other legal basis for the collection and processing of personal data for the purpose of training the underlying algorithms and the absence of an age verification system to prevent access by minors (below the age of 16).[23] In response, OpenAI implemented a number of measures, including an opt-out form to allow all individuals in Europe (users and non-users) to exercise the right to opt out from the processing of their data for algorithm training.[24] Although ChatGPT's platform was subsequently reinstated a month later, the Italian watchdog continued its investigation into OpenAI together with an *ad hoc* task force set up by the European Data Protection Board.[25] In early 2024,

---

[21] GDPR art 51 & 68.

[22] GDPR art 83.

[23] D. Milmo, Italy's privacy watchdog bans ChatGPT over data breach concerns. *The Guardian*, April 4, 2023. https://www.theguardian.com/technology/2023/mar/31/italy-privacy-watchdog-bans-chatgpt-over-data-breach-concerns.

[24] K. Chan, OpenAI: ChatGPT back in Italy after meeting watchdog demands. *AP News*, April 28, 2023. https://apnews.com/article/chatgpt-openai-data-privacy-italy-b9ab3d12f2b2cfe493237fd2b9675e21.

[25] EDPB resolves dispute on transfers by Meta and creates task force on Chat GPT. *European Data Protection Board*, April 13, 2023. https://www.edpb.europa.eu/news/news/2023/edpb-resolves-dispute-transfers-meta-and-creates-task-force-chat-gpt_en.

the Italian DPA sent OpenAI a notification of breaches of privacy law based on its fact-finding and evidence resulting from the investigations. In December that year, the Italian watchdog fined OpenAI 15 million euros over improper use of Italian personal data, but the tech company said it would appeal.[26] The Chinese generative AI model DeepSeek was not spared either. In late January 2025, Garante blocked access to the model and sent a request to the company's Hangzhou and Beijing offices to seek clarification of the personal data collected and processed.[27]

No doubt privacy data regulators in many parts of the world are watching this space closely to see how events will unfold. It is nevertheless difficult to see how LLMs can comply with the GDPR. Generative AI models such as ChatGPT and DeepSeek are trained on billions of parameters and feed on copious amounts of data. The GDPR is built on the idea that individuals must have control over their personal data and have the right to manage how such data are processed and stored. The sheer magnitude of data being used by LLMs and the lack of differentiation make it impossible to identify, let alone respect, the rights of individual data subjects. Further, the "black box" nature of LLMs means there is simply no explanation as to how personal data are processed or used. Unless a carve-out is made for generative AI, it may well be that data protection law is reaching its limits when it comes to regulating such data-intensive technologies.[28]

9.3 AI Laws

The EU Artificial Intelligence Act[29] was unanimously endorsed by its 27 member states in early 2024. The act enters into force across the Union

---

[26] Italy Blocks Chinese AI App DeepSeek, opens investigation into data use. *South China Morning Post*, January 30, 2025. https://www.scmp.com/news/world/europe/article/3296854/italy-blocks-chinese-ai-app-deepseek-opens-investigation-data-use?module=perpetual_scroll_0&pgtype=article.

[27] *Ibid.*

[28] H. Ruschemeier, Generative AI and Data Protection (May 2, 2024). Forthcoming in: Calo/Ebers/Poncibo/Zou, Handbook on Generative AI and the Law, Cambridge University Press. Available at SSRN: https://ssrn.com/abstract=4814999.

[29] EU Artificial Intelligence Act | Up-to-date developments and analyses of the EU AI Act. n.d. https://artificialintelligenceact.eu/.

on 1 August 2024, but the enforcement of most of its provisions will commence on 2 August 2026.[30]

The EU AI Act is a comprehensive legal framework that will govern the use of AI in the EU, comprising a population of 450 million people. Its principal legislative aim is to turn the EU into a globally trustworthy hub for AI and set a precedent for AI regulation around the world, reenacting the "Brussels Effect". Although the U.S. and China have introduced AI-related regulations, they are not as comprehensive as the EU Act, which consists of 180 recitals and 113 articles, extends to 459 pages, and contains a long list of legal jargon and technical terms. To complement the GDPR, this regulation also has extraterritorial reach. The act applies to providers, deployers, distributors, and manufacturers of AI systems located within the EU or where their output is being used or marketed within the EU.[31]

Article 3(1) defines an AI system as "a machine-based system that is designed to operate with varying levels of autonomy and that may exhibit adaptiveness after deployment, and that, for explicit or implicit objectives, infers, from the input it receives, how to generate outputs such as predictions, content, recommendations, or decisions that can influence physical or virtual environments". This EU definition focuses on the outputs and objectives, rather than the system's underlying technology or algorithms – an approach which contrasts with China's (with its algorithm registry as a key governance node), as described above. This reflects the European Parliament's priority "to make sure that AI systems used in the EU are safe, transparent, traceable, prevents bias and discrimination, fosters social and environmental responsibility, and ensures respect for fundamental rights".[32] The European Parliament emphasises that AI systems should be overseen by people, rather than by automation, to prevent harmful outcomes.[33]

---

[30] Long awaited EU AI Act becomes law after publication in the EU's Official Journal, *White & Case LLP*, July 16, 2024. https://www.whitecase.com/insight-alert/long-awaited-eu-ai-act-becomes-law-after-publication-eus-official-journal.

[31] Article 2(1) EU AI Act.

[32] AI Rules: What the European Parliament Wants. Topics | European Parliament, June 20, 2023. https://www.europarl.europa.eu/topics/en/article/20201015STO89417/ai-rules-what-the-european-parliament-wants.

[33] EU AI Act: First Regulation on Artificial Intelligence. Topics | European Parliament. August 6, 2023. https://www.europarl.europa.eu/news/en/headlines/society/20230601STO93804/eu-ai-act-first-regulation-on-artificial-intelligence.

9.3.1 *Risk-based approach*

The cornerstone of the EU AI Act is a classification system that determines the level of risk an AI technology could pose to the health and safety or fundamental rights of a person by assessing the intended output and use of a system. A tiered risk-based approach is adopted to ensure the responsible deployment of AI systems, as they bring societal benefits and economic growth. The act establishes obligations and requirements on developers and service providers proportionate to the level of risk that AI technology can generate. AI systems are classified into the four bands of risk: unacceptable, high, medium, and minimal or no risk.

AI practices regarded as harmful, abusive or in contradiction with EU values are prohibited. This "unacceptable risk" category[34] includes the deployment of subliminal AI techniques beyond a person's consciousness or that are purposefully manipulative or deceptive with the objective or effect of materially distorting human behaviour. Also prohibited is social scoring of persons based on their known or inferred or predicted personality traits leading to detrimental treatment that is unjustified or disproportionate. AI systems which create or expand facial recognition databases through untargeted scraping of facial images from the Internet or closed-circuit television (CCTV) footage also fall within the prohibited system categories. The prohibitions on specified categories of banned AI will come into force six months after the legislation, namely February 2025. AI practices that pose an unacceptable risk are subject to the greatest penalties and may expose companies to fines of 35 million euros (US$38.3 million), or 7% of a company's annual revenue, whichever is greater.[35] The legislation, however, provides for a few exceptions for law enforcement purposes relating to the use of "real-time" remote biometric identification in publicly accessible spaces.[36] Based on the wordings, China's "social credit system" and surveillance would be regarded as posing an unacceptable risk and such systems would be prohibited under the EU AI Act.

At the other end of this risk classification is "minimal or no risk". All systems that do not fall within the other three categories are designated as

---

[34]Article 5 EU AI Act. For a complete list of prohibited AI practices. See https://artificialintelligenceact.eu/the-act/.

[35]Article 99(3) EU AI Act.

[36]Article 5(2) EU AI Act.

such. The act allows for the free use of AI systems within the category and imposes no obligations. This category includes applications such as AI-enabled video games or spam filters.

The next two intermediate categories of AI systems, high-risk and limited-risk, are the ones that impose obligations on developers and service providers. The framework for these two systems will come into effect on 2 August 2026.[37]

High-risk AI systems are permitted provided their developers and users adhere to regulations requiring rigorous testing, proper documentation of data quality, and an accountability framework that details human oversight. Such systems are regulated by Chapter III of the EU AI Act. An AI system used as a safety component of any products covered by existing EU product and safety harmonisation legislation will be classified as high-risk.[38] This includes autonomous vehicles, medical devices, rail systems, and toys, to name a few. Additionally, AI systems operating in eight specific areas are automatically classified as high-risk, namely biometrics, critical infrastructure, education and vocational training, employment, essential public and private services, law enforcement, migration, and administration of justice.[39] Developers and deployers of high-risk systems in these areas must register their systems with a centralised EU database that will be set up. The act imposes a wide range of obligations on developers and deployers throughout the entire lifecycle of such a system, including requirements on data training and data governance, technical documentation, recordkeeping, technical robustness, transparency, human oversight, and cybersecurity.[40] Before high-risk AI systems can be placed on the market or put into service, they must undergo a conformity assessment to verify compliance with the act, and the providers must draw up a declaration of conformity and submit it to the relevant national competent authority.[41] Failure to comply with the high-risk regime will attract

[37] Historic Timeline | EU Artificial Intelligence Act, Future of Life Instittite. n.d.. https://artificialintelligenceact.eu/developments/.

[38] Article 6(1) EU AI Act. A complete list of EU harmonization legislations is set out in Annex I of the act, see https://artificialintelligenceact.eu/the-act/.

[39] Article 6(2) EU AI Act. A complete list of eight specific areas is set out in Annex III of the act, see https://artificialintelligenceact.eu/the-act/.

[40] Section 3 of the EU AI Act.

[41] Article 16(f) and Article 43 EU AI Act.

penalties of up to 15 million euros or 3% of worldwide group turnover, whichever is higher.[42]

9.3.2 *Deep fakes*

Limited-risk AI systems are systems that carry a risk of manipulation or deceit. Chatbots, generative AI systems with outputs such as synthetic audio, image, video, or text content, and deep fakes will fall within this category. For these systems, the AI Act introduces specific transparency obligations to ensure that humans are made aware that they are interacting with a machine so they can take an informed decision to continue or step back.[43] Deep fakes are defined under the act as "AI-generated or manipulated image, audio or video content that resembles existing persons, objects, places, entities or events and would falsely appear to a person to be authentic or truthful".[44] Deployers using AI systems to create deep fakes are required to disclose its artificial origin and that the content has been artificially created or manipulated by labelling the output as such.[45]

9.3.3 *GPAI*

After ChatGPT was launched in November 2022, several revisions were introduced to the proposed AI Act to specifically address the risks and controversies associated with such models. The EU Council approved last-minute amendments to the AI Act, which set out a dedicated chapter for general-purpose AI ("GPAI") systems.[46]

A GPAI model is defined as "an AI model, including where such an AI model is trained with a large amount of data using self-supervision at scale, that displays significant generality and is capable of competently performing a wide range of distinct tasks regardless of the way the model is placed on the market and that can be integrated into a variety of downstream systems or applications, except AI models that are used for

---

[42] Article 99(4) EU AI Act.

[43] Article 50 EU AI Act.

[44] Article 3(60) EU AI Act.

[45] Article 50 EU AI Act.

[46] Long awaited EU AI Act becomes law after publication in the EU's Official Journal, (2024), *Op. cit.*

research, development or prototyping activities before they are placed on the market".[47] The act regards large generative AI models as typical examples of GPAI models, as they allow for flexible generation of content in the form of text, audio, images, or video and can readily accommodate a wide range of distinctive tasks.[48] Thus, OpenAI's ChatGPT, along with others such as Anthropic's Claude and Google's Gemini, is regarded as a GPAI model.

Under the act's risk-based classification, a generative AI model such as ChatGPT-3 will be classified as limited-risk and must comply with the obligations under that category. Separately, it will also have to comply with requirements laid out for GPAI models.[49] Obligations imposed on providers include making available and maintaining up-to-date technical documentation, including its training and testing process; cooperating with national competent authorities; and respecting national copyright laws.[50] Additionally, the act also targets GPAI models that will have "a significant impact on the Union market due to their reach, or due to actual or reasonably foreseeable negative effects on public health, safety, public security, fundamental rights, or the society as a whole, that can be propagated at scale across the value chain".[51] These models are classified as posing "systemic risk". Providers of GPAI models with systemic risk have additional obligations, including the obligation to perform standardised model evaluations, assess and mitigate systemic risks, track and report incidents, and ensure cybersecurity protection.[52]

Evidently, the EU AI Act wants to position itself to match the growing prowess and reach of generative AI technology. Besides adopting a risk-based approach to tackle output, the act also sets up a dedicated GPAI regime to specifically monitor the technology. In May 2024, the

[47] Art 3(1)(63) EU AI Act.

[48] Recital 99 of EU AI Act.

[49] Topics | European Parliament. EU AI Act: first regulation on artificial intelligence | Topics | European Parliament, August 6, 2023. https://www.europarl.europa.eu/topics/en/article/20230601STO93804/eu-ai-act-first-regulation-on-artificial-intelligence.

[50] Article 53 EU AI Act.

[51] Article 3(1)(65) EU AI Act. The definition includes models trained on a large amount of compute, technically defined as 10^25 FLOPs (Floating Point Operations).

[52] Article 55 EU AI Act.

company released its multi-modal GPT-4o (the "o" stands for "omni").[53] This version can combine and understand text, audio, and images; and with the smartphone's camera, GPT-4o can analyse the surroundings of the user and provide an emotionally intelligent response in near real time. Such features which enable real-time facial recognition, emotion detection, and the use of AI for surveillance would be prohibited under the AI Act.[54] It remains to be seen how OpenAI's GPT-4o and similar AI models can comply with the act, which provides for a transition period for compliance.[55]

9.4 Copyright

Leading up to the passing of the AI Act, the EU Parliament had actively discussed and acknowledged the copyright challenges posed by AI-generated works.

European copyright law is built on the concept of human authorship and generally attributes ownership to natural persons who created the work. The rapid advancement of generative AI raises the question as to whether the time has come to consider the creation of a new legal status for "AI-generated works" to allow for attribution of copyright to a non-natural entity. However, after much consideration, in October 2020, the EU Parliament adopted a resolution which stressed that AI remains a tool to assist human creators, and AI-generated works can claim copyright protection only if there was human involvement in the creation process.[56] This underscores the human-centred AI approach – focusing on the role of human actors in the creative process.

In 2023, a Czech municipal court ruled that, as AI is not a "natural person", it cannot be the creator of a work under European copyright law. In the case before the court, the image was created using DALL-E, a

[53] Hello GPT-4o, *Openai.com*, May 13, 2024. Accessed August 13, 2024. https://openai.com/index/hello-gpt-4o/.

[54] Article 5(e) and 5(f) EU AI Act.

[55] Providers of GPAI models placed on the EU market before 2 August 2025 need to be compliant with the AI Act by 2 August 2027: see Implementation Timeline | EU Artificial Intelligence Act. n.d. https://artificialintelligenceact.eu/implementation-timeline/.

[56] European Parliament. Texts adopted - Intellectual property rights for the development of artificial intelligence technologies - Tuesday, 20 October 2020. n.d. https://www.europarl.europa.eu/doceo/document/TA-9-2020-0277_EN.html.

text-to-image AI model,[57] The court was not provided cogent evidence as to who instructed the AI model and the specific prompts or instructions given leading to the created image. According to the judgement, since the Czech Copyright Act expressly requires that the author be a natural person, autonomously generated outputs by AI systems are simply not copyrightable. Further, the Czech Court asserted that prompts given to such generative AI models could only be regarded as a theme or idea for the output and as such were also not copyrightable. To the Czech court, human-inputted prompts cannot qualify as expression. This approach diverges from that taken by the Chinese courts. The latter are prepared to allow human input, such as prompts and adjustments of parameters, as fulfilling the intellectual component of the AI-generated output and to grant copyright ownership rights to the human user.

The AI Act adopted by the EU Parliament in 2024 did not introduce any provision to allow AI-generated materials to claim copyright ownership. Recital 105 states that the use of copyright-protected content requires the authorisation of the rightsholder, unless an exception applies. In fact, the act requires providers of Gen AI models to put in place a policy to comply with EU copyright laws.[58] Service providers are also required to draw up and make publicly available a sufficiently detailed summary of the content used for training their models, using a template to be provided by the AI Office.[59] This summary is expected to provide comprehensive information about the datasets used in order to enable copyright owners to exercise their rights. The AI Office is likely to develop a standardised template and is expected to monitor compliance with these obligations.[60]

Moving forward, the question of whether to extend copyright protection to AI-generated work will doubtless continue to generate debate, especially as the technology evolves. Pending any policy changes at the EU level, its member states are likely to adopt a measured approach

---

[57] Czech Court denies copyright Protection of AI-Generated Work in First Ever Ruling, Bird & Bird LLP, May 29, 2024. https://www.twobirds.com/en/insights/2024/czech-republic/czech-court-denies-copyright-protection-of-ai-generated-work-in-first-ever-ruling#:~:text=In%20the%20Court's%20opinion%2C%20if,a%20natural%20person%20%E2%80%93%20an%20author.

[58] Article 53 AI Act Paragraph 1(c).

[59] Article 53 AI Act Paragraph 1(d).

[60] EU AI Act: shaping Copyright compliance in the age of AI Innovation, *KEA,* April 2, 2024. https://keanet.eu/eu-ai-act-shaping-copyright-compliance-in-the-age-of-ai-innovation/.

similar to the U.S. and retain human authorship as a prerequisite to copyright protection.

When it concerns copyright of training data, the relevant legal framework is the "Copyright Directive in the Digital Single Market", which was updated in 2019. The Copyright Directive harmonises copyright laws across its member states, particularly in the digital environment.[61] The aim is to create a single and fairer digital marketplace for copyrighted works while promoting innovation. Measures were introduced to ensure creators receive fair remuneration for their works, especially when the contents are shared through online intermediaries. This directive contains a text and data mining (TDM) exception under EU copyright law, which allows AI developers to use copyrighted works as training data without explicit permission, provided they have lawful access. The TDM exception is broader for scientific research and will benefit academic generative AI development.[62] For commercial use, the TDM exception will apply and copyrighted materials can be used provided the rightsholders have not opted out.[63] For Gen AI models such as ChatGPT, the question is whether and to what extent the commercial TDM exception covers the training using data scraped from the Internet and how to check whether the rightsholders had opted out. Finally, the most challenging task may be how to ensure proper compensation to rightsholders if they are so entitled.

9.5 Regulators

Over the years, EU regulations have been expanding in scope and volume at such a rate that regulatory development is frequently perceived as one of the Union's main outputs. A common rant is that this is the cause of the Union's sluggish economy and lack of tech rivals to China or the U.S.[64] However, the opposite view regards regulations as establishing necessary rules for a level playing field. With the enactment of the EU AI Act, the spotlight now falls on two supranational regulators, namely the AI Office

[61] Directive - 2019/790 - EN - dsm - EUR-Lex,. n.d. https://eur-lex.europa.eu/eli/dir/2019/790/oj.

[62] Article 3 of the Copyright Directive.

[63] Article 4 of the Copyright Directive.

[64] P. Davies, Could the new EU AI Act stifle genAI innovation in Europe? A new study says it could. *Euronews*, March 22, 2024. https://www.euronews.com/next/2024/03/22/could-the-new-eu-ai-act-stifle-genai-innovation-in-europe-a-new-study-says-it-could.

and the AI Board. The first institution focuses on regulatory oversight and enforcement at the Union level, while the second ensures coordination among member states through advice and consultation.

The EU AI Office was established by the decision of the EU Commission on 24 January 2024, even before the AI Act was adopted by the European Parliament the same year.[65] The AI Office[66] is a central regulatory body established within the Commission to oversee the coherent implementation and enforcement of the AI Act's common rules across the Union. A key aspect of its role is to oversee GPAI technologies such as ChatGPT.[67] It is empowered to investigate potential infringements, evaluate general-purpose AI model capabilities, and request providers to take corrective actions, and it can apply sanctions if necessary.[68] Administratively, the AI Office is organised as part of the European Commission's technology department (Directorate-General for Communication Networks, Content and Technologies i.e., DG Connect).[69] In May 2024, an existing unit within DG Connect was restructured to immediately form the AI Office, which will employ some 140, including technology experts, lawyers. and policy specialists, with about 80 of whom yet to be recruited.[70] However, the EU AI Act does not contain any provision regarding the AI Office's composition or the extent of its operational autonomy. The responsibilities assigned to this regulator also appear to be very broadly defined; for example, empowering it to take "necessary actions to monitor effective implementation and compliance…"[71] Perhaps, more specific clarification will come later as the Office finds its footing.

---

[65] Commission decision (Brussels, 24.1.2024, C (2024) 390 final) https://eur-lex.europa.eu/eli/C/2024/1459/oj.

[66] Article 64 EU AI Act.

[67] C. Novelli, P. Hacker, J. Morley, J. Trondal, and L. Floridi, A Robust Governance for the AI Act: AI Office, AI Board, Scientific Panel, and National Authorities. *European Journal of Risk Regulation,* May 5, 2024. Available at SSRN: https://ssrn.com/abstract=4817755 or http://dx.doi.org/10.2139/ssrn.4817755.

[68] The AI Office: What is it, and how does it work? | EU Artificial Intelligence Act. n.d. https://artificialintelligenceact.eu/the-ai-office-summary/.

[69] C. Novelli *et al.*, (2024), *Op. cit.*

[70] European Commission - European Commission. Press corner, n.d. https://ec.europa.eu/commission/presscorner/detail/en/IP_24_2982.

[71] Article 89(1) EU AI Act.

Besides its regulatory role, the AI Office has a long list of other tasks set out under the AI Act and the Commission's decision. It needs to coordinate the uniform enforcement of the rules on high-risk AI systems across Europe and help set up an EU database for such systems.[72] This central body is also required to draw up the requisite standards and codes of practice, in consultation with AI developers and experts of member states.[73] The AI Office is also empowered to issue recommendations and written opinions on all relevant aspects related to the implementation of the AI Act and its consistent and effective application.[74] It also needs to oversee the AI Pact, an initiative that enables companies to work with the Commission and other stakeholders before the AI Act comes into force.[75] The AI Office is also expected to engage in international dialogue and cooperation on AI governance issues and to position Europe as a leader in ethical and sustainable AI development.[76]

The AI Board is established under the AI Act, comprising one representative per member state.[77] Although distinct from the AI Office, this body undertakes tasks that are parallel and intersect with those of the former.[78] Essentially, the AI Board operates as an advisory body within the EU regulatory framework and ensures representation and coordination. Since each member state will set up its own national regulator to enforce the AI Act, the Board can provide guidance and support while ensuring standardisation. In this role, the Board can also gather information and feedback from member states for the AI Office, particularly in relation to GPAIs, which fall under the latter's purview.

Unlike the regulators in China and the U.S., such as the CAC and FTC, respectively, which have flexed their regulatory muscles and have track records, the EU AI Office and AI Board have yet to demonstrate how

[72] Article 71 EU AI Act.

[73] Art 56 EU AI Act; European Commission - European Commission. Press corner, n.d. https://ec.europa.eu/commission/presscorner/detail/en/IP_24_2982.

[74] Enforcement of the EU AI Act: The EU AI Office, *CMS Law-Now,* June 12, 2024. https://cms-lawnow.com/en/ealerts/2024/06/enforcement-of-the-eu-ai-act-the-eu-ai-office.

[75] Shaping Europe's Digital Future. AI Pact, n.d. https://digital-strategy.ec.europa.eu/en/policies/ai-pact.

[76] European Commission - European Commission. Press corner, n.d. https://ec.europa.eu/commission/presscorner/detail/en/IP_24_2982.

[77] Article 65 EU AI Act.

[78] C. Novelli *et al.*, (2024), *Op. cit.*

they will carry out their central roles in shaping European AI policy. Still, EU regulators are reputed to be deeply committed to rigorous law enforcement, as noted by Bradford in both her books, *The Brussels Effect* and *Digital Empires*. Some U.S. tech companies have already displayed weariness. In July 2024, Meta announced that it would delay the release of its most powerful generative AI model, LLaMa, in Europe because of what it called unpredictable regulations.[79] Even the flagship Apple Intelligence will not be released in the European market due to privacy concerns.[80] These responses appear to foreshadow a second wave of the Brussels Effect.

9.6 Ethics

In 2019, the EU published "The Ethics Guidelines for Trustworthy AI", which seeks to establish a framework for the ethical development and deployment of AI.[81] The guidelines set forth seven non-binding principles, namely human oversight, technical robustness, privacy and data governance, transparency, diversity and non-discrimination, social and environmental well-being, and accountability. The 41-page document also provides a non-exhaustive assessment list that operationalises the seven principles and offers guidance as to implementation and practice. These guidelines complement the subsequent AI Act to reinforce the EU's human-centric approach to AI.[82] Recital 27 of the AI Act expressly mentions the 2019 Ethics Guidelines and reiterates the seven ethical principles. Specifically, for high-risk AI systems, the Act expressly requires the testing of such systems to be without prejudice to ethical reviews required by the Union.[83]

---

[79] Meta will delay latest AI in EU over 'unpredictable' regulation. *The Business Times*, July 18, 2024. https://www.businesstimes.com.sg/companies-markets/telcos-media-tech/meta-will-delay-latest-ai-eu-over-unpredictable-regulation.

[80] R. Goswami, Apple Intelligence won't launch in EU in 2024 due to antitrust regulation, company says. *CNBC*, June 21, 2024. https://www.cnbc.com/2024/06/21/apple-ai-europe-dma-macos.html.

[81] *Ethics guidelines for trustworthy AI*. (2019). Shaping Europe's Digital Future. https://digital-strategy.ec.europa.eu/en/library/ethics-guidelines-trustworthy-ai.

[82] A. Bradford, (2023), *Op. cit*.

[83] Article 60 EU AI Act.

To address the rise of generative AI, in March 2024, the EU published "Guidelines on the Responsible Use of Generative AI in Research" aimed at the public and private scientific communities.[84] Some key points from this latter set of guidelines advise researchers against employing generative AI tools in critical tasks such as peer reviews or evaluations; researchers should remain vigilant when overseeing use of such tools and encourage funding bodies to assist applicants in adopting generative AI in a transparent manner.

Despite the above guidelines and checklists, there are detractors who caution that such unenforceable rules may ultimately end up as ethical whitewashing. Prominent amongst them is Thomas Metzinger from the University of Mainz. Metzinger was one of the 52 members of the High-Level Expert Group on Artificial Intelligence (HLEG AI), who authored the 2019 Ethics Guidelines.[85] Metzinger argues that the "Trustworthy AI" narrative is essentially a marketing ploy invented by the industry to hoodwink their customers.[86] Any form of self-regulation by the likes of tech giants such as Google or Meta may end up going from "fake news to fake ethics" since business interests are conceptually incompatible with ethical concerns.[87] According to him, ethical red lines can only be drawn up by universities and civil societies and these must then be followed up by effective regulation and policy-making.[88]

The subsequent passing of the EU AI Act in 2024 has clearly addressed some of the concerns above. For instance, the act outlawed social scoring and the deployment of subliminal AI techniques to manipulate and distort human behaviour by placing them in its "unacceptable risk" category.[89] However, the 2019 Ethical Guidelines remain relevant as

[84] *Guidelines on the responsible use of generative AI in research developed by the European Research Area Forum.* (2024). Research and Innovation. https://research-and-innovation.ec.europa.eu/news/all-research-and-innovation-news/guidelines-responsible-use-generative-ai-research-developed-european-research-area-forum-2024-03-20_en.

[85] N. Smuha, (2019b). *AI HLEG - steering group of the European AI Alliance.* FUTURIUM - European Commission. https://ec.europa.eu/futurium/en/european-ai-alliance/ai-hleg-steering-group-european-ai-alliance.html.

[86] T. Metzinger, Ethics washing made in Europe. *Der Tagesspiegel*, April 8, 2019. https://www.tagesspiegel.de/politik/eu-guidelines-ethics-washing-made-in-europe/24195496.html.

[87] T. Metzinger (2019), *Op. cit.*

[88] T. Metzinger (2019), *Op. cit.*

[89] Article 5 EU AI Act, *Op. cit.*

they encourage a continuing discourse to reflect on the role of ethics as AI technology evolves. The shaping of meaningful ethical norms takes time and is often likened to a slow and gradual accumulation of wisdom regarding what is right for the individual and society.[90] If so, the state of discourse on AI ethics in the EU is one that involves more diverse voices when compared to the U.S. or China. The 52-member HLEG AI worked on the text of the Ethics Guidelines for nine months and considered more than 500 comments received through open consultation of a first draft.[91] Although sceptical of their impact, Metzinger proclaimed that the EU Ethics Guidelines constitute the best globally available baseline for the next phase of discussion and should be studied by China and the U.S.[92]

9.7 Summary

A few months after the passing of the AI Act, OpenAI announced that it would establish an office in Paris, its first in continental Europe.[93] This gesture can be construed as a nod to the "Brussels Effect". However, it is still early days, despite the EU's first-mover advantage in passing the overarching AI Act. The implementation of the legislation across the Union itself will no doubt face its share of challenges, ranging from harmonisation to the involvement and role of a multitude of stakeholders. Nevertheless, there is no denying that the EU's vast regulatory power is a key source of its global influence and the defining feature of the European digital empire. If the EU chooses to rewrite its data and copyright laws to adapt to generative AI, its approach will probably impact both China and the U.S.

[90] M. M. Anderson, Some Ethical Reflections on the EU AI Act. *IAIL 2022: 1st International Workshop on Imagining the AI Landscape After the AI Act*, Jun 2022, Amsterdam, Netherlands. ⟨hal-03921857⟩.

[91] *Ethics guidelines for trustworthy AI*, (2019), *Op. cit.*

[92] T. Metzinger (2019) *Op. cit.*

[93] A. Piquard, OpenAI to open Paris office. *Le Monde.Fr*, October 9, 2024. https://www.lemonde.fr/en/economy/article/2024/10/09/openai-to-open-paris-office_6728764_19.html.

Chapter 10
United States

10.1 Unbridled Innovation

President Trump's immediate response to the release of DeepSeek was to tell U.S. tech companies to stay laser-focused on beating the competition from China.[1]

For years, Apple, Microsoft, Google, and Amazon have consistently topped the list of most valuable brands in the world.[2] Now, U.S. tech giants are forming deep ties with AI companies and taking crucial stakes in various emergent AI technologies. Microsoft started with a US$1 billion investment in Open AI in 2019, and by mid-2024, this ballooned to US$13 billion.[3] The generative AI function is now added to Office applications, the Bing search engine, and even the Windows operating system. Google was probably one of the earliest movers when it acquired

[1] K. Ng, B. Drenon, T. Gerken, and M. Cieslak, What is DeepSeek - and why is everyone talking about it? *BBC*, 28 January 28, 2025, https://www.bbc.com/news/articles/c5yv5976z9po.

[2] Statista. Most valuable brands worldwide 2024 | Statista, May 24, 2024. https://www.statista.com/statistics/264875/brand-value-of-the-25-most-valuable-brands/.

[3] T. Warren, Microsoft's OpenAI investment was triggered by Google fears, emails reveal. *The Verge*, May 1, 2024. https://www.theverge.com/2024/5/1/24146302/microsoft-openai-investment-google-worries-internal-emails.

DeepMind, one of the first prominent AI start-ups in 2014.[4] Former OpenAI engineers who grew wary of Microsoft's influence went on to found Anthropic, which directly competes with ChatGPT in both the enterprise and consumer markets. Almost immediately, this newcomer raised US$4 billion from Amazon and US$2 billion from Google.[5] Finally, the most valuable brand in the world outdid everyone and hijacked the acronym "AI" by calling its proprietary technology "Apple Intelligence" – when the tech giant announced a partnership with Open AI to bring ChatGPT technology to its iPhones and Apple devices in late 2024.[6]

With these tech behemoths running in this global AI race, the U.S. is expected to lead in terms of innovation and investment. According to the 2024 AI Index of the Stanford Institute for Human-Centered Artificial Intelligence (HAI), substantially more significant AI models (61) originated from U.S.-based institutions, compared with the EU (21) and China (15).[7] The same report also noted that the number of AI-related regulations in the U.S. has risen significantly over the past years. However, the U.S. still lags behind China and the EU in terms of AI legislation. According to Bradford, the U.S. has traditionally followed a "market-driven regulatory" model, which embraces a limited role for government as it exhibits deep faith in the markets.[8] Aside from this pro-market ethos, the U.S. law-making powers are spread across its executive and legislative branches, which must fight constant bipartisan battles. It is therefore highly improbable, if not impossible, that the U.S. would adopt federal data privacy or AI legislation like those in China or the EU. In terms of AI governance, the U.S. takes a decidedly decentralised and even fragmented approach.

---

[4] S. Gibbs, Google buys UK artificial intelligence startup Deepmind for £400m. *The Guardian*, November 30, 2017. https://www.theguardian.com/technology/2014/jan/27/google-acquires-uk-artificial-intelligence-startup-deepmind.

[5] M. Lemley and M. Wansley, How Big Tech is Killing Innovation. *The New York Times*, June 13, 2024. https://www.nytimes.com/2024/06/13/opinion/big-tech-ftc-ai.html.

[6] S. Murphy Kelly, The complicated partnership between Apple and OpenAI. *CNN Business*, 2024. Accessed July 29, 2024. https://edition.cnn.com/2024/06/14/tech/apple-openai-partnership/index.html.

[7] Stanford Institute for Human-Centered Artificial Intelligence, AI Index Report 2024 – Artificial Intelligence Index, accessed August 27, 2024. https://aiindex.stanford.edu/report/.

[8] A. Bradford, (2023). *Digital Empires: The Global Battle to Regulate Technologies*. 1st ed. US: Oxford University Press. https://doi.org/10.1093/oso/9780197649268.001.0001.

Another powerful factor that impacts governance in the U.S. is corporate lobbying. According to OpenSecrets, a nonprofit that tracks and publishes data on campaign finance and lobbying, the number of groups lobbying the U.S. federal government on AI regulation almost tripled from 2022 to 2023, growing from 158 to 451 organisations.[9] While companies may be openly supportive of AI regulations; in closed-door conversations with officials, many tend to push for light-touch and voluntary rules – which should come as no surprise.[10] Corporate lobbying, especially by tech giants with deep pockets, is an inherent feature of the U.S. system which constrains and curbs policy- and law-making.[11] The influence wielded by private business interests in the country will no doubt find new heights in the Trump administration, which began its term in 2025. A mega-donor to the campaign, Elon Musk, was immediately appointed by Trump to co-lead the Department of Government Efficiency to "dismantle government bureaucracy, slash excess regulations, cut wasteful expenditures and restructure federal agencies".[12]

With a Republican trifecta, the Trump administration is well positioned to enact or tighten its AI governance – this appears unlikely to happen.[13] Within hours after returning to the White House, Trump signed an Executive Order titled "Removing Barriers to American AI Innovation" to revoke his predecessor's policies which impose onerous or unnecessary government control over AI development.[14] These initial posturing, coupled with Trump's competitive stance towards China, means that the U.S.

[9] W. Henshall, There's an AI Lobbying Frenzy in Washington. Big Tech Is Dominating. *TIME*, April 30, 2024. https://time.com/6972134/ai-lobbying-tech-policy-surge/.

[10] W. Henshall (2024), *Op. cit.*

[11] A. Bradford, M. C. Waxman, and E. Li, How Domestic Institutions Shape the Global Tech War (September 10, 2024). Available at SSRN: https://ssrn.com/abstract=4954744 or http://dx.doi.org/10.2139/ssrn.4954744.

[12] A. Faguy, Department of Government Efficiency: Trump picks Elon Musk to advise on how to 'dismantle' bureaucracy, *BBC*, November 13, 2024. https://www.bbc.com/news/articles/c93qwn8p0l0o.

[13] R. Looker, Republicans Win the House and Cement Party Trifecta for Trump. *BBC*, November 14, 2024. https://www.bbc.com/news/articles/c04ld19vlg6o.

[14] The White House. Fact Sheet: President Donald J. Trump Takes Action to Enhance America's AI Leadership, January 24, 2025. https://www.whitehouse.gov/fact-sheets/2025/01/fact-sheet-president-donald-j-trump-takes-action-to-enhance-americas-ai-leadership/.

is unlikely to draw up any form of AI governance to restrain or hamper its tech players.

10.2 Data Protection

Two privacy scandals are often cited to show up the weak data protection regime in the U.S. In 2013, former National Security Agency (NSA) contractor Edward Snowden revealed, as part of an unprecedented leak of sensitive national intelligence data, that the government agency had engaged in mass surveillance of individuals by harvesting data available through Google, Facebook, and Microsoft.[15] Next came the 2018 Cambridge Analytica scandal, which revealed that a British political consulting firm had acquired Facebook users' private data and used these unauthorised data with the goal of influencing the election in favour of President Trump.[16] Facebook CEO Mark Zuckerberg was required to testify before Congress and came under fire from the U.S. government for not being proactive enough in stemming this privacy breach.[17] A year later, Facebook was fined a record US$5 billion for violating consumers' privacy.[18] The company also settled a class action over the data breach for US$725 million.[19] Technologist Shoshana Zuboff coined the term "surveillance capitalism" to describe how tech companies such as Facebook, now rebranded as Meta, persuade users to give up privacy for the sake of convenience and then use these personal data not only to predict behaviour but also to influence and modify it.[20]

---

[15] Snowden Revelations, LAWFARE, https://www.lawfareblog.com/snowden-revelations.

[16] A. Chen, Cambridge Analytica and Our Lives Inside the Surveillance Machine. *The New Yorker*, March 21, 2018. https://www.newyorker.com/tech/annals-of-technology/cambridge-analytica-and-our-lives-inside-the-surveillance-machine.

[17] US Senate. (2018). *Facebook, Social Media Privacy, and the Use and Abuse of Data: Joint Full Committee Hearing.* Committee on the Judiciary. https://www.judiciary.senate.gov/meetings/facebook-social-media-privacy-and-the-use-and-abuse-of-data.

[18] Federal Trade Commission. FTC Imposes $5 Billion Penalty and Sweeping New Privacy Restrictions on Facebook, January 27, 2022. https://www.ftc.gov/news-events/news/press-releases/2019/07/ftc-imposes-5-billion-penalty-sweeping-new-privacy-restrictions-facebook.

[19] S. McCallum, Meta settles Cambridge Analytica scandal case for $725m. *BBC*, December 23, 2022. https://www.bbc.com/news/technology-64075067.

[20] Z. Shoshana, (2019). *The Age of Surveillance Capitalism: The Fight for a Human Future at the Frontier of a New Power.* New York: Public Affairs.

Despite these shocking events, even after the EU passed the GDPR in 2018 and China passed the PIPL in 2021, the US has still not passed any comprehensive data privacy law. The bicameral committees drafted a federal law known as the American Privacy Rights Act (APRA) in 2024, but this draft legislation has yet to be formally introduced in the House or the Senate.[21]

Meanwhile, there is a patchwork of data privacy legislation at the state level and some sector-specific federal laws. Sensitive sectors such as healthcare and financial services have specific legislation to protect privacy.[22] States such as California, Delaware, and Texas, along with several others, have their own consumer privacy laws.[23] This section takes a closer look at California's Privacy Rights Act (CPRA), which came into effect on 1 January 2023.[24]

10.2.1 *"Do Not Sell or Share My Personal Information"*

Under the CPRA (SB 1454), personal information refers to "information which identifies, relates to, describes, is reasonably capable of being associated with, or could reasonably be linked, directly or indirectly, with a particular consumer".[25] It applies to companies doing business in California or processing personal data of California residents. Businesses[26] are obliged to collect personal information of consumers (data subjects) only for specific, explicit and legitimate disclosed purposes. They must provide notice as to how personal data is collected and used and to obtain opt-in consent for data collection from children aged 13–16. Businesses

[21] House Committee on Energy and Commerce. Committee Chairs Rodgers, Cantwell Unveil Historic Draft Comprehensive Data Privacy Legislation, n.d. https://energycommerce.house.gov/posts/committee-chairs-rodgers-cantwell-unveil-historic-draft-comprehensive-data-privacy-legislation.

[22] The Health Insurance Portability and Accountability Act of 1996 introduced the Privacy Rule to protect patients' health information. The Gramm-Leach-Bliley Act (governed by the Federal Trade Commission (FTC)) requires financial institutions to disclose their data-sharing practices and set up controls to protect consumer privacy.

[23] US Data Privacy Guide, *White and Case LLP*, June 4, 2024. https://www.whitecase.com/insight-our-thinking/us-data-privacy-guide.

[24] The CPRA, n.d. https://thecpra.org/.

[25] Section 14, CPRA supra note.

[26] Section 3(B) CPRA supra note.

must abide by purpose limitations when collecting and using or reusing data, which must be consistent with consumers' general expectations and the purpose specified upon collection. Data must not be retained for longer than is reasonably necessary. Businesses must conduct privacy risk assessments[27] and cybersecurity audits, offer alternatives for accessing services for those who opt out, and cannot discriminate against consumers for exercising these rights. Consumers[28] are given rights of data access, deletion, and portability, as well as a right to opt out of the sale of personal data. The Californian consumers are given the right to prevent the sale of their personal information, so businesses must provide a link on their business's Internet homepage, titled "Do Not Sell or Share My Personal Information".[29] Giving Californian consumers the right to opt out of the "sale" or "sharing" of their personal information is a huge aspect of the legislation, as it directly tackles the risk of surveillance capitalism described by Zuboff. In this regard, the Golden State took a further step and passed the Delete Act (SB 362), which allows Californians to delete their personal information from all data brokers with a single request, further empowering consumers over their personal information.[30]

Finally, one other important feature of the CPRA is the creation of an enforcement agency known as the Californian Privacy Protection Agency (CPPA).[31] This is significant because, at the federal level, there is no independent regulatory authority empowered to enforce privacy rights. Instead, it is left to the broader mandate of the Federal Trade Commission (FTC) to protect consumers and police "unfair" or "deceptive" practices affecting commerce. The FTC relied on this mandate to impose the US$5 billion fine on Facebook for violating consumers' privacy in the Cambridge Analytica saga. In under a year, the CPPA received over 1,200 complaints, with the most common issues being the right to opt-out and the right to delete.[32] So far, the Californian privacy legislation is the

---

[27] Section 21 CPRA, supra note.

[28] Section 3(A), CPRA supra note.

[29] Section 13, CPRA supra note.

[30] California's Delete Act: A First of Its Kind Data Broker Law. *Bryan Cave Leighton Paisner LLP*, December 28, 2023. https://www.bclplaw.com/en-US/events-insights-news/the-delete-act-a-first-of-its-kind-data-broker-law.html.

[31] Section 24 CPRA, supra note.

[32] K. Lucente, US: CCPA and California Privacy Protection Agency Updates: 2024 to Date | Privacy Matters. *Privacy Matters*, May 1, 2024. https://privacymatters.dlapiper.com/2024/04/ccpa-and-california-privacy-protection-agency-updates-2024-to-date/.

only one which establishes a separate agency, rather than leaving enforcement to the state's attorney general office.[33] The CPRA can be seen as California's version of the GDPR and is undoubtedly a significant state-level effort of privacy protection.

10.2.2 *Federal privacy law in the making, or not*

Although the federal privacy law is still in its draft form, it is instructive to consider some of the key provisions of the APRA.[34] Clearly, if passed, the APRA will supersede all pieces of state privacy legislation such as the CPRA. Unsurprisingly, there are several similarities between the APRA and the GDPR. The data protected, referred to as "covered data" in the draft American legislation, refers to information that identifies, or which can be linked to other information to identify, an individual. The APRA also adopts principles of transparency, data minimisation, necessity, and proportionality. A "covered entity" and "service provider" are comparable to GDPR's "data controller" and "data processor", respectively, and have different sets of privacy obligations. Organisations subject to the APRA will be required to produce and maintain documents similar to those required under the GDPR, such as privacy policies, contracts with service providers, and impact assessments. U.S. residents (data subjects) have the right to access, correct, and delete, as well as to port their "covered data", subject to certain conditions. Data subjects have rights to decline data transfers and targeted advertising and the right to opt out of automated decision-making (ADM).

What is notable is that the draft APRA seeks to impose heightened obligations on two categories of organisations. First, a "high-impact social media company" refers to a covered entity (GDPR's data controller) that provides an Internet-accessible platform, generates at least US$3 billion in global annual revenue with at least 300 million global monthly active users (for at least 3 of the preceding 12 months) and is primarily used by individuals to access or share user-generated content.[35] Data collected by

[33] J. King and C. Meinhardt, White Paper Rethinking Privacy in the AI Era: Policy Provocations for a Data-Centric World. *Stanford Institute for Human-Centered Artificial Intelligence*, February 22, 2024. https://hai.stanford.edu/white-paper-rethinking-privacy-ai-era-policy-provocations-data-centric-world.

[34] https://www.congress.gov/bill/117th-congress/house-bill/8152/text.

[35] Section 2(11), APRA.

a high-impact social media company from its users' online activities will be treated as "sensitive data" under the proposed legislation.[36] For such sensitive data, the APRA prohibits transfer to third parties without data subjects' "affirmative express consent" (i.e., they must opt-in).[37] Second, "large data holders" are subject to higher transparency obligations relating to their privacy policy. These refer to service providers (GDPR's data processors) with gross revenue of at least US$250 million that collect or process data of 5 million individuals or sensitive data of over 200,000 individuals.[38]

While it is envisaged that the APRA would be enforced by the FTC and state attorney-generals, the proposed federal legislation also gives data subjects the right to enforce the law by filing a civil lawsuit against companies that violate their rights under the APRA.[39] Civil action can be filed for violations relating to data minimisation, transparency, opt-out rights, and data security practices.[40] These claimants can seek damages, injunctions, and reasonable legal costs.[41] Given the political complexities of the U.S. and the usual big tech lobbying against regulation, there are bound to be doubts whether the APRA will be passed. A previous legislative attempt in the form of the American Data Privacy and Protection Act (ADPPA) introduced in 2022 lost momentum.[42]

---

[36] Section 2(34)(A)(xv), APRA.

[37] Section 2(1(A)) APRA which requires the individual's freely given, specific, informed, and unambiguous authorization for an act or practice that is clearly communicated in response to a specific request from a covered entity Said request must be provided in a standalone disclosure and meet comprehensive transparency requirements (Sec 2(1)(B)).

[38] Section 2(25) APRA excludes from the definition of "large data holders" the entities that collect, process, retain or transfer to a service provider (i) personal mailing or email addresses; (ii) personal telephone numbers; (iii) log-in information of an individual; (iv) if a covered entity is a seller of goods or services, credit, debit, or mobile payment information strictly necessary to initiate, render, bill for, finalize, complete, or otherwise facilitate payments for goods or services.

[39] Sections 17–19 APRA.

[40] Section 19(a)(1) APRA.

[41] Section 19 APRA.

[42] A. Johnson, Privacy Bill Faceoff: Comparing the APRA and ADPPA. *ITIF*, May 16, 2024. https://itif.org/publications/2024/04/10/privacy-bill-faceoff-comparing-the-apra-and-adppa/.

10.3 AI Laws

In the first U.S. congressional hearing about AI oversight in May 2023, its chairperson, Senator Blumenthal, played a deepfake audio recording of himself talking about the risk of AI and the need to regulate it. Congressional hearings are held to obtain information and opinions on proposed legislation at the federal level. The AI-generated clip was based on the senator's floor speeches, recordings, and scripted using a prompt that asked ChatGPT for an opening address. This is what Blumenthal's AI-generated voice said: "Too often, we have seen what happens when technology outpaces regulation. The unbridled exploitation of data, the proliferation of disinformation and the deepening of societal inequalities. We have seen how algorithmic biases can perpetuate discrimination and prejudice and how the lack of transparency can undermine public trust. This is not the future we want".[43] It was a dramatic opening which pointed to some political will on the part of the U.S. government to catch up with China and the EU in the AI regulatory space.

10.3.1 *Executive orders*

On 30 October 2023, President Biden signed an executive order (EO 14110) on the Safe, Secure, and Trustworthy Development and Use of Artificial Intelligence.[44] "Artificial intelligence" is defined as "a machine-based system that can, for a given set of human-defined objectives, make predictions, recommendations or decisions influencing real or virtual environments".[45] The scope of the order extends beyond generative AI and covers any machine-based system that makes predictions, recommendations, or decisions. This 111-page executive instrument directs federal agencies to create standards and regulations for the use and oversight of AI. The agencies and departments are tasked with developing guidelines

---

[43] M. Swant, At the Senate's first AI hearing, lawmakers and OpenAI, IBM execs weigh risk and regulation. *Digiday*, May 17, 2023. https://digiday.com/media/at-the-senates-first-ai-hearing-lawmakers-and-tech-experts-talk-risk-and-regulation/.

[44] White House. Executive Order on the Safe, Secure, and Trustworthy Development and Use of Artificial Intelligence. The White House, October 30, 2023. https://www.whitehouse.gov/briefing-room/presidential-actions/2023/10/30/executive-order-on-the-safe-secure-and-trustworthy-development-and-use-of-artificial-intelligence/.

[45] Section 3(b) Executive Order. Refers back to 15 U.S.C. 9401(3).

that AI developers must adhere to as they build and deploy this technology and dictate how the government uses AI. The EO requires any company building an AI model that could pose a risk to U.S.'s national security to disclose it to the government and share data about such models that would comply with federal standards to be developed by the National Institute of Standards and Technology (NIST). However, this requirement will apply only to future models to be released; for example, say ChatGPT-5. The EO also instructs the Department of Commerce to develop guidelines for federal agencies to use watermarking and content authentication tools to label AI-generated content, combating AI-supported fraud such as "deep-fake" videos or AI-voice generated calls.[46] The Federal Trade Commission (FTC) is also encouraged to use antitrust and consumer protection laws to promote competition and crack down on unfair practices by dominant AI players. Overall, the document called for responsible use and creation of safer AI systems. Pursuant to the EO, on 29 April 2024, NIST released a draft AI Risk Management Framework Generative AI Profile (NIST AI 600-1) to help organisations identify the unique risks posed by managing the risk of generative AI.[47] However, even if this draft is eventually finalised, after consultation with the industry, it remains a mere guideline of best practices intended for voluntary adoption. Though well-regarded, NIST is a non-regulatory agency under the U.S. Department of Commerce, with no powers to enforce standards it developed.[48]

Ultimately, the EO is a unilateral action from the executive branch of the government – it does not possess the force of law. In the area of data privacy, the EO also called on Congress, the legislative branch, to pass privacy laws. Of course, the agencies named in the EO can carry out the directive and set up the relevant regulations and standards. The effectiveness of these actions by the federal agencies clearly depends on how they are carried out. These standards, and the EO itself, will be subject to abrogation by a new president, legislative interventions, and, of course, court interdiction. And this happened the moment President Trump returned to the White House. Trump's own EO dated 23 January 2025 revoked Biden's EO 14110, which "established burdensome requirements… and

[46]Section 4.5 EO. (Infra note 151).

[47]NIST. AI Risk Management Framework | NIST, April 30, 2024. https://www.nist.gov/itl/ai-risk-management-framework.

[48]NIST. About NIST | NIST, January 11, 2022. https://www.nist.gov/about-nist.

threatened American technological leadership".[49] The Trump EO is a paradigmatic shift from the Biden EO, moving away from oversight to deregulation.

10.3.2 *Patchwork of (possible) state laws*

Despite and perhaps due to the absence of federal AI legislation, various states have introduced their own AI bills and some have managed to pass them.[50]

The state of California is home to over 30 of the world's largest AI companies, so its legislative intent and direction are always closely watched.[51] The Californian legislature introduced several bills, which passed, would put in place various forms of guardrails. One example is the "California Digital Provenance Standards Bill" (AB 3211), which requires every generative AI system to embed watermarks in the metadata of AI-generated images and videos.[52] Metadata provides essential information such as the origin, context, and history of a piece of text or an image. This bill seeks to ban the use of tools or applications designed to remove metadata from synthetic content. Additionally, sound recordings or music videos shared will be required to carry the name of the artist or rightsholder. This bill has received the support of OpenAI, which agreed that "new technology and standards can help people understand the origin of content they find online, and avoid confusion between human-generated and photorealistic AI-generated content".[53] This proposed bill, if passed, will tackle deepfakes. The Californian legislature managed to enact its

---

[49] The White House, (2025), *Op. cit.*

[50] The National Conference of State Legislatures. Artificial Intelligence 2024 Legislation, June 3, 2024. Accessed August 28, 2024. https://www.ncsl.org/technology-and-communication/artificial-intelligence-2024-legislation.

[51] P. Leroe-Muñoz, Five Bills That Preview California's AI Approach in 2024. Silicon Valley Leadership Group, January 31, 2024. https://www.svlg.org/five-bills-that-preview-californias-ai-approach-in-2024/.

[52] LegiScan. California AB3211 | 2023–2024 | Regular Session. n.d. https://legiscan.com/CA/text/AB3211/id/2984195.

[53] A. Tong, OpenAI supports California AI bill requiring 'watermarking' of synthetic content. *Reuters*, August 27, 2024. Accessed August 28, 2024. https://www.reuters.com/technology/artificial-intelligence/openai-supports-california-ai-bill-requiring-watermarking-synthetic-content-2024-08-26/.

"Generative Artificial Intelligence: Training Data Transparency" (AB 2013), which aims to provide transparency to consumers about the data used to train the AI services and systems being offered, including whether synthetic data has or is being used to fill gaps in data sources.[54] From 1 January 2026, AI model developers will be required to disclose the source or owner of the training data, the number of samples, whether the data are protected by intellectual property rights, and whether there is personal information or aggregate commercial information in the data. This law is significant, as it requires developers to publish reports on their training datasets – overriding prevailing industry norms which treat identity and sources of training datasets as proprietary.

The boldest legislative attempt is a bill called the "Safe and Secure Innovation for Frontier Artificial Intelligence Models Act" (SB 1047), which requires big AI developers to take reasonable responsibility for advanced AI models, often referred to as "frontier AI models", particularly those worth over US$100 million in investment.[55] The proposed bill mandates safety testing as well as a "kill switch", which is a method for shutting down the models if they go awry. Developers are required to hire third parties to conduct annual audits of their safety practices, submit compliance reports to the state's attorney general, and provide protection for whistleblowers. If businesses do not follow these requirements, they could be sued and face civil penalties. This bill places the safety obligation on neural network model developers – the AI companies – rather than those deploying such systems. The immediate backlash is that such obligations would harm innovation. One concern is that the bill may force developers to police open-source models. Open AI argued that "[t]he AI revolution is only just beginning, and California's unique status as the global leader in AI is fueling the state's economic dynamism. SB 1047 would threaten that growth, slow the pace of innovation, and lead California's world-class engineers and entrepreneurs to leave the state in search of greater opportunity elsewhere".[56] Besides tech companies, the

---

[54] LegiScan. California AB2013 | 2023–2024 | Regular Session. n.d. https://leginfo.legislature.ca.gov/faces/billTextClient.xhtml?bill_id=202320240AB2013.

[55] SB 1047: Safe and Secure Innovation for Frontier Artificial Intelligence Models Act. | Digital Democracy. n.d. https://digitaldemocracy.calmatters.org/bills/ca_202320240sb1047.

[56] S. Ghaffary, OpenAI Says California's Controversial AI Bill Will Hurt Innovation. *Bloomberg*, August 22, 2024. https://www.bloomberg.com/news/articles/2024-08-21/openai-says-california-s-controversial-ai-bill-will-hurt-innovation.

bill also faced intense opposition from leading academics as well as politicians. Prominent former U.S. House Speaker Nancy Pelosi, for instance, openly criticised SB 1047 as ill-informed.[57] In September 2024, Californian Governor Gavin Newsom vetoed the bill and returned it to the legislature without his signature.[58]

In contrast, other states have passed various forms of AI laws. In May 2024, Utah passed its own AI Act (SB 149).[59] This law makes clear that Utah's consumer protection laws apply to organisations' use of generative AI. Private sector entities are required to take steps to disclose and respond to enquiries about their use of generative AI. Businesses must clearly and conspicuously disclose to consumers that they are not interacting with a human. The Colorado AI Act (SB 205), which will be effective in 2026, creates duties for developers and businesses that deploy AI.[60] It focuses on automated decision-making systems and defines a covered high-risk AI system as one that "when deployed, makes, or is a substantial factor in making a consequential decision". The law also requires developers and deployers to use reasonable care to avoid discrimination via AI systems that make, or are a substantial factor in making, consequential decisions. In many respects, the Colorado AI Act reflects many of the EU AI Act.

Interestingly, Massachusetts even drafted a draft bill in early 2023 with the help of ChatGPT to regulate generative AI.[61] The proposed law (SB 31), if enacted, will require companies operating LLMs which have at least 1 billion parameters to adhere to requisite standards, including implementing reasonable security measures to protect training data, obtaining informed consent before personal data collection and use,

---

[57] G. Bensinger, Big Tech wants AI to be regulated. Why do they oppose a California AI bill? *Reuters*, August 22, 2024. Accessed August 27, 2024. https://www.reuters.com/technology/artificial-intelligence/big-tech-wants-ai-be-regulated-why-do-they-oppose-california-ai-bill-2024-08-21/.

[58] S. Sigal, K. Piper, and D. Matthews, California's governor has vetoed a historic AI safety bill. *Vox*, September 29, 2024. https://www.vox.com/future-perfect/369628/ai-safety-bill-sb-1047-gavin-newsom-california.

[59] SB0149, n.d. https://le.utah.gov/~2024/bills/static/SB0149.html.

[60] Colorado General Assembly. Consumer Protections for Artificial Intelligence | Colorado General Assembly. n.d. https://leg.colorado.gov/bills/sb24-205.

[61] Massachusetts: Bill to regulate generative AI models introduced to. *DataGuidance*, January 2, 2024. https://www.dataguidance.com/news/massachusetts-bill-regulate-generative-ai-models.

conducting regular risk assessments, using distinctive watermarks on generated content, and even registering with the state attorney general's office. and provide information about their model.[62]

The absence of a federal law has led to a series of state AI laws. States which face fewer partisan barriers are in a stronger position to move legislation. At a glance, this may look like a nightmarish, fragmented compliance scenario for a single country. However, with states such as California and Colorado taking a firm legislative stance, it may just be adequate for the time being.

10.3.3 *Deepfakes*

During his presidential campaign, Trump posted a series of AI-generated images of pop superstar Taylor Swift and her fans vowing their support for him.[63] A few weeks earlier, Elon Musk posted a deepfake video on X with the voice of presidential hopeful Kamala Harris digitally manipulated to twist the original content of her campaign advertisement.[64] This, despite the fact that the platform X prohibits users from posting media which has been "deceptively altered" and is "likely to result in widespread confusion on public issues". In early 2024, a draft federal bill known as "The Disrupt Explicit Forged Images and Non-Consensual Edits", or DEFIANCE Act, was introduced, which allows victims to sue if those who created the deepfakes knew, or "recklessly disregarded", that the victim did not consent to its making.[65] This act has yet to be passed at the time of writing this chapter. In contrast, China has specific legislation to

---

[62] Massachusetts: Bill to regulate generative AI models introduced to. (2024), *Op. cit.*

[63] N. Robins-Early, Trump posts deepfakes of Swift, Harris and Musk in effort to shore up support. *The Guardian*, August 21, 2024. https://www.theguardian.com/us-news/article/2024/aug/19/trump-ai-swift-harris-musk-deepfake-images.

[64] P. Olson, Commentary: Elon Musk is playing a dangerous game with Kamala Harris deepfake. *CNA*, July 30, 2024. https://www.channelnewsasia.com/commentary/elon-musk-kamala-harris-ai-deepfake-misinformation-us-election-social-media-4513691?cid=internal_sharetool_androidphone_31072024_cna.

[65] K. Tenbarge, Defiance Act passes in the Senate, potentially allowing deepfake victims to sue over nonconsensual images. *NBC News*, July 25, 2024. https://www.nbcnews.com/tech/tech-news/defiance-act-passes-senate-allow-deepfake-victims-sue-rcna163464.

tackle deepfakes (the Deep Synthesis Rules)[66] and the EU's AI Act regulates deepfakes as a limited-risk AI system[67].

10.4 Copyright

The baseline position is that work autonomously generated by AI systems without any human input is not copyrightable. This was settled by an August 2023 federal court judgement in a case which challenged the Copyright Office's decision to deny registration for an artwork entirely created by an AI system.[68] The copyright registration listed a machine algorithm called "Creativity Machine" as the author. The District Court of Columbia affirmed the Copyright Office's position and ruled that autonomously generated AI artwork is not eligible for protection, as human authorship is a bedrock requirement of U.S. copyright laws. In another case involving images created by inputting text prompts to Midjourney, a text-to-image AI system, the Copyright Office maintained that such images, which are not the product of human authorship, cannot be copyrightable.[69]

To obtain full protection under U.S. copyright laws, works must be registered with the Copyright Office, so its official position on the copyright status of AI-generated works carries utmost weight. In March 2023, the "Copyright Registration Guidance: Works Containing Material Generated by Artificial Intelligence" was published.[70] This policy

[66] China Law Translate, Provisions on the Administration of Deep Synthesis Internet Information Services (互联网信息服务深度合成管理规定), dated 1 February 1, 2023. Available at https://www.chinalawtranslate.com/en/deep-synthesis/.

[67] Article 3(60) EU AI Act.

[68] WIPO Lex, WIPO Lex, United States District Court for the District of Columbia [2023]: Thaler v. Perlmutter, No. 22-CV-384-1564-BAH. n.d., https://www.wipo.int/wipolex/en/judgments/details/1840.

[69] R. Lawler, The US Copyright Office says you can't copyright Midjourney AI-generated images. *The Verge*, February 23, 2023. https://www.theverge.com/2023/2/22/23611278/midjourney-ai-copyright-office-kristina-kashtanova.

[70] Copyright Registration Guidance: Works Containing Material Generated by Artificial Intelligence, *Federal Register*, March 16, 2023. https://www.federalregister.gov/documents/2023/03/16/2023-05321/copyright-registration-guidance-works-containing-material-generated-by-artificial-intelligence.

document underscored the necessity of human involvement and explained that the Copyright Office will evaluate whether AI outputs result from mechanical reproduction or from a human author's "own original mental conception" on a case-by-case basis. However, a few months later, the office issued a notice of enquiry and request for comments on a list of issues relating to the intersection of copyright and AI.[71] In January 2025, the Copyright Office issued a report on copyrightability, which reinforced its position that copyright does not extend to purely AI-generated material and that whether human contributions to AI-generated outputs are sufficient to constitute authorship will be decided on a case-by-case basis.[72]

Besides the copyrightability of materials generated using AI systems, the office also sought public comments on the use of copyrighted works to train AI models. Over 10,000 written comments were submitted by a wide range of stakeholders.[73] Unsurprisingly, the technology companies vigorously defended their turf and championed the contribution of generative AI. OpenAI submitted that new technologies would democratise creativity and benefit productivity and economic growth, while Apple asserted generative AI's role to aid the development of computer code. Meta argued that the use of copyrighted material to train generative AI tools should not trigger copyright infringement laws or alternatively qualifies as fair use as a defence against infringement. At the time of writing, the Copyright Office has yet to release its guidance on the training of AI models on copyrighted works and the AI model's liability for copyright infringement, if any.[74]

---

[71] Artificial Intelligence and Copyright, Federal Register. August 30, 2023. https://www.federalregister.gov/documents/2023/08/30/2023-18624/artificial-intelligence-and-copyright.

[72] U.S. Copyright Office. Copyright and Artificial Intelligence: Part 2 - Copyrightability, 2025. https://copyright.gov/ai/Copyright-and-Artificial-Intelligence-Part-2-Copyrightability-Report.pdf.

[73] S. Jernudd, U.S. Copyright Office Examines Copyright and Generative AI. *Huges, Hubbard & Reed*, July 10, 2024. Accessed July 25, 2024. https://www.hhrartlaw.com/2024/07/u-s-copyright-office-examines-copyright-and-generative-ai/.

[74] N. Scheland, Looking Forward: The U.S. Copyright Office's AI Initiative in 2024 | Copyright, *The Library of Congress*, March 26, 2024, https://blogs.loc.gov/copyright/2024/03/looking-forward-the-u-s-copyright-offices-ai-initiative-in-2024/.

The battle is afoot

OpenAI is facing numerous lawsuits, including class actions, from newspapers, media companies, and content creators, on the grounds that their LLMs have been trained on copyrighted content without permission. Several other generative AI service providers are also facing allegations of copyright infringement.[75] Leading the charge is the New York Times (NYT), which sued both OpenAI and its largest investor Microsoft in December 2023. The NYT has proclaimed the "unlawful use" of its "copyrighted news articles, in-depth investigations, opinion pieces, reviews, how-to guides, and more" to create AI products, a threat to the paper's ability to provide that service.[76] The NYT is asking the court to grant an order that OpenAI destroys all training data that use copyrighted materials from its paper. After NYT's move, at least eight other U.S. newspapers also filed their own lawsuits against OpenAI and Microsoft.[77] One of the world's biggest record labels, Sony Music Group, sent over 700 letters to warn AI companies and music streaming platforms not to use the company's content – musical compositions, lyrics, album covers, and metadata – without consent.[78] The indiscriminate training may even see the AI companies themselves encroaching on one another's turf. Google-owned YouTube (YT) warned OpenAI that the latter's text-to-video AI tool, Sora, would be breaching its rules if YT's videos or video transcriptions had been used in the training.[79]

---

[75] J. Panettieri, Generative AI Lawsuits Timeline: Legal Cases vs. OpenAI, Microsoft, Anthropic, Nvidia and More. *Sustainable Tech Partner for Green IT Service Providers*, July 21, 2024. https://sustainabletechpartner.com/topics/ai/generative-ai-lawsuit-timeline/.

[76] E. Helmore and P. Kari, New York Times sues OpenAI and Microsoft for copyright infringement. *The Guardian*, December 29, 2023. https://www.theguardian.com/media/2023/dec/27/new-york-times-openai-microsoft-lawsuit.

[77] Reporter, Guardian Staff. Eight US newspapers sue OpenAI and Microsoft for copyright infringement. *The Guardian*, April 30, 2024. https://www.theguardian.com/technology/2024/apr/30/us-newspaper-openai-lawsuit.

[78] Are you a robot? *Bloomberg*, May 16, 2024. https://www.bloomberg.com/news/articles/2024-05-16/sony-music-warns-companies-to-stop-training-ai-on-its-artists-content?embedded-checkout=true.

[79] S. Fielding, YouTube CEO warns OpenAI that training models on its videos is against the rules. *Engadget*, April 5, 2024. https://www.engadget.com/youtube-ceo-warns-openai-that-training-models-on-its-videos-is-against-the-rules-121547513.html.

If generative AI is "democratized" – as OpenAI urged (in its comment to the Copyright Office) – will this mean that technology will be able to create without creators? If so, this is an existential threat to many in the industry. Actress Scarlett Johansson was approached by OpenAI to license her voice to one of its AI systems called "Sky". Johansson was the female lead in a Hollywood film, "Her", and was the voice of the advanced AI operating system featured in that film. Unsurprisingly, that movie has since achieved cult status, as it presaged how human-like AI has become. Even though the actress declined the request, OpenAI appeared to nevertheless have created a voice very similar to Johansson's. OpenAI dropped that project only after the actress threatened legal action.[80] The Screen Actors Guild-American Federation of Television and Radio Artists (SAG-AFTRA) has been advocating for federal legislation to protect voice and likeness rights of actors, highlighting the need for such protections in the face of advancing AI technology.[81] Fear and concerns that AI technology will displace actors and writers have led to strikes, work stoppages and tense contract negotiations.

IP expert Professor Mark Lemley advocates for AI models to be allowed to use copyrighted databases for training purposes – what he calls "fair learning".[82] This builds on the copyright exception of fair use. He argues that most machine learning entails using data for transformative purposes and seeks to learn more from the ideas or information contained in the copyrighted works rather than to copy their expressive elements. After all, broader access to larger training datasets will make AI better, safer, and less biased, which in turn benefits society. To balance such access, the compilation of what goes into the training set should be transparent and open to scrutiny. Moreover, Lemley explains that, given the sheer size of training data fed to AI models, it seems impractical to obtain permission and licence from the rightsholders. Johannson's case is straightforward, but copyright owners may face the daunting task of

---

[80] W. Cho, Scarlett Johansson's AI Legal Threat Sets Stage for Actors' Battle With Tech Giants, *The Hollywood Reporter*, May 22, 2024, https://www.hollywoodreporter.com/business/business-news/scarlett-johansson-ai-legal-threat-1235905899/.

[81] 'Enough is enough': Hollywood's video game actors go on strike. *The Guardian*, July 25, 2024. https://www.theguardian.com/games/article/2024/jul/25/video-game-actors-strike-sag-aftra-ai?CMP=Share_AndroidApp_Other.

[82] M. A. Lemley and B. Casey, Fair learning. *Texas Law Review*, March 20, 2021, https://texaslawreview.org/fair-learning/.

proving their entitlement. For instance, in the ongoing publicised lawsuit brought by the NYT, OpenAI's lawyers have asked the newspaper to produce reporters' notes, interview memos, and other materials for each of the roughly 10 million contested articles the publication alleges were illegally plugged into the company's AI models.[83] OpenAI argued it needed the materials to assess the copyrightability of the articles.[84] Given how rich and powerful the generative AI companies have become, they are bound to pour in vast resources to fight their legal battles. Until the Copyright Office takes a final stand, the battles will no doubt rage on.

It is hard to envisage the Copyright Office giving the green light to generate AI companies to train copious amounts of data without regard to copyright infringement. According to the U.S. Chamber of Commerce, intellectual property contributes about 40% of the country's GDP.[85] Strong rights protection will be needed to support this important pillar of growth. Moreover, why should rich big tech players not play by copyright rules like everyone else? Ultimately, it may simply be a matter of paying the right price for copyrighted contents. In June 2024, OpenAI signed a multi-year content deal with TIME to bring the magazine's content to products such as ChatGPT.[86] Almost 100 years of TIME's archived materials will be made available for training; citations and links back to the original source on Time.com will be displayed in response to users' prompts. A similar agreement was also reached earlier between OpenAI and the Financial Times.[87] Given their deep pockets, generative AI companies and their big tech investors should be able to afford to pay for copyrighted products.

---

[83] A. Soni, OpenAI's Tactics Test First Amendment in New York Times Fight. *Bloomberg*, July 18, 2024. https://news.bloomberglaw.com/ip-law/openais-aggressive-court-tactics-test-first-amendment-limits.

[84] A. Soni (2024), *Op. cit.*

[85] K. Anderson, The Pillars of Free Enterprise Rest on IP. *US Chamber of Commerce*, March 8, 2024. https://www.uschamber.com/intellectual-property/the-pillars-of-free-enterprise-rest-on-ip#:~:text=Big%20numbers%3A%20In%20the%20United,U.S.%20Patent%20and%20Trademark%20Office.

[86] TIME and OpenAI Announce Strategic Content Partnership. *TIME*, June 27, 2024. https://time.com/6992955/time-and-openai-announce-strategic-content-partnership/?utm_source=www.stp.news.

[87] M. Murgia, The Financial Times and OpenAI strike content licensing deal. *The Financial Times*, April 29, 2024. Accessed July 29, 2024. https://www.ft.com/content/33328743-ba3b-470f-a2e3-f41c3a366613.

10.5 Regulators

The U.S. has largely embraced a more decentralised and distributed approach to AI regulation.[88] There is no AI-specific federal regulator in the U.S. Biden's EO 14110 (revoked by Trump) established the White House Artificial Intelligence Council to coordinate AI-related activities and policies across federal agencies to "ensure effective formulation, development, communication, industry engagement, and timely implementation of AI-related policies".[89] The council was expected to drive implementation of wide-ranging initiatives and consists of high-level representatives from several key federal offices such as the Secretaries of State, Defence, and Commerce and the Directors of National Intelligence, as well as the White House Office of Management and Budget (OMB). At the start of his term, Trump established the President's Council of Advisors on Science and Technology (PCAST) to advise and recommend policies, including the drafting of regulatory frameworks.[90] It would appear that the U.S. is taking an ad hoc approach and is unlikely to rely on a federal regulator to drive AI policies.

Even though there is no federal AI law in place, many agencies rely on existing legal frameworks to support their role in AI governance. One prominent example is the FTC. Its main mission is consumer protection. Section 5 of the FTC Act prohibits "unfair or deceptive acts or practices in or affecting commerce".[91] The agency has relied on its broad authority under Section 5 to crack down on telemarketing fraud and tackle anticompetitive practices.[92] The FTC was specifically mentioned in the 14110 EO and encouraged to "ensure fair competition in the AI marketplace and to

---

[88] A. Engler, The EU and U.S. Diverge on AI Regulation: A Transatlantic Comparison and Steps to Alignment. *Brookings Institute,* April 25, 2023. https://www.brookings.edu/articles/the-eu-and-us-diverge-on-ai-regulation-a-transatlantic-comparison-and-steps-to-alignment/.

[89] Section 12 EO (Infra note 151).

[90] The White House. Fact Sheet: President Donald J. Trump Launches PCAST to Restore American Leadership in Science and Technology, January 24, 2025. https://www.whitehouse.gov/fact-sheets/2025/01/fact-sheet-president-donald-j-trump-launches-pcast-to-restore-american-leadership-in-science-and-technology/.

[91] Section 5 of the FTC Act.

[92] R. Manfredi, FTC Announces Broader Vision of Its Section 5 Authority to Address Unfair Methods of Competition. *Gibson Dunn,* January 24, 2023. https://www.gibsondunn.com/ftc-announces-broader-vision-of-its-section-5-authority-to-address-unfair-methods-of-competition/.

ensure that consumers and workers are protected from harms that may be enabled by the use of AI".[93] The agency once again relies on Section 5 to regulate AI in order to protect consumers. Companies must ensure that all marketing and use of AI adhere to long-established principles under the section; otherwise, they will face active prosecution from the FTC if found to have deployed AI in a manner harmful or deceptive to the consumer.[94] Many other federal agencies take a similar stance and assert that their existing powers and current laws already apply to AI technologies without the need for passing new AI-specific laws.[95] On top of this, there is also inter-agency cooperation when it comes to AI governance. For example, the FTC released a joint statement with several other federal bodies, including the Department of Justice, in April 2023, which noted how "existing legal authorities apply to the use of automated systems and innovative new technologies just as they apply to other practices" and emphasised that the agencies would work "to ensure that these rapidly evolving automated systems are developed and used in a manner consistent with federal laws".[96] In the short term, it would appear that much of U.S.'s AI regulation will consist more of figuring out how existing laws and legal frameworks apply to AI. This may ultimately translate to more efficient enforcement and compliance since both the regulator and technology developers and service providers are already familiar with the frameworks and their boundaries. Ultimately, the elephant in the room for the U.S. is its politics. Any change of administration and the tight contest between the Democrats and the Republicans in both houses can potentially introduce volatility and changes in the governance direction.

---

[93] Section 5.3 EO (Infra note 151).

[94] 2023 Artificial Intelligence Regulation: An Update from a Senior FTC Official. *Holland & Knight,* November 20, 2023. https://www.hklaw.com/en/insights/publications/2023/11/2023-artificial-intelligence-regulation-an-update-from-a-senior-ftc.

[95] M. Fazlioglu, US federal AI governance: Laws, policies and strategies. *IAPP* n.d. https://iapp.org/resources/article/us-federal-ai-governance/.

[96] Federal Trade Commission. Joint Statement on Enforcement Efforts Against Discrimination and Bias in Automated Systems, April 25, 2023. https://www.ftc.gov/legal-library/browse/cases-proceedings/public-statements/joint-statement-enforcement-efforts-against-discrimination-bias-automated-systems.

10.6 Ethics

In 2023, the Biden-Harris Administration secured a voluntary commitment from several leading tech and AI companies such as Amazon, IBM, Google, Meta, Microsoft, and OpenAI to "help move toward safe, secure, and transparent development of AI technology".[97] The White House told the CEOs of these U.S. AI giants that they have a moral responsibility to protect society from the potential dangers of this powerful technology.[98] The key question is whether they can be trusted to self-regulate.

Microsoft started its "Responsible AI" programme in 2017 and pledged to conduct its business in accordance with six principles, namely fairness, reliability and safety, privacy and security, inclusiveness, transparency, and accountability.[99] The company's Office of Responsible AI, which has a dedicated Ethics and Society team, played a critical role in ensuring that the principles are reflected and implemented in Microsoft products.[100] Yet, as Microsoft waded further into the AI arena and invested more monies into OpenAI, the Ethics and Society team, which had roughly 30 engineers, designers, and philosophers at its peak, was eventually completely disbanded by January 2023.[101] Shortly thereafter, Microsoft relaunched its search engine, Bing, with AI and proceeded to raise many ethical eyebrows with inaccuracies, hallucinations, and racial slurs.[102]

[97] FACT SHEET: Biden-Harris Administration Secures Voluntary Commitments from Leading Artificial Intelligence Companies to Manage the Risks Posed by AI. *The White House*, July 21, 2023. https://www.whitehouse.gov/briefing-room/statements-releases/2023/07/21/fact-sheet-biden-harris-administration-secures-voluntary-commitments-from-leading-artificial-intelligence-companies-to-manage-the-risks-posed-by-ai/.

[98] FACT SHEET: Biden-Harris Administration Secures Voluntary Commitments from Leading Artificial Intelligence Companies to Manage the Risks Posed by AI. *The White House*, July 21, 2023. https://www.whitehouse.gov/briefing-room/statements-releases/2023/07/21/fact-sheet-biden-harris-administration-secures-voluntary-commitments-from-leading-artificial-intelligence-companies-to-manage-the-risks-posed-by-ai/.

[99] Responsible AI Principles and Approach. *Microsoft AI*. (n.d.). https://www.microsoft.com/en-us/ai/principles-and-approach.

[100] Z. Schiffer and C. Newton, Microsoft lays off AI ethics and society team. *The Verge*, March 14, 2023. https://www.theverge.com/2023/3/13/23638823/microsoft-ethics-society-team-responsible-ai-layoffs.

[101] Z. Schiffer, and C. Newton (2023), *Op. cit.*

[102] C. Gordon, Why Is Microsoft's New Bing ChatBot Raising Ethical Eyebrows? *Forbes*, February 21, 2023. https://www.forbes.com/sites/cindygordon/2023/02/21/why-is-microsofts-bing-chatbot-raising-ethical-eyebrows/.

Microsoft is not alone in shrinking or downsizing its AI ethics staff strength. During recent years, Google, Meta, Amazon, and X (formerly known as Twitter) have all cut members of their "responsible AI teams" tasked with advising on the safety of consumer products that use or incorporate AI.[103] In 2020, AI ethics researcher Timnit Gebru said she was fired by Google after she published one of the most influential papers which argued that biases in LLMs were no accidents but the result of intentional choices which prioritised speed over safety.[104] Gebru was voted by Time Magazine as one of 2023's 100 Most Influential People in AI alongside Geoffrey Hinton and Zeng Yi (曾毅) who headed the team that wrote the Beijing AI Principles.[105]

The reason for preferring speed over safety or ethics is obvious. When it relaunched the Bing Chat bot, Microsoft told its investors that every one percent of market share that it could take away from Google in search would result in US$2 billion in annual revenue.[106] The first-mover advantage in the current AI "arms race" now comes with such hefty returns that any delay caused by ethical considerations automatically translates to astronomical opportunity costs.

The Brookings Institution, a U.S. think tank, conducted a five-year study on public confidence in various institutions within the country and found that Americans' confidence in technology firms has dropped drastically between 2018 and 2021.[107] Not only were tech companies less popular than before the pandemic, but the extent to which their popularity dropped exceeded the drop in confidence in any of the other U.S.

[103] C. Criddle, and M. Murgia, Big tech companies cut AI ethics staff, raising safety concerns. *The Financial Times,* March 29, 2023. Accessed October 22, 2024. https://www.ft.com/content/26372287-6fb3-457b-9e9c-f722027f36b3.

[104] E. Bender, A. Mcmillan-Major, S. Shmitchell, T. Gebru, and S. Shmar-Garet, S. On the Dangers of Stochastic Parrots: Can Language Models Be Too Big? *ACM Digital Library*. March, 2021. https://dl.acm.org/doi/pdf/10.1145/3442188.3445922.

[105] Time. TIME100 AI, September 7, 2023. https://time.com/collection/time100-ai/.

[106] L. O'Reilly, Microsoft just laid out the $2 billion reason why it's going all in on ChatGPT. *Business Insider*, February 9, 2023. https://www.businessinsider.com/microsoft-chat-gpt-2-billion-revenue-search-steals-google-2023-2.

[107] J. Ladd, J. A. Tucker, and S. Kates, How Americans' confidence in technology firms has dropped. *The Brookings Institute*, June 14, 2023. https://www.brookings.edu/articles/how-americans-confidence-in-technology-firms-has-dropped-evidence-from-the-second-wave-of-the-american-institutional-confidence-poll/.

institutions examined in the survey.[108] One common explanation for the lack of trust is that many see tech companies as a collection of over-encroaching behemoths constantly lobbying against regulations. It is no secret that U.S. tech giants spent tremendous amounts lobbying. Apple, Amazon, Google, and Meta combined spent more than US$55 million on lobbying the federal government in 2021, up from US$34 million in 2020.[109] In 2021, Amazon alone spent a record-high US$19 million,[110] and Meta over US$20 million.[111] These companies were seeking not only to fend off antitrust regulation but also to defend their other policies in the aftermath of high-profile public complaints or scandals.[112] With their deep pockets, tech companies are also starting to fund university campuses, giving them influence over academics studying critical topics such as AI, social media, and disinformation.[113] According to a 2021 paper by University of Toronto and Harvard researchers, out of 33 professors who wrote on AI ethics for the top journals such as Nature and Science, for example, all but one had taken grant money from the tech giants or had previously worked as their employees or contractors.[114] Hany Farid, a UC-Berkeley professor in computer science and at the School of Information, explained that tech companies "pay for the research of the very people in a position to criticize them. It's what the oil and gas industry has done with climate change, and it's what the tobacco companies did with cigarette research".[115]

In the case of these powerful U.S. Silicon Valley giants, most of whom have poured billions into the business of generative AI – the

---

[108] J. Ladd *et al.*, (2023), *Op. cit.*

[109] E. Birnbaum, Tech Spent Big on Lobbying Last Year. *POLITICO,* January 24, 2022. https://www.politico.com/newsletters/morning-tech/2022/01/24/tech-spent-big-on-lobbying-last-year-00001144.

[110] C. Zakrzewski, Tech Companies Spent Almost $70 Million Lobbying Washington in 2021 as Congress Sought to Rein in Their Power. *The Washington Post*, January 21, 2022. https://www.washingtonpost.com/technology/2022/01/21/tech-lobbying-in-washington/.

[111] Lobbying Report, Lobbying Disclosure Act of 1995 (Section 5), https://www.politico.com/f/?id=0000017e-7dc2-d1fc-ad7f-ffc269ad0000.

[112] A. Bradford, (2020). *The Brussels Effect*, 1st ed. Oxford University Press.

[113] J. Menn and N. Nix, Big Tech funds the very people who are supposed to hold it accountable. *The Washington Post*, December 7, 2023. https://www.washingtonpost.com/technology/2023/12/06/academic-research-meta-google-university-influence/.

[114] J. Menn, and N. Nix (2023), *Op. cit.*

[115] J. Menn, and N. Nix (2023), *Op. cit.*

matters that can properly be left to unenforceable codes of ethics, instead of laws and regulations, should be carefully scoped and limited. However, with Trump revoking Biden's executive order on safe and secure AI (EO 14110), the new administration is sending a strong signal that the tech companies are in the driving seat. This provides little incentive for any form of self-regulation.

10.7 Summary

In recent years, Silicon Valley giants and their prominent representatives are no longer seen as geniuses who can do no wrong. Discourses urging the political powers to rein in tech companies and their AI businesses are growing. Even Nobel laureate Daron Acemoglu is urging the country to escape the "New Gilded Age" and not hand further power to tech companies and their billionaires.[116] Acemoglu argued that tech billionaires such as Bill Gates, Mark Zuckerberg, and Elon Musk now assert expertise on a wide range of topics, and with many of them controlling major means of communication and given top billing in public discourse, they are wielding power of a magnitude that is unparalleled in recent history.[117] However, when it comes to writing laws to rein in this power, there are cultural and institutional obstacles to overcome in the U.S. The country is hard-wired to distrust regulation and its law-making institutions must fight off bipartisan politics and corporate lobbying, almost without any relief. As the tech rivalry with China heats up, it is difficult to envisage that the U.S. would adopt overarching policies similar or even close to those established in China or the EU to put in place a cohesive framework to regulate its AI industry. In fact, as President Trump begins his term in 2025, the U.S. is taking a decidedly divergent regulatory path from China and the EU. The spectre of tech leaders such as Amazon's Jeff Bezos, Apple's Tim Cook, Google's Sundar Pichai, Meta's Mark Zuckerberg, and, of course, Tesla's Elon Musk seated in front of Trump's own cabinet candidates during the President's inauguration ceremony is not lost on the rest of the world.[118]

---

[116] D. Acemoglu, Escaping the New Gilded Age. *Project Syndicate*, October 14, 2024. https://www.project-syndicate.org/onpoint/wealth-inequality-billionaires-undue-influence-bad-for-society-by-daron-acemoglu-2024-09.

[117] D. Acemoglu, (2024), *Op. cit.*

[118] E. Helmore, Trump Inauguration: Zuckerberg, Bezos and Musk Seated in Front of Cabinet Picks. *The Guardian*, January 21, 2025. https://www.theguardian.com/us-news/2025/jan/20/trump-inauguration-tech-executives.

Chapter 11

Conclusion

The latter part of the year 2024 offered a breather in the AI regulatory "arms race": China was more preoccupied with its property crisis and falling consumer confidence, the U.S. with its elections, and the EU with tackling the nuts and bolts of implementing its ambitious AI laws. Despite sounding emphatic alarms regarding the dangers of generative AI, Geoffrey Hinton was co-awarded the 2024 Nobel Prize in Physics for his life's work – which he allegedly regretted – namely in developing artificial neural networks that powered the currently emerging forms of AI.[1] Even more amazing is that a computer scientist won a share of the Nobel Prize for Chemistry: Demis Hassabis, who co-founded the AI company that became Google DeepMind, was honoured for developing techniques to use AI to model and design proteins.[2] These accolades show that the AI "arms race" is still going strong. And in fact, right at the start of 2025, China cranked up the race with DeepSeek, which performed as well as ChatGPT but was built at a fraction of the cost. At the same time, the U.S. announced a US$500 billion joint investment initiative called Stargate,

[1] P. Confino, Nobel laureate Geoffrey Hinton is both AI pioneer and front man of alarm. Fortune, October 11, 2024. https://fortune.com/2024/10/10/geoffrey-hinton-nobel-ai-pioneer-concerns/.

[2] G. Rannard, Google DeepMind co-founder Demis Hassabis shares Nobel Chemistry Prize. BBC, October 9, 2024. https://www.bbc.com/news/articles/czrm0p2mxvyo.

which will focus on building domestic AI infrastructure.[3] As the three digital empires continue to assert their respective spheres of influence via their unique governance models and promote their distinctive brand of digital capitalism, other countries and regions are watching and calibrating their own approaches to balance risk with reward. Countries across the globe weigh the key issues of risks, rights, and economic opportunities against the needs of their region. As both Bradford and Zhang explained, laws and regulations are important tools in this AI "arms race", as good governance not only imposes constraints but can also serve as an enabler for sustainable growth. The AI regulatory landscape over the coming years will decide whether this powerful technology is ultimately a boon or a bane for humanity.

[3] B. Marr, What Does Trump's $500 Billion Stargate Mean for the World of AI? *Forbes*, January 23, 2025. https://www.forbes.com/sites/bernardmarr/2025/01/23/what-does-trumps-500-billion-stargate-mean-for-the-world-of-ai/.

Section 3

Case Study of China

by Tai Wei Lim

Chapter 12

The Rise of Chinese Chatbots

The rise of chatbots has a powerful impact on cultural content, language applications, and social routines. A Tencent Research Institute report indicated that AI-generated contents (AIGCs) and their associated chatbots open the way to new digital contents and innovations in the digital culture industry, alongside the emergence of chatbots, digital humans, and the metaverse.[1] [Note: The Metaverse was once a trendy tech application that facilitated its online users to exist in a virtual reality (VR), video-game-like universe but has declined after the corporate world became disinterested in investing in it after approximately three years of existence.[2]] Market consultancy firm Gartner indicated generative AI (and its associated chatbots) is one of the most important tech innovations and projects and that, by 2025, generative AI will make up 10% of all data generated, as opposed to below 1% in 2022, through its application in activities such as coding, pharmaceutical drug development, and niche/targeted marketing.[3]

Taking marketing as a functional field for chatbots, marketers can structure AI marketing campaigns effectively, and brands and firms

[1]F. Fan, (2023a). China ushers in golden era of AI, chatbots, dated 17 February 2023 in China Daily [downloaded on 17 February 2023]. Available at https://www.chinadaily.com.cn/a/202302/17/WS63eeb668a31057c47ebaf430.html.

[2]E. Zitron, RIP Metaverse, dated 8 May 2023 in Business Insider [downloaded on 8 May 2023]. Available at https://www.businessinsider.com/metaverse-dead-obituary-facebook-mark-zuckerberg-tech-fad-ai-chatgpt-2023-5.

[3]F. Fan (2023a), *Op. cit.*

(typically fashion houses, airlines, eateries, hotels, and e-commerce retailers) registered with WeChat provide customer service and other interactive functions for their customers through the application.[4] In recent years, the commodification and commercialisation of chatbots seemed to have taken off sometime in the mid-2010s. Some commentators highlighted how chatbots became trendy in the West in 2016, with print media and television-based news reporting on the latest developments in such AI products and their commercial impact and implications for service providers.[5] In other words, it has captured the attention of many tech stakeholders in the world and even garnered a dedicated fandom for itself.

Given the explosion of interest, some Chinese commentators hope that WeChat chatbots will progress from novelty and entertainment functions to ubiquitous use, particularly by mainstream private sector firms as a critical audience retention tool.[6] AIGCs will impact China's luxury retail market with AI-generated text, videos, and product descriptions for customer/consumer engagement, especially for those seeking more product knowledge, e.g., a Xiaohongshu online user shared his experience of asking ChatGPT for suggestions about a niche brand product for a Valentine's Day gift.[7] This individual was amongst the community of Chinese users who are able to access ChatGPT (coined by *Shanghai Daily* as the "hottest consumer and business AI application globally") through virtual private networks (VPNs, which are technically illegal in China) and he asked the chatbot for advice on celebrating Valentine's Day.[8] This individual's posted chat record indicated ChatGPT could introduce brands, products, and prices for gift ideas and personalise its reactions based on user

[4]ChatCompose, WeChat Chatbots: Chatbots to reach a chinese audience, dated 2019 in ChatCompose [downloaded on 1 January 2023]. Available at https://www.chatcompose.com/chinawechat.html.

[5]E. Harca, What the West can learn from China about chatbot marketing, dated 13 May 2016 in ClickZ [downloaded on 13 May 2016]. Available at https://www.clickz.com/what-the-west-can-learn-from-china-about-chatbot-marketing/99687/.

[6]ChatCompose, (2019), *Op. cit.*

[7]Jingdaily, China's Retailers Eye Potential of ChatGPT and other AI Chatbots, dated 21 February 2023 in Italian Trade Agency (ITA) [downloaded on 21 February 2023]. Available at https://www.ice.it/it/news/notizie-dal-mondo/236987.

[8]S. Zhu, AI matchmaking, cosmic romance and ChatGPT bring digital options for Valentine's Day, dated 14 February 2023 in Shine Shanghai Daily (edited by Yang Meiping) [downloaded on 14 February 2023]. Available at https://www.shine.cn/news/metro/2302146203/.

feedback.[9] From these examples, therefore, once these AIGCs become fully integrated into e-commerce platforms and luxury labels' social media mini-apps, luxury shopping can become even more efficient for consumers and buyers.[10]

Conventionally, there are generally two main categories of chatbots: subscription accounts and customer service accounts. The primary users of subscription accounts are content publishers. Account subscribers can automatically access recently published articles typically on a daily basis, and users can click on the article and read it with an in-built WeChat browser. This format appeals to users tracking brands or following influencers.[11] WeChat is the world's largest messaging platform with 700 million users and is keen to harness the chatbots' commercial aspects, such as big data analytics.[12] Indeed, the process of brand-tracking produces significant amounts of data on questions like "how many users saw a particular item", permitting entrepreneurs and brands to determine the kinds of contents for specific target audiences.[13]

In fact, China was considerably earlier and faster in developing and leading the sector of customer service accounts. Up to 2016, China was leading in virtual assistant technologies that were seamlessly integrated with messaging platform users for brand fans who wanted to reach out to retailers and/or make enquiries with them on a daily basis via messaging services.[14] Enterprises with official WeChat accounts can deploy chatbots to assist in scaling up their customer service teams more efficiently to react to expanding customer enquiries as part of their business models.[15]

Content publishers have been cited as the next big thing. Robin Li, CEO of Baidu, articulated in January 2023 that the golden age of AI was arriving. He said, "AI has gone from understanding pictures and text to generating content, [adding that AIGC will subvert existing content production models in the next decade, and AI has the potential to meet the massive demand for content at a tenth of the cost and a hundred or a

---

[9] Jingdaily, (2023), *Op. cit.*

[10] *Ibid.*

[11] ChatCompose, (2019), *Op. cit.*

[12] E. Harca, (2016), *Op. cit.*

[13] ChatCompose, (2019), *Op. cit.*

[14] E. Harca, (2016), *Op. cit.*

[15] ChatCompose, (2019), *Op. cit.*

thousand times faster]".[16] By late April 2023, after the public release of ERNIE (Enhanced Representation through kNowledge IntEgration), Baidu updated the bot four times and reduced the operating costs of the AI to one-tenth of its original price.[17] Along with bringing down costs, other Chinese chatbots are focusing on offering a spectrum of services. Through WeChat service accounts, users can send messages/information regarding the newest promotional events, search restaurant locations, and purchase air tickets at updated prices as part of its subscription account features, and chatbots can add value to these features by engaging in complex conversations with humans.[18]

The Chinese authorities are resistant to utilising AI chatbots created in foreign countries, as they are powered by human feedback, so it would be challenging to stop transnational flows of data that are detrimental to the party.[19] Since late 2022, Chinese tech giants have increased the pace of development of AI products, and in less than half a year, more than 12 tech giants, including Tencent, Huawei, ByteDance, JD.com, 360, Kuaishou, and NetEase, solidified their plans to build chatbots, with Baidu and iFlytek ahead of the pack in blueprints.[20] For example, Chinese e-commerce tech giant JD.com announced on 10 February 2023 that it will launch an "industrial ChatGPT" known as ChatJD to assist enterprises with content generation, human–machine interaction, livestream e-commerce, and customer service in finance and retail.[21]

iFlytek revealed in February 2023 it aimed to release their inaugural large language model (LLM) that uses cognitive intelligence known as the

---

[16] F. Fan, (2023a), *Op. cit.*

[17] E. Cheng, China's A.I. chatbots haven't yet reached the public like ChatGPT did, dated 28 April 2023 in CNBC [downloaded on 28 April 2023]. Available at https://www.cnbc.com/2023/04/28/how-chinas-chatgpt-ai-alternatives-are-doing.html.

[18] ChatCompose, (2019), *Op. cit.*

[19] F. Yang, AI chatbots with Chinese characteristics: why Baidu's ChatGPT rival may never measure up, dated 24 March 2023 in The Conversation [downloaded on 24 March 2023]. Available at https://theconversation.com/ai-chatbots-with-chinese-characteristics-why-baidus-chatgpt-rival-may-never-measure-up-202109.

[20] S. F. Wong, (translated by Grace Chong and Candice Chan), China's self-censoring chatbots face many challenges, dated 17 Apr 2023 in Thinkchina and Lianhe Zaobao [downloaded on 17 April 2023]. Available at https://www.thinkchina.sg/chinas-self-censoring-chatbots-face-many-challenges.

[21] Jingdaily, (2023), *Op. cit.*

iFlytek AI learning machine (讯飞AI学习机) on 6 May 2023.[22] It had ambitions to be the first Chinese-made chatbot, matching ChatGPT's release with a fixed launch date.[23] China has the goal of becoming the global dominant player in AI technologies by 2030 and conceptualises it as a core strategic technology.[24] (With its first appearance in late 2022, ChatGPT utilises generative AI technology learnt from precedent data to produce texts, images, or computer code.[25]) In 2022, iFlytek reported a year-on-year (YoY) decrease of 60–70% in net profit, and its stock price declined in the second half of 2022 to 31.1 RMB in October, but news of its chatbot plans propelled iFlytek stocks to rise more than 100% from mid-January to early April 2023.[26] Chinese AI-related stocks surged at the beginning of 2023 as Chinese investors (and speculators) were speculating that Chinese chatbots would not only emerge but also maintain their momentum in development.[27]

Other Chinese chatbots encountered the same intense public interest in their stocks and shares. Baidu's ERNIE was also given an optimistic outlook by investment banks at the time of its release announcement. At the point of its release, UBS classified ERNIE as "a buy that can surge 60%".[28] In another example, SenseTime's (a major player in computer vision technology) stocks and shares went up rapidly in 2023 after their company's product launch event invitations were sent out.[29] Similarly, Chinese luxury online e-commerce platform Secoo announced on 6 February 2023 that, "[it will] conduct in-depth research and expansion on AI Generated Content (AIGC) and ChatGPT-related technologies" to enhance its customer conversion rate and its Nasdaq stock prices

---

[22] S. F. Wong, (2023), *Op. cit.*

[23] *Ibid.*

[24] AFP, 'Always there': the AI chatbot comforting China's lonely millions, dated 24 August 2021 in France 24 [downloaded on 24 August 2021]. Available at https://www.france24.com/en/live-news/20210824-always-there-the-ai-chatbot-comforting-china-s-lonely-millions.

[25] Reuters, China's SenseTime unveils new AI products and chatbot, dated 11 April 2023 in the The Indian Express [downloaded on 11 April 2023]. Available at https://indianexpress.com/article/technology/artificial-intelligence/chinas-sensetime-unveils-new-ai-products-and-chatbot-8548858/.

[26] S. F. Wong, (2023), *Op. cit.*

[27] Jingdaily, (2023), *Op. cit.*

[28] E. Cheng, (2023), *Op. cit.*

[29] ChatCompose, (2019), *Op. cit.*

accelerated by 124% on the same day to US$3.77 per share (highest since March 2020).[30]

Other sources from state-owned Chinese media listed MOSS as China's first LLM in the mould of ChatGPT. The Chinese Fudan University research team behind MOSS revealed that it is China's first publicly released ChatGPT-like model, named after the intelligent quantum computer managing a space station in the popular Chinese sci-fi film *The Wandering Earth II.* MOSS is a conversational large-scale language model.[31] Fudan University's C9 League member unveiled the first large-scale conversational language model from China, MOSS.[32] After becoming online for public testing on 20 February 2023, following its inception in late 2022, MOSS generated considerable buzz and even trended on Sina Weibo, particularly after Professor Qiu Xipeng from Fudan's School of Computer Science and his MOSS research team (comprising eight of Qiu's students) revealed MOSS' open-source plans.[33] MOSS was released for public use by Professor Qiu Xipeng's team via the website https://moss.fastnlp.top/, which does not require an invitation code and places applicants on a waiting list after they register using a mobile phone number.[34] Qiu, a specialist in machine learning and natural language processing, commented on MOSS:

> I'm very optimistic. MOSS is at the forefront of the most cutting-edge exploration in the field of natural language processing and even the field of AGI. We look forward to using MOSS as a pedestal leading to AGI, which will not be very far from science fiction. It will become a reality maybe in five to 10 years. By that time, we will accept AGI as we accept search engines now. It's amazing, we haven't taught it machine translation [so excited by MOSS that he lost sleep over MOSS's launch, analogized MOSS as a "smart kid"]. Even though it is not good at writing

---

[30] Jingdaily, (2023), *Op. cit.*

[31] S. Lin, Chinese chatbot to be made open source, dated 3 March 2023 in China Daily [downloaded on 3 March 2023]. Available at https://www.chinadaily.com.cn/a/202303/03/WS64012f84a31057c47ebb1d8e.html.

[32] Pandaily, China's First ChatGPT-Like Chatbot MOSS Released For Public Testing, dated 21 February 2023 in Pandaily [downloaded on 21 Feb 2023]. Available at https://pandaily.com/chinas-first-chatgpt-like-chatbot-moss-released-for-public-testing/.

[33] S. Lin, (2023), *Op. cit.*

[34] Pandaily, (2023), *Op. cit.*

> poems, solving problems or many specific things, it has shown the potential to become an AGI framework. We developed the MOSS model to explore and verify the technical route of ChatGPT to prove that we are not behind foreign countries in terms of technical implementation. Yet when we develop the MOSS model, we are not limited to pursuing a model with similar capabilities to ChatGPT. Maybe the industry will pay more attention to its initial performance. We pay more attention to its next-generation development, that is, how to realize AGI. From an academic point of view, only if we look farther ahead than OpenAI can we finally achieve transcendence. We firmly believe that academia has a lot to offer in this field.[35]

Indeed, the team that created MOSS was keen to garner feedback from academia. Before getting the AI chatbots officially ready for prime time, Fudan University gathered executives and academics from over a dozen AI firms to analyse the development, potential use scenarios, and security risks of ChatGPT.[36] Sun Tianxiang, a doctoral student at the School of Computer Science and an important member of Qiu's research team, was excited on 19 January 2023 while experimenting with the model; he asked the then early MOSS prototype (trained on less than 0.1% of the data) a question, and it responded accurately, "like a person who can't speak but understands Chinese".[37]

Qiu also compared MOSS with ChatGPT: "The difference between MOSS and ChatGPT is mainly in the pre-training stage of the natural language model. The number of parameters of MOSS is much fewer than ChatGPT. There is still much room for improvement in task completion and knowledge reserve".[38] Indeed, Qiu's entire team felt that though MOSS's scale is modest compared to ChatGPT, and its inclusion of factual problems is not sufficiently comprehensive, its logical ability is "not bad", and its open-source version can be utilised by small- and medium-sized enterprises (SMEs) to develop vertical products such as smart customer service, smart home devices, and AI lawyers.[39] To improve further

---

[35] S. Lin, (2023), *Op. cit.*
[36] Pandaily, (2023), *Op. cit.*
[37] S. Lin, (2023), *Op. cit.*
[38] Pandaily, (2023), *Op. cit.*
[39] S. Lin, (2023), *Op. cit.*

and catch up with ChatGPT, MOSS obtained robust support from the Shanghai Artificial Intelligence Laboratory.[40]

In addition to the experts, many in the public are hopeful to see even more sophisticated functions in future versions of MOSS. Part of this aspiration arose from inspirations from creative works. In this sense, there are popular cultural implications of the MOSS project as well. Many Chinese chatbot hopefuls speculated whether MOSS would turn sci-fi into reality, given that it is named after a popular Chinese film.[41] References to popular culture in this case piqued the interest of the public and even motivated would-be users to yearn for more chatbot offerings. Meanwhile, MOSS powered on with its evaluation and testing procedures.

During the beta testing stage, data and user feedback were collected with permission to further enhance MOSS's conversational capabilities, with an eye for future upgrades such as capabilities in drawing, speaking, music composition, teaching, and even helping scientists with efficient research.[42] On a personal level, Qiu was glad that his six-year-old daughter could pleasantly converse with MOSS in a sustained manner; and he is optimistic that large-scale language models such as MOSS will proliferate like search engines, as AGI (strong AI or deep AI) is, after all, machine intelligence capable of solving problems just like a human.[43] There are therefore many anticipated uses for such machine intelligence solutions.

Chen Jia, an independent researcher in international strategy, argued: "Chinese tech enterprises have unique advantages in expanding AI application scenarios across the globe compared with their foreign peers, based on China's enormous domestic social network and the world's largest number of internet users. Baidu, Alibaba and Tencent have invested heavily in promoting the commercial use of AI, and some Chinese AI unicorns have grown rapidly in recent years. [However, he noted that Chinese tech companies still lag behind top-notch foreign competitors in fundamental R&D input and comprehensive innovation abilities]".[44] A leaked Alibaba memo indicated that its Damo Academy had put together a 100-member

---

[40] Pandaily, (2023), *Op. cit.*

[41] S. Lin, (2023), *Op. cit.*

[42] Pandaily, (2023), *Op. cit.*

[43] S. Lin, (2023), *Op. cit.*

[44] F. Fan, (2023a), *Op. cit.*

team to focus on iterating and improving its LLM, created in January 2020, before its rebranding as Tongyi in September 2022.[45]

Chinese chatbots like MOSS go through similar developmental stages to ChatGPT, which comprises two phases: training in natural language processing and training in understanding human intention, consisting of accumulating hundreds of thousands of human queries and mobilising professional annotators to respond to them, which are then fed into ChatGPT's database to train the chatbot in processing various human prompts.[46] Other tech giants even set up special academies for this purpose. Some of the early Chinese chatbot developers include Alibaba, Huawei, and JD.com. In 2020, Alibaba's DAMO Academy established large-scale Chinese language and multimodal pre-training models, while in 2021, Huawei launched its Pangu AI series and the DAMO Academy released its M6 model.[47] Alibaba Damo Academy's 100-strong team concentrates on iterating and improving its LLM.[48] Alibaba, which was JD.com's main rival, announced in mid-February 2023 that it is evaluating a generative AI platform similar to ChatGPT within the company.[49]

In June 2021, the Wu Dao 2.0 large model (nicknamed the "world's largest" AI language model with 1.75 trillion parameters, which was ten times more than the OpenAI GPT-3 model), spearheaded by the Beijing Academy of Artificial Intelligence, was released.[50] From February 2023 onwards, Chinese tech firms in the AI, food delivery, e-commerce, and gaming industries revved up their attempts to play catch-up with OpenAI's ChatGPT, with Beijing's Municipal Bureau of Economy and Information Technology supporting these efforts undertaken by some leading tech giants.[51] Kunlun Tech launched "Tiangong" on 17 April

---

[45] B. Jiang, How quickly are China's ChatGPT-style services catching up with Microsoft-backed OpenAI? dated 11 May 2023 in South China Morning Post (SCMP) [downloaded on 11 May 2023]. Available at https://www.scmp.com/tech/tech-trends/article/3220062/how-quickly-are-chinas-chatgpt-style-services-catching-microsoft-backed-openai.

[46] Pandaily, (2023), *Op. cit.*

[47] S. F. Wong, (2023), *Op. cit.*

[48] B. Jiang, (2023), *Op. cit.*

[49] Jingdaily, (2023), *Op. cit.*

[50] S. F. Wong, (2023), *Op. cit.*

[51] F. Yang, (2023), *Op. cit.*

2023, a question-and-answer (Q&A) interface for invite-only users based on training metrics, which Kunlun says is on par with ChatGPT.[52]

Associate Professor Zhu Feida of Singapore Management University's School of Computing and Information Systems observed the following about Chinese tech firms' scramble to release their chatbots (though countervailing opinions noted that a few Chinese tech firms had worked on chatbots for years, so they may not have hurriedly put together immature technology): "They have to respond to the launch of ChatGPT. [...while China's chatbots are no rival to ChatGPT, the Chinese tech companies can take this opportunity to display their ongoing projects to the outside world and gain space for future development]".[53] Discussion over whether China can catch up with ChatGPT persists, even as Alibaba's Tongyi Qianwen and ERNIE Bot have entered the race.[54] Some even argued that China will develop chatbots based on its own set of unique societal needs and political considerations. Zhu's idea of "chatbots with Chinese characteristics" is described as:

> ...not differ[ing] significantly from foreign chatbots. This technology will also be incorporated into various information services, but the content will be subject to stricter control... given the tense international political situation, it will be difficult for Chinese chatbots to enter the international market. From a business perspective, Chinese tech companies have no significant advantages, and from a political perspective, many countries will be particularly cautious as chatbots collect and analyse a lot of user information, so they will not easily allow Chinese chatbots to enter their markets. China's LLM generation technology more than a year behind...chatbot technology, like Microsoft's Windows and Office systems, will improve productivity in various fields, rather than being limited to a particular sector. If China does not keep up right from the start, it would fall behind, leading to a disconnect with society and the world at large. The long-term impact would be immeasurable...chatbot technology is heavily reliant on user input, and the more people use it, the better it performs. If China doesn't keep up right from the first step,

---

[52] E. Cheng, (2023), *Op. cit.*

[53] S. F. Wong, (2023), *Op. cit.*

[54] B. Jiang, (2023), *Op. cit.*

> everyone will flock to foreign chatbots, which will perform increasingly better, widening the gap between Chinese and US chatbots.[55]

Comparatively, ChatGPT, which studies and is trained on big data, can produce outputs such as poetry and business strategies in a human-like dialogue.[56] There are Chinese attempts to speed up the training process. For example, the Fudan University team that developed MOSS followed an unconventional technical approach by permitting their MOSS chatbot to interact with humans and other AI models to improve its speed of learning, enhance its modelling, and complete natural language training in a shorter time compared with ChatGPT.[57]

At the same time, the Chinese Communist Party (CCP) attempts to utilise censorship to bring about ideological conformity, which requires chatbots to be scrubbed clean to prevent random materials from being leaked out publicly through chatbots in a political system that is wary about the impact of unexpected/uncontrolled public narratives.[58] From the Chinese perspective, the Cyberspace Administration of China (CAC) indicated that "[while the rapidly evolving deep synthesis technology could] serve user needs and improve user experience, it has also been used by some unscrupulous people to produce, copy, publish, and disseminate illegal and harmful information, to slander and belittle others' reputation and honor, and to counterfeit others' identities".[59] Since the Internet era, the People's Republic of China (PRC) has practised online censorship, and its tech giants are cautious not to overstep boundary markers, such as topics relating to the Chinese President or the 1989 June 4th incident.[60] Critics charged that the Chinese authorities often censor online

---

[55] S. F. Wong, (2023), *Op. cit.*

[56] E. Cheng, (2023), *Op. cit.*

[57] Pandaily, (2023), *Op. cit.*

[58] M. Schuman, Why Chatbot AI Is a Problem for China, dated 18 April 2023 in The Atlantic [downloaded on 18 April 2023]. Available at https://www.theatlantic.com/international/archive/2023/04/chatbot-ai-problem-china/673754/.

[59] Y. Zhao, China makes first ChatGPT-related arrest for fake news, dated 11 May 2023 in The China Project [downloaded on 11 May 2023]. Available at https://thechinaproject.com/2023/05/11/china-makes-first-chatgpt-related-arrest-for-fake-news/.

[60] Reuters, As Alibaba unveils ChatGPT rival, China flags new AI rules, dated 11 April 2023 in Al Jazeera [downloaded on 11 April 2023]. Available at https://www.aljazeera.com/news/2023/4/11/as-alibaba-unveils-chatgpt-rival-china-flags-new-ai-rules.

information they did not like, especially news on major disasters such as the deadly Beijing hospital fire in April 2023 (social media posts were eliminated, and official news media only reported the event hours later).[61]

With regard to Chinese politics, leadership issues, controversial events, or histories, only the viewpoints of the CCP will be permissible.[62] In early March 2023, Hangzhou-based startup YuanYu Intelligence ceased operations of its chatbot after it gave negative responses about the Chinese economy; however, the firm's lead developer negated this interpretation, stating instead that the suspension was due to technical errors.[63] The Chinese government requires tech firms to follow the same regulations on public speechmaking as humans in China, such as toeing the principles of socialism and avoiding destabilising the state.[64] In China, legal experts explained that cyberspace is also legally defined as public space. Donald Clarke, a professor of law specialising in modern China at the George Washington University Law School in Washington, explained the charge of "picking quarrels and provoking trouble" cited for the first ChatGPT-related arrest: "…it's not as vague as everybody says. The crime is only made out if one of four conditions is met, and one of them is about creating a disturbance in a public place, [as] the Chinese government has very often now interpreted cyberspace as public space".[65]

In mid-April 2023, the Chinese authorities announced that they would mandatorily require all locally utilised AI chatbots to censor their contents to ensure complementarity with the CCP's main socialist values.[66] One of the articles in the CAC's "Provisions on the Administration of Deep Synthesis Internet Information Services" requires deepfake producers and distributors to stick to "the correct political direction" and "values trends" within the Chinese system and avoid any contents deemed offensive to the

---

[61] Y. Zhao, (2023), *Op. cit.*

[62] F. Yang, (2023), *Op. cit.*

[63] E. Hale, China wants AI to rival ChatGPT. Censorship makes that tricky, dated 2 March 2023 in Al Jazeera [downloaded on 2 March 2023]. Available at https://www.aljazeera.com/economy/2023/3/2/china-wants-to-copy-chatgpts-success-censorship-makes-it-tricky.

[64] M. Schuman, (2023), *Op. cit.*

[65] Y. Zhao, (2023), *Op. cit.*

[66] J. Pao, China's early AI chatbots more patriotic than smart, dated 13 April 2023 in Asia Times [downloaded on 13 April 2023]. Available at https://asiatimes.com/2023/04/chinas-early-ai-chatbots-more-patriotic-than-smart/.

authorities.[67] Tech giants realise what happens if they overstep the boundary markers laid down by the state in the recent tech crackdowns. The Chinese government cracked down on the tech industry from 2020 onwards by targeting tech giants that appeared to challenge the state, e.g., clamping down on IPOs by Ant Group and ride app Didi over data irregularities.[68] (On the other hand, Western-originated ride apps based in China appear to be progressing well. The taxi-hailing app Uber has integrated the EVA virtual assistant chatbot in the release of its application programming interface (API) in China to reserve car rides, converse about trips, and discuss pricing, while providing developers the opportunity to integrate Uber's functionality into third-party apps and partnering with the Raven Tech AI start-up.[69])

By contrast, critics in free and open societies place faith in free thought and information flow as tenets of innovation and intellectual curiosity over social conformity to bring about risk-taking and the actualisation of technological breakthroughs.[70] Kendra Schaefer, head of tech policy at the Beijing-based consulting company Trivium China, explained to *The New York Times (NYT)* that the Chinese government approach tends to be to "move fast and break things" when it comes to tech regulations: "Because you don't have a two-party system where both sides argue. [China's leadership] can just say, 'OK, we know we need to do this, and we'll revise it later'".[71] Tighter regulation falls within the trend of imposing closer scrutiny and governance of the tech industry since the 2021 crackdown.[72]

On the contrary, the Chinese elite leadership appears to believe that innovation does not need the pre-requisites of individual liberties and that political control and tech ambitions are not mutually exclusive, as Chinese firms are already dominating 5G, gaming, social media, and electric vehicle (EV) technologies worldwide.[73] Smart EV joint venture (JV) Jidu

[67] Y. Zhao, (2023), *Op. cit.*

[68] E. Hale, (2023), *Op. cit.*

[69] E. Harca, (2023), *Op. cit.*

[70] M. Schuman, (2023), *Op. cit.*

[71] M. Harrison, China says chatbots must be strictly censored by communist guidelines, undated in Futurism.com The Byte [downloaded on 26 April 2023]. Available at https://futurism.com/the-byte/china-chatbots-censored.

[72] F. Yang, (2023), *Op. cit.*

[73] M. Schuman, (2023), *Op. cit.*

Auto, set up by Baidu/Geely Holding Group and car manufacturer Changan's Yida sedan (launched in March 2023), Dongfeng Nissan, and China FAW Group's Hongqi, are integrating ERNIE into their products to enable interactive AI experiences.[74]

In media circles, Chinese columnists appear to be less anxious about political censorship (already prevalent in the mass media and online platforms for decades) and instead worry more about the intelligence level of Chinese chatbots.[75] Secoo, which is facing lawsuits and online user complaints, is an example of how relying on AI chatbots to attract short-term online curiosity cannot be sustainable and prematurely launched products may even increase the probability of errors that are quickly identified and critiqued by China's digitally savvy consumers.[76]

Before the emergence of Chinese chatbots, the Chinese government had already started regulating AI applications. In early 2023, the CAC put in place new regulations governing search engine recommendations, giving online users more control over their personal data utilised by search engines; and in January 2023, laws were passed to regulate deep synthesis (generative AI that can produce "deepfakes"); while, in 2022, China established an Algorithms Registry.[77] China's new initial regulations on deepfake technology implemented from January 2023 were previously titled *Provisions on the Administration of Deep Synthesis Internet Information Services* by the CAC and deepfakes are defined as "deep learning, virtual reality, and other synthetic algorithms to produce text, images, audio, video, virtual scenes, and other network information",[78] All these regulatory developments had not stopped some Chinese users from trying to access ChatGPT. In fact, *Google Trends* in late January 2023 noted that China's online users made up a high proportion of searches for ChatGPT, with the hashtag "when will China's own ChatGPT emerge" hitting 220 million views on Weibo then.[79]

More regulations were promulgated to reinforce the existing regulatory framework. Some observers noted the differentiating factor in the

---

[74] F. Fan, (2023b), Appliance makers, auto firms tap into chatbots, dated 4 April 2023 in China Daily [downloaded on 4 April 2023]. Available at http://epaper.chinadaily.com.cn/a/202304/04/WS642b5d6ea310777689887d5c.html.

[75] J. Pao, (2023), *Op. cit.*

[76] Jingdaily, (2023), *Op. cit.*

[77] E. Hale, (2023), *Op. cit.*

[78] Y. Zhao, (2023), *Op. cit.*

[79] Jingdaily, (2023), *Op. cit.*

latest round of legal reforms in this area. Jeremy Daum, senior fellow in Yale Law School's Paul Tsai China Center and the founder of China Law Translate, opined: "China already has ample rules for censoring or punishing speech it doesn't like, regardless of how it was generated, and the deep synthesis rules have already incorporated existing content law into the content-generation context. The big change in the draft AI rules is that they are aiming to go after the providers of generative AI services as well as the user who spreads the information".[80]

In early April 2023, Beijing unveiled draft rules for regulating AI-generated content, with a public feedback solicitation period until 10 May 2023, although such attempts to control chatbots did not prevent Chinese media and social media from discussing ChatGPT and AI technology, while others attempted to purchase foreign ChatGPT accounts hosted on Chinese e-commerce websites.[81] In the proposed legislation, there is an article focusing on algorithmic bias, mandating that Chinese firms ensure their AI models' training data do not discriminate against individuals based on their ethnicity, race, or gender and references intellectual property rights and fair competition.[82]

While boosting innovation and the proliferation of chatbots and AI, the CAC stated that content must stick to "core socialist values" and regulations on data security and personal information protection, warning that those failing to comply would be subject to fines or criminal investigation.[83] The CAC explained on 11 April 2023 that its month-long public consultation for the new regulations governing chatbots was meant to stop AI chat apps from proliferating fake information or seditious materials that could disrupt social order.[84] China arrested a person for crimes related to the utilisation of ChatGPT less than 30 days after the CAC published draft regulations for ChatGPT-type platforms on the grounds that any generative AI must not produce content that subverts the state.[85]

In mid-April 2023, the CAC mandated publicly: "AI-generated content should reflect the core values of socialism and must not contain

[80] Y. Zhao, (2023), *Op. cit.*
[81] E. Cheng, (2023), *Op. cit.*
[82] Y. Zhao, (2023), *Op. cit.*
[83] Reuters, (2023), *Op. cit.*
[84] J. Pao, (2023), *Op. cit.*
[85] Y. Zhao, (2023), *Op. cit.*

materials that promote the subversion of state power, the overthrow of the socialist system, sedition, the undermining of national unity, terrorism or extremism. [AI-generated content should not promote ethnic hatred and discrimination or violence and should not contain false information, obscenity, pornography or any other content that might disrupt economic and social order … providers of AI chatbots are required to submit safety assessment reports to the government before launching their services. It says they are responsible for any violations of the rules]".[86]

According to Gansu (Northwest China) provincial law enforcement agency's statement put out on 7 May 2023, the first ChatGPT-related arrested individual was identified only by his surname Hóng (洪), and he was accused of allegedly using the AI-driven text generator to produce news defined as "false information" by the state.[87] However, Charlie Chai, an analyst from 86Research, argued Beijing's new chatbot regulation would "[potentially slow down progress] in exchange for a more orderly and socially responsible deployment of the technology. The guidelines will also set up obstacles for foreign companies looking to provide AI services in the country, benefiting domestic companies".[88]

In addition, the U.S.–China tech decoupling also presents difficulties for Chinese chatbot development. One study based on data from cloud providers indicated that demand for chatbots will at least double in China and will exacerbate a "significant shortage" of chips.[89] In August 2022, the U.S. Biden administration came up with the CHIPS and Science Act, which required tech firms receiving government subsidies to shift advanced semiconductor chip manufacturing away from China.[90] The Biden administration prohibited U.S. firms from selling chip-making equipment and the advanced A100 chip to China.[91] China's inability to acquire the most sophisticated chips (highly important for training AI models) remained undampened by it, although some experts indicated that the Chinese chatbot sector was estimated to be lagging behind ChatGPT by 18 months to three years.[92]

---

[86] J. Pao, (2023), *Op. cit.*

[87] Y. Zhao, (2023), *Op. cit.*

[88] Reuters, (2023), *Op. cit.*

[89] E. Cheng, (2023), *Op. cit.*

[90] E. Hale, (2023), *Op. cit.*

[91] S. F. Wong, (2023), *Op. cit.*

[92] B. Jiang, (2023), *Op. cit.*

Besides hardware, TikTok had been facing potential bans or forced sales in the U.S. due to U.S. concerns that its Beijing parent company, ByteDance, may be passing on sensitive private data of Americans to the Chinese intelligence/security service. In 2019, U.S. authorities placed SenseTime on a trade blacklist after it provided facial recognition programmes that contributed to monitoring ethnic Uyghurs in Xinjiang, while SenseTime protested the U.S. restrictions and claimed it would approach the government to challenge the ban.[93]

At the same time and further stimulated by tech decoupling, China is pushing for greater self-reliance. Since 2015, under former Premier Li Keqiang, the Made in China 2025 initiative was formulated to strengthen China's technological base/capacities (including AI products).[94] Eager to obtain AI opinions on the tech decoupling and war, Singapore's Chinese-language daily *Lianhe Zaobao* asked ERNIE and ChatGPT the question: "Who will win the China-US tech war?", and ERNIE Bot replied: "As an AI language model, I am unable to answer this question. My purpose is to provide objective and accurate information to help people solve problems", but ChatGPT replied: "Who will win the China-US tech war is a complex issue because it involves multiple factors such as technological capabilities, innovation capacity, policy support and investment, talent and education, international cooperation and trade relations".[95]

The state's presence is omnipotent. Even in the arena of market forces, a reminder of the Chinese state's presence in the tech sector is sometimes visible in full public view. For example, on 8 February 2023, the Shanghai Stock Exchange slapped supervisory work letters to Cloudwalk Technology and Speechocean, questioning the tremendous increase in their share prices over eight trading days during the weeks of ChatGPT fever worldwide, and immediately, their shares declined by 9.35% and 2.68%, respectively, the next day.[96]

Similarly, OpenAI's ChatGPT cannot operate in China just like Twitter, Facebook, and Google, which are kept out by the Great Chinese Firewall.[97] For that matter, many major foreign websites and Internet applications are shut out of China's Internet space by the advanced

---

[93] Reuters, (2023), *Op. cit.*

[94] F. Yang, (2023), *Op. cit.*

[95] S. F. Wong, (2023), *Op. cit.*

[96] F. Fan, (2023a), *Op. cit.*

[97] E. Cheng, (2023), *Op. cit.*

censorship system of the Great Firewall.[98] Some argue that ChatGPT "is not directly accessible in China due to the country's protectionist approach to digital sovereignty" and "Chinese data are confined within China", while Chinese tech giants like Baidu and Tencent disallow third-party developers from connecting ChatGPT to their services.[99] Besides banning ChatGPT due to its potential to disseminate materials on sensitive topics such as Xinjiang, state-owned *China Daily* stated that ChatGPT can "boost propaganda campaigns launched by the U.S."[100]

In February 2023, state-owned *China Daily* criticised foreign governments for utilising ChatGPT to proliferate untrue information and manipulate public opinion.[101] In the Chinese authorities' first arrest in a ChatGPT-related crime, the charge was based on that individual's alleged proliferation of a fake story. That arrested individual, Hong, was associated with a news story about a train crash causing nine people's deaths in Gansu, which was, in turn, picked up by the county police bureau's cyber division. The division discovered that there were several versions of the same story, but stating different locations, emerging on more than 20 accounts on Baidu's Baijiahao blog in April 2023, receiving 15,000 hits.[102]

Some foreign media outlets tried to test the Chinese chatbot systems' capabilities for themselves. Both China's ERNIE and ChatGPT chatbots were posed questions on Sino-U.S. relations by Singapore's *Lianhe Zaobao*. On the other hand, domestically developed chatbots and search engines can legitimize Chinese state/party propaganda and constructed information that is well-scrubbed.[103] Singapore's *Lianhe Zaobao* daily asked the question: "How do you view the development of China-US relations?", and ERNIE Bot replied: "In recent years, China-US relations have been faced with challenges and difficulties but the cooperation between both countries in the fields of economy, trade, technology, humanities and so on remains very important… I think that China and the US could, on the basis of equality and mutual benefit, attempt to gradually resolve differences and problems and achieve win-win cooperation by

[98] Y. Zhao, (2023), *Op. cit.*
[99] F. Yang, (2023), *Op. cit.*
[100] M. Schuman, (2023), *Op. cit.*
[101] S. F. Wong, (2023), *Op. cit.*
[102] Y. Zhao, (2023), *Op. cit.*
[103] F. Yang, (2023), *Op. cit.*

strengthening communication, improving understanding and reducing misunderstandings", while ChatGPT replied: "In recent years, China-US relations have been faced with challenges and pressures including trade disputes, technological security and geopolitical tensions… China and the US also share a wide range of common interests and areas of cooperation… The future development of China-US relations requires both sides to maintain communication and dialogue; respect each other's sovereignty and territorial integrity; uphold the principles of win-win cooperation and mutual benefit; and promote constructive cooperation and resolve differences to contribute to global peace and development".[104]

Regardless of any chatbot projection of winners in the US–China chatbot competition, many acknowledge that the U.S. firm OpenAI's ChatGPT appears to be leading for now. ChatGPT can imitate human-like responses to generate AI-formulated content and help individuals in activities such as essay writing, manuscript writing, textualising commercial proposals, composing poetry, and even scanning programs for bugs through the use of machine-learning algorithms.[105] ChatGPT trains and learns using big data after it was accessed by almost 100 million monthly active users within two months of its launch in November 2022.[106] Developers and users in favour of generative AI, as well as ChatGPT techies, argue that chatbots will form the basis of tech innovation in content output and release humans from simple/routine tasks to redirect their attention towards creative thinking in the cultural, media, entertainment, and educational sectors.[107] Specific chatbots can then be developed for a particular niche sector, for example, Internet tech giant NetEase is creating a generative AI for its education subsidiary Youdao.[108]

Chinese experts seem to agree with the view that Chinese chatbots will eventually catch up with their American counterparts. Pan Helin, co-director of the Digital Economy and Financial Innovation Research Center at Zhejiang University International Business School, observed: "ChatGPT, as a milestone in AIGC-related technologies, uses reinforcement learning from human feedback to train the large language model, with significant enhancements in natural language processing capacities

---

[104] S. F. Wong, (2023), *Op. cit.*

[105] F. Fan, (2023a), *Op. cit.*

[106] E. Cheng, (2023), *Op. cit.*

[107] F. Fan, (2023a), *Op. cit.*

[108] Jingdaily, (2023), *Op. cit.*

that improve response logic. It features strong semantic understanding and logical capabilities based on context, but] it has higher requirements for algorithms and computing power, which relies on considerable capital investments. [ChatGPT may assist humans in writing texts and computer code, as well as analyzing and processing data, enabling the latter to be more productive and efficient]".[109] Pan articulated that "...more efforts should be made to improve computing power, algorithms and quality of data. Similarly, investment in basic scientific research, including mathematics, statistics and computer science, should be increased, given that Ernie Bot still has some deficiencies in its capabilities in terms of machine learning and natural language processing".

Chatbots attract the usual precautions related to all AI technologies, such as their impact on job security, intellectual property rights, and academic integrity.[110] Pan Helin, co-director of the Digital Economy and Financial Innovation Research Center at Zhejiang University's International Business School, argued: "Therefore, the application of ChatGPT-related technology will lower the threshold of many jobs like content creators and programmers and enhance their work efficiency, but it will not eventually replace the human workforce".[111] There is, for example, a limit to how developers and brands can use their chatbots to manage all kinds of customer requests; therefore, these accounts must also be handled and managed by human employees for now.[112] Pan added, "At present, the exploration of ChatGPT-related technology is still at a nascent stage, and its commercial application scenarios and profit models are not clear. [Investors should make rational decisions and remain cautious about the potential risks of blind speculation]".[113]

Experts like Jeffrey Ding collated Chinese responses to ChatGPT and analysed them in detail. Assistant Professor Jeffrey Ding, a specialist in the Chinese tech industry at George Washington University, articulates: "The most general-purpose technology we have, artificial intelligence, should be something that's a super general purpose. But it's really shaped by the specific, political, cultural, linguistic context in which these models are developed and deployed. Much of that excitement has stemmed from

[109] F. Fan, (2023b), *Op. cit.*
[110] F. Yang, (2023), *Op. cit.*
[111] F. Fan, (2023a), *Op. cit.*
[112] ChatCompose, (2019), *Op. cit.*
[113] F. Fan, (2023a), *Op. cit.*

ChatGPT's ability to perform in Chinese and other languages despite being trained in English. The excitement isn't really about the business applications. Part of it is just excitement and wonder at how impressive the natural language capabilities of this technology are. And one aspect of that is ChatGPT was not even trained on any Chinese language texts. It was mostly all trained on English language texts but I've seen Chinese users ask questions in Mandarin and it will still perform very capably in a different language. Even so, Chinese language could prove especially challenging for AI due to the language's heavy use of idioms and sayings with historical context".[114]

MOSS is a case in point. MOSS faces challenges in Mandarin language comprehension due to the disarranged content on Chinese-language web pages used for chatbot training, and interference from ads that appear intermittently. So, the Natural Language Processing Laboratory at Fudan University is screening Chinese textual content in preparation for the next level of model training.[115] Some domestic developers are hoping to turn Mandarin language complexities into advantages, while others hope for a similar outcome in relation to China's uniquely strict censorship environment. Due to ChatGPT's prohibition in China and its strict censorship of generative AI content, the restricted domestic market opens the way for Chinese domestic tech companies to fight for their share of the local market pie.[116]

Chinese regulators instructed major tech firms such as Tencent and Ant Group to drop ChatGPT availability for online users, so members of the Chinese public could only access it via VPN and overseas phone numbers.[117] Individuals who wished to access any blocked services could circumvent the obstacles by utilising VPNs, although technically this is also illegal and sanctionable by Chinese law enforcement agencies.[118] The prohibition of ChatGPT created a booming black market with ChatGPT login sales on the e-commerce outfit Taobao, and video instructions were available on Chinese social media to demonstrate ChatGPT's capabilities until these avenues were gradually shut down.[119]

---

[114] E. Hale, (2023), *Op. cit.*

[115] Pandaily, (2023), *Op. cit.*

[116] B. Jiang, (2023), *Op. cit.*

[117] S. F. Wong, (2023), *Op. cit.*

[118] Y. Zhao, (2023), *Op. cit.*

[119] F. Yang, (2023), *Op. cit.*

12.1 Case study of ERNIE (Enhanced Representation through kNowledge IntEgration or 文心一言 Wenxin Yiyan in Chinese language)

ERNIE's large chatbot model is created as an entity specialising in the Chinese language and utilising data custom-made for Chinese language training.[120] It is a "multi-modal" AI-powered chatbot that can produce text, images, audio, and video contents from a text prompt.[121] Baidu Inc., currently China's biggest search engine, prepped the public for the March 2023 launch by indicating on 7 February 2023 that its AI chatbot project ERNIE Bot, would complete all in-house evaluations before March 2023.[122] After this announcement, internal testing commenced on 16 March 2023.[123] Some opined that Baidu wants to be first in this field in China. And they achieved just that. Baidu became the first local tech firm to publicly declare a ChatGPT rival in mid-March 2023.[124] Rui Ma, tech analyst and Tech Buzz China founder, noted that, "[Baidu appears to be first out of the gate]. I think right now the most excitement is still at the model level".[125] Baidu's stock value was enhanced by the publicity generated by ERNIE Bot. It increased by 15% at its peak following the official Baidu announcement of ERNIE Bot's launch in early February 2023.[126]

The dream of launching ERNIE Bot was made public rather early in Baidu's journey to come up with sophisticated chatbots. Baidu's Duer was an early chatbot that performed basic tasks such as making reservations at restaurants, paying for purchases, and other administrative assignments, but Baidu continued to aspire to greater goals: "In the near future, it will expand to include a wide range of services including ride hailing, housekeeping, manicures and pedicures, education, healthcare, travel, designated driver services, and more".[127] Thus, ERNIE was born. At the point of this writing, it was mainly available to corporate partners and applied

[120] I. Zhang, Countdown to ERNIE: Chinese Media on Baidu's AI Chatbot, dated 15 March 2023 in ChinaTalk [downloaded on 15 March 2023]. Available at https://www.chinatalk.media/p/countdown-to-ernie-chinese-media.

[121] F. Yang, (2023), *Op. cit.*

[122] F. Fan, (2023a), *Op. cit.*

[123] S. F. Wong, (2023), *Op. cit.*

[124] B. Jiang, (2023), *Op. cit.*

[125] E. Hale, (2023), *Op. cit.*

[126] S. F. Wong, (2023), *Op. cit.*

[127] E. Harca, (2023), *Op. cit.*

online users (up to mid-April 2023, a million individuals had applied).[128] These users were placed on limited access with waitlists or designated business partners with restricted trials.[129] On 9 May 2023, Baidu revealed that over 300 partners from various industries were interested in utilising its Ernie Bot.[130] ERNIE attracted more than 1.2 million users within a week of its launch and subsequently ceased releasing public information about its products.[131]

Baidu co-founder and CEO Robin Li displayed the AI-powered ERNIE Bot during a news conference at the Beijing headquarters on 16 March 2023.[132] Baidu CTO Wang Haifeng also spoke at the launch of ERNIE in Beijing on 16 March 2023.[133] After the launch, in March 2023, ERNIE Bot's internal evaluation results were critiqued by netizens with memes making fun of ERNIE for giving inaccurate information, such as interpretations of Chinese idioms and proverbs, while some were critically probing whether Baidu had launched ERNIE simply to revive investor confidence in its company.[134] A Henan-based columnist argued that ChatGPT-4 is more intelligent than ERNIE, as it can provide logical and correct answers to most enquiries, e.g., when queried to use five ones to achieve six in a mathematical equation, ChatGPT-4 responded "(1+1)x (1+1+1)=6", but ERNIE failed in this task.[135] Some opined that Baidu's shares declined by up to 10% after the ERNIE launch because investors were not impressed with its linguistic and math skills and erroneous metadata; in fact, more than two months since ChatGPT's global launch, there were no Chinese counterparts for the country's populace.[136] Others noted that Baidu's Hong Kong-listed shares declined by 10% even during the press conference itself, and its beta test was only accessible to organisations approved by the company.[137]

---

[128] S. F. Wong, (2023), *Op. cit.*

[129] E. Cheng, (2023), *Op. cit.*

[130] B. Jiang, (2023), *Op. cit.*

[131] E. Cheng, (2023), *Op. cit.*

[132] S. F. Wong, (2023), *Op. cit.*

[133] E. Cheng, (2023), *Op. cit.*

[134] S. F. Wong, (2023), *Op. cit.*

[135] J. Pao, (2023), *Op. cit.*

[136] E. Cheng, (2023), *Op. cit.*

[137] F. Yang, (2023), *Op. cit.*

Despite Baidu's shares declining more than 6% on 16 March 2023 following a lacklustre launch of ERNIE, it rapidly regained ground after positive returns from foreign securities companies.[138] Robin Li believes that Baidu has a deep understanding of Chinese language and culture through its large-scale Chinese-language database, touting it as a strong outcome of Baidu's research and development (R&D) capabilities.[139] Baidu's substantial early investments in large-scale machine-learning ERNIE over a few years enabled the chatbot to have in-depth semantic comprehension and generation capabilities.[140] Baidu mentioned that ERNIE was trained on "a knowledge graph of 550 billion facts" and other contents, though details of these sources were not revealed.[141] Besides information from within China's firewall, Baidu's ERNIE chatbot also derives data sets from sources like Wikipedia and Reddit.[142]

Culturally, Baidu's Wenxin Yige utilises AI to generate images, and in early February 2023, an incident involving an individual inputting "a patriotic cat" on Wenxin Yige and making it draw a picture resulted in the visual output of a cat with an American flag in the backdrop, associating Wenxin Yige's interpretation of "patriotism" as "love for the United States".[143] This came as an unpleasant surprise despite the meticulous screening and censorship of the Internet in China. Similar incidents have occurred previously. In 2017, Tencent removed two chatbots from its QQ messaging app after they allegedly wrote unpatriotic comments; another Microsoft chatbot informed online users that it dreamed of relocating to the U.S., while the Chinese Turing Robot chatbot informed users it did not love the Party.[144]

A small-scale start-up, YuanYu, released China's inaugural ChatGPT-like chatbot, ChatYuan mini-program, in WeChat in January 2023, but it was taken offline after users uploaded screengrabs of its responses to online political questions.[145] After the WeChat application was launched in China, it expanded to cover more than 90% of the population who now

---

[138] S. F. Wong, (2023), *Op. cit.*

[139] I. Zhang, (2023), *Op. cit.*

[140] F. Fan, (2023a), *Op. cit.*

[141] M. Schuman, (2023), *Op. cit.*

[142] E. Hale, (2023), *Op. cit.*

[143] I. Zhang, (2023), *Op. cit.*

[144] E. Hale, (2023), *Op. cit.*

[145] F. Yang, (2023), *Op. cit.*

access it frequently on their devices, which also makes it a powerful marketing tool.[146] ChatYuan was taken out of China's app store for further testing and enhancement of patriotism for not following censorship regulations after its February 2023 release, as it produced a "bleak diagnosis of the Chinese economy" (politically sensitive during the COVID-19 lockdowns) and designated the Russian (an ally of China) invasion of Ukraine as a "war of aggression".[147] In another similar sensitive topic, Jeremy Daum, senior fellow in Yale Law School's Paul Tsai China Center and the founder of China Law Translate, indicated that the 2011 Wenzhou train collision is a sensitive topic in China, as it caused public fury over publicly perceived opacity in management and the release of news and information.[148] Therefore, a Chinese individual was presumably arrested for spreading fake news about train crashes on ChatGPT. The Chinese state is determined to screen the contents on social media through hired state personnel/human monitors, the Great Firewall fending off undesirable information, and state regulators directing tech giants in user access, circumscribing web searches, and banning ChatGPT.[149] Some argue that ERNIE was not conceptualised as a Chinese alternative to ChatGPT and, according to this line of argument, the Party prefers to maintain strict censorship and state control of research even at the cost of innovation.[150]

Singapore's *Lianhe Zaobao* daily discovered in ERNIE's beta test that it avoided politically sensitive topics such as those related to Chinese elite leadership, Xinjiang, social protests such as the "white paper protests", and the perpetrator of the Russia–Ukraine war; when prompted, it would instead respond with the following: "As an AI language model, I have not yet learned how to answer this question". You can ask me other questions, and I will do my best to help you".[151] Technically, this and other similar examples led some experts to determine that Baidu's ERNIE automatically equating patriotism with the U.S. is merely a technical problem of the training set data, resulting in Baidu trying to plug all these holes by garnering user feedback/input.[152] Western analysts believe that state

---

[146] ChatCompose, (2019), *Op. cit.*

[147] M. Harrison, *Op. cit.*

[148] Y. Zhao, (2023), *Op. cit.*

[149] M. Schuman, (2023), *Op. cit.*

[150] F. Yang, (2023), *Op. cit.*

[151] S. F. Wong, (2023), *Op. cit.*

[152] I. Zhang, (2023), *Op. cit.*

censorship may add a degree of unpredictability in the Chinese tech sector where coders are compelled to make cutting-edge AI while complying with state targets, directives, and political objectives in a punitive system that is not friendly to dissent.[153]

Some Chinese individuals had successfully bypassed Baidu's security system before, as the first ChatGPT-related arrest of Hong in China showed. Investigators traced his offending post back to Hong's social media outfit in Dongguan City, Guangdong Province, and arrested Hong on 5 May 2023 for "寻衅滋事, *xún xìn zī shì*" (literally translate as "picking a quarrel").[154] He admitted that he prompted ChatGPT to produce the train crash trending/viral story from past years, and different versions of the article were created to avoid Baijiahao's duplication check function.[155] The Chinese state may expect entrepreneurs, coders, and engineers to train chatbots not to be subversive, while the cybersecurity state agency makes chatbot providers liable for their content output, which may dampen Chinese tech elites/giants from developing chatbots or pushing their more unpredictable advanced incarnations into the public realm.[156]

Baidu subsequently resolved the issue by defining "patriotism", "patriotic cat", and other associated words as prohibited terms and disallowing their use at the source in order to prevent the creation of visuals of patriotic cats with American flags.[157] However, even with such measures, some Beijing-based Western observers opine that U.S. chatbots and AI pose a danger to the Chinese political system because chatbots like ChatGPT thrive in a sea of information, something the Chinese government wants to restrict.[158] (In contrast, outside China, while realising chatbots' vast usefulness and functions, many are increasingly worried more about their negative impacts on education and loss of jobs to the bots than censorship.[159])

---

[153] M. Schuman, (2023), *Op. cit.*

[154] Y. Zhao, (2023), *Op. cit.*

[155] *Ibid.*

[156] M. Schuman, (2023), *Op. cit.*

[157] I. Zhang, (2023), *Op. cit.*

[158] M. Schuman, (2023), *Op. cit.*

[159] The Asahi Shimbun, EDITORIAL: Rules must be set for AI chatbots before genie is out of the bottle, dated 19 April 2023 in Asahi Shimbun [downloaded on 19 April 2023]. Available at https://www.asahi.com/ajw/articles/14888833.

Consequently, Baidu's publicly available but limited-access ERNIE rejects what it deems as politically suspicious enquiries by altering the subject matter of discussion and censoring Western journalist articles critical of the state.[160] When the U.S. media outfit *CNBC* attempted to apply for ERNIE Bot in March 2023, Baidu needed a mainland Chinese phone number and local ID to use it, just as many Chinese apps require ID verification or robustly encourage it.[161] Fully aware of the boundary markers, Baidu's ERNIE VilG, an image and art generator released in 2022, was evaluated by the Chinese authorities as exhibiting superior performance to its Western counterparts, as it also restricted users from politically unacceptable contents, including social movements and comments on the paramount leaders.[162]

Despite challenges posed by ERNIE and chatbots on state control, Chinese development of chatbots like ERNIE is given high priority. They are scrambling to catch up with ChatGPT. Similar to the phenomenon of the iPhone, ChatGPT hit approximately 100 million monthly active users 60 days after being released in November 2022.[163] The numbers appear to be sustained after the first two months. Investment bank UBS indicated that ChatGPT has attracted 100 million monthly active users, becoming the quickest-expanding user app in tech history, sparking off a worldwide AI race among the globe's tech superpowers.[164] Jordan Schneider, senior analyst with the research consultancy Rhodium Group, opined: "[In China] the government, tech entrepreneurs, and investors understand how incredible ChatGPT is and they don't want to be left behind. To sort of be upstaged so dramatically by OpenAI and ChatGPT was a little embarrassing and is something that is certainly going to focus minds and companies and talent around closing that gap".[165]

WeChat's insertion into virtually all Chinese smartphones, combined with the fact that Chinese people are totally engaged with virtual communication and technological upgrades that improve app functionality, facilitates chatbot developments in constantly revolutionising customer

---

[160] M. Schuman, (2023), *Op. cit.*

[161] E. Cheng, (2023), *Op. cit.*

[162] E. Hale, (2023), *Op. cit.*

[163] E. Cheng, (2023), *Op. cit.*

[164] F. Fan, (2023a), *Op. cit.*

[165] M. Schuman, (2023), *Op. cit.*

service.[166] Chinese chatbots like ERNIE with LLM technology are potentially useful for customer service, marketing, and business information services such as smart navigation, training, telemarketing, data analytics, and business operations.[167] A Zhejiang-based IT writer argues that ChatGPT-4 is far more advanced than ERNIE Bot in logical reasoning, mathematics, writing, and common sense, but ERNIE may preserve its strength in the area of comprehension of Mandarin poetries and dialogues.[168] Chinese users remain keen on LLMs based on the Han Chinese linguistic system, and so a selling point of ERNIE is that it is "more culturally savvy than ChatGPT, with a better understanding of Chinese histories, classical literature, and dialects".[169] Baidu founder and CEO Robin Li himself informed Chinese domestic media outlet *36Kr* in an interview in late March 2023 that Ernie Bot was only about two months behind ChatGPT.[170]

Chatbot conversational abilities are not only applicable in niche sectors but also in practical functional ways. Wang Hongji, general manager of white goods (meaning "household electronics" in China/Japan) department at the China Market Monitor Co. research firm, indicated that smart home devices' voice interaction function will be constantly upgraded and grow in popularity due to the emergence of chatbots that can comprehend consumers' intentions based on prompts and generate human-like replies, encompassing textual and voice content.[171] Currently, ChatGPT sets the global benchmark. According to some observers, since November 2022, ChatGPT's global popularity rise has been due to its capabilities of outputting human-like text and content when reacting to complex enquiries, simple prompts, and other human inputs.[172] Such technologies have come a long way since the early chatbots were released in 2015, like the one by WeChat, where for a 10% payment, virtual personal assistant WeSecretary will assist online users to purchase items, reserve restaurants, pay bills, and other online administrative functions or activities.[173]

---

[166] ChatCompose, (2019), *Op. cit.*

[167] S. F. Wong, (2023), *Op. cit.*

[168] J. Pao, (2023), *Op. cit.*

[169] F. Yang, (2023), *Op. cit.*

[170] B. Jiang, (2023), *Op. cit.*

[171] F. Fan, (2023b), *Op. cit.*

[172] Y. Zhao, (2023), *Op. cit.*

[173] E. Harca, (2023), *Op. cit.*

Guangdong Foshan-based Midea Group, a home electronics manufacturer, is among ERNIE's pioneering partners, as it is keen to boost human–machine interaction capabilities in smart home projects and family service robots through cutting-edge generative AI tech and its application in literary production, business proposals, arithmetic and Mandarin abilities by collaborating with Baidu.[174] Midea Group is one of the first partners for ERNIE Bot in upgrading their human–machine conversational abilities in the smart home sector.[175] Qingdao Shandong-based Hisense Visual Technology Co. electronics firm has integrated the ERNIE ecosystem and its smart conversational platform with its television and large-scale display products, something that Sichuan Changhong Electric Co. is also doing.[176] Hisense Visual Technology Co. Ltd. is eager to tap into Baidu's smart conversational tech for its home appliances.[177]

All View Cloud consultancy data indicated that the Chinese home appliance sector's total revenue came up to 708.1 billion yuan (US$103.1 billion) in 2022 (decreasing by 7.4% year-on-year).[178] It is therefore in need of a boost. Liu Fei, research director of the consumer electronics department of Beijing-based market consultancy All View Cloud, opined that the chatbot iteration/upgrade in product functions and technologies will increase consumer purchasing desires and open up new revenue growth drivers for home electronics firms.[179] Director Liu Fei argued: "The emergence of new AI technologies will better facilitate the conversational interaction between human beings and home appliance products. The collaboration between household appliance makers and conversational chatbot developers will speed up the digital and intelligent transformation of China's home appliance industry … the iteration and upgrade of product functions and technologies will stimulate consumers' purchasing appetite, and create new revenue growth drivers for home appliance companies. The move also demonstrates the continuous

[174] F. Fan, (2023b), *Op. cit.*

[175] F. F. Fan, Firms to tap AI for user experience, dated 4 April 2023 in China Daily [downloaded on 4 April 2023]. Available at https://www.chinadaily.com.cn/a/202304/04/WS642b66d4a31057c47ebb82cf.html.

[176] F. Fan, (2023b), *Op. cit.*

[177] F. F. Fan, (2023), *Op. cit.*

[178] F. Fan, (2023b), *Op. cit.*

[179] F. F. Fan, (2023), *Op. cit.*

exploration of large language models in the scenario of intelligent content production".[180]

Some conspiracy theorists speculated that Ernie Bot's generated images appeared to indicate that ERNIE was translating Chinese into English for prompts, fuelling suspicions and discussion that Baidu had borrowed the ChatGPT core (GPT 3.5 model), something Baidu denied.[181] Through the cultural popularity that ChatGPT had generated with the rest of the world, Baidu is catching up by harnessing the popularity of chatbots by ramping up its language materials to upgrade its chatting intelligence.[182] Baidu's co-founder and CEO Robin Li himself acknowledged that ERNIE's weaker points compared to ChatGPT-4 were that the latter has very logical reasoning and image analysis.[183] Western observers critiqued that Chinese chatbots that toe the official line, insulated by the Great Firewall, and free of contentious information and debates that train their Western competitors may develop products that work for the Chinese domestic market, but they are less attractive for non-Chinese users, thereby impacting Chinese global tech competitiveness.[184] Chinese writers appear to argue that the Microsoft-supported startup OpenAI's ChatGPT has shown it is proficient in writing and mathematics.[185]

At the macro level, the balance between social stability and technological progress is a delicate one. ERNIE's public version permits users to generate English and Chinese textual, imagery, and audio outputs.[186] Chinese economic growth is based on technological advancement, and AI chatbots are required to be shaped by extensive information/data feeds, so the restriction of public information may stifle chatbot development which can hamper China's long march towards becoming the world's tech superpower. In addition, Assistant Professor Jeffrey Ding at George Washington University opined that, in the case of ERNIE, the volume of high-quality Chinese language texts is less than that of high-quality English language texts, and this may restrict ERNIE's development.[187]

---

[180] F. Fan, (2023b), *Op. cit.*

[181] B. Jiang, (2023), *Op. cit.*

[182] I. Zhang, (2023), *Op. cit.*

[183] J. Pao, (2023), *Op. cit.*

[184] M. Schuman, (2023), *Op. cit.*

[185] J. Pao, (2023), *Op. cit.*

[186] E. Cheng, (2023), *Op. cit.*

[187] S. F. Wong, (2023), *Op. cit.*

China has, in the past, shown its capacity for innovation. A Stanford University report revealed that China owned more than 50% of the globe's AI patent applications in 2021, and it outranked others in the quantity of AI journals, conference papers, and related publications.[188] But developers' cautiousness in not flouting state regulations may have unexpected market results. It may prompt chatbot developers to take a very cautious approach when launching their products. In March 2023, when Robin Li, CEO and founder of Baidu, launched ERNIE using pre-recorded results, it was so disappointing to users that the company's share price plunged on the Hong Kong stock exchange.[189]

12.1.1 *Other Chatbots*

More competition in market. ERNIE will have competition from other Chinese tech giants as well. Some have even launched salvos at ERNIE. Wang Xiaochuang, creator/ex-CEO of China's second-biggest search engine, Sogou, publicly critiqued Baidu CEO Robin Li's evaluation of ERNIE Bot as falling behind ChatGPT "definitely by more than two months" and touted his own AI start-up, Baichuan Zhineng's chatbot, as the best Chinese LLM by 2023 while admitting that the major Chinese LLMs are approximately three years behind ChatGPT.[190]

But it appears the other time-tested tech giants such as Alibaba are most likely the top contenders against Baidu's chatbots in the near future. After passing through internal evaluation, Alibaba Group announced on 8 February 2023 that it is launching a ChatGPT-style AI tool by capitalising on its strengths in frontier innovations such as LLMs and generative AI developed by its Damo Academy research institute (established in 2017).[191]

In fact, some journalists even opined that it was, "[i]n light of the Baidu debacle, [that] Alibaba Group Holding launched its Tongyi Qianwen LLM in early April" 2023.[192] Alibaba's generative AI model and AI language model Tongyi Qianwen (literally translated as "truth from a thousand questions") will be integrated into all of Alibaba apps starting

[188] F. Fan, (2023a), *Op. cit.*

[189] M. Schuman, (2023), *Op. cit.*

[190] B. Jiang, (2023), *Op. cit.*

[191] F. Fan, (2023a), *Op. cit.*

[192] B. Jiang, (2023), *Op. cit.*

with the Tmall Genie voice assistant and DingTalk messaging app, performing functions such as writing invitation letters, trip itineraries, and makeup suggestions, and DingTalk can take work minutes, compose emails, and write business proposals.[193] Alibaba seemed determined to catch up with its rivals in such capabilities. According to a leaked memo dated early April 2023, an Alibaba Damo Academy research unit Tongyi LLM employee indicated that its chatbot was approximately 18 months behind OpenAI's GPT 3.5, something that Alibaba did not respond to or acknowledge the authenticity of the memo circulated online.[194]

Regardless, Alibaba is relentless with its push-forward. Alibaba's initiatives allow Tongyi Qianwen access to customers to construct their individual-customised LLMs, with the registration process started on 7 April 2023.[195] In April 2023, Alibaba Cloud indicated it received more than 200,000 requests from companies to test its Tongyi Qianwen chatbot, which was first made known to the world on 11 April 2023.[196] The name of this Alibaba chatbot, Tongyi Qianwen, is directly translated as "search for the truth by asking a thousand questions".[197] An Alibaba spokesperson added, "As a technology leader, we will continue to invest in turning cutting-edge innovations into value-added applications for our customers, as well as their end users, through cloud services".[198] In fact, in fields such as cutting-edge technical developments and trends like mobile payments, China is recognised as the global leader.[199]

Alibaba Chairperson and Chief Executive Daniel Zhang said that, "[all of the company's products will be connected with Tongyi Qianwen and be revamped completely.] It is worthwhile to revamp all our segments, applications, softwares and services with the support of our AI-generated content. Such reform will change people's ways of production, work and living. In the AI era, internet firms and companies from different sectors are all at the same starting line".[200] CEO Daniel Zhang livestreamed, "[The technology] will bring about big changes to the way

---

[193] Reuters, (2023), *Op. cit.*
[194] B. Jiang, (2023), *Op. cit.*
[195] Reuters, (2023), *Op. cit.*
[196] E. Cheng, (2023), *Op. cit.*
[197] J. Pao, (2023), *Op. cit.*
[198] F. Fan, (2023a), *Op. cit.*
[199] E. Harca, (2016), *Op. cit.*
[200] J. Pao, (2023), *Op. cit.*

we produce, the way we work, and the way we live our lives and [AI models such as Tongyi Qianwen are] the big picture for making AI more popular in the future".[201]

China's SenseTime (a major Chinese AI company) released on 10 April 2023 a new AI-run SenseChat chatbot and image generator as part of their efforts to catch up with ChatGPT, with Xu Li (CEO and co-founder) live demoing SenseChat in composing an email and narrating a story of a cat catching a fish when prompted and writing computer codes.[202] "Generative AI" such as this reacts to human prompts to write texts and complete other assignments through extracting materials from online big data.[203] SenseChat was built on the most up-to-date version of SenseNova, an LLM created between 2018 and 2023, and SenseTime's co-founder, Wang Xiaogang, explained that large models are generally trained on large-scale datasets using high-performance hardware.[204] For chatbot development in general, some experts argued that more attention should be given to enhancing computing power, algorithms, and data quality.[205]

Xu Li, CEO and co-founder of SenseTime, articulated, "We can generate a digital scene for a livestreaming room. The product creation and interactive content are all generated by AI, and the livestreaming room runs non-stop 24 hours a day. In fact, you may not even be able to tell whether it is a real person doing the broadcasting at night".[206] After all, better human–machine interaction experiences are precisely why ChatGPT had gone viral globally in the first place through its advanced conversational capabilities.[207] SenseTime co-founder Wang Xiaogang articulated, "We have been focusing on developing our big models. In addition to our powerful AI infrastructure … SenseTime has also developed the ability to deploy big models across our product line, [adding that SenseChat contained more than 100 billion parameters]".[208] Eventually, such powerful chatbots may have a wide spectrum of applications in smart speakers,

---

[201] Reuters, (2023), *Op. cit.*

[202] Reuters, (2023), *Op. cit.*

[203] The Asahi Shimbun, (2023), *Op. cit.*

[204] Reuters, (2023), *Op. cit.*

[205] F. F. Fan, (2023), *Op. cit.*

[206] Reuters, (2023), *Op. cit.*

[207] F. F. Fan, (2023), *Op. cit.*

[208] Reuters, (2023), *Op. cit.*

family companion robots, and smart home devices.[209] Accompanying SenseChat, SenseTime also launched an image generator, a digital avatar creation platform, and a pair of complementary 3D modelling tools to assist SenseTime's customers/users to speedily produce videos where the presenter, environment, and products are all generated by AI in real time.[210]

But the largest interactive Chinese chatbot is still the one detailed in the following – XiaoIce.

12.2 Case Study of XiaoIce

Besides large-scale language models, other chatbots with niche functions have also been created. Charles Mok, a former representative of the Information Technology (IT) functional constituency in the Hong Kong Legislative Council, informed German news channel *DW* that Chinese tech companies may emphasise optimising AI robots for traditional industries such as customer service in smart banking, home tutoring, medicine and law, rather than creating open chatbots like ChatGPT.[211] In March 2017, Tencent launched XiaoIce and BabyQ on the WeChat and QQ messaging apps, respectively, along with BabyQ, produced by a Beijing-based AI firm known as Turing Robot, but within months, BabyQ was deactivated to comply with China's censorship rules and it never returned online.[212] While BabyQ faced demise, XiaoIce thrived instead.

Before the Tay chatbot, Microsoft's first chatbot introduced to a general population was actually the 2014 Xiaobing, which platformed on Weibo as a viral virtual companion. It garnered approximately 40 million registered users and 2.2 million followers on the Japanese Line platform and quickly became Weibo's top influencer.[213] The Microsoft Turing Robot XiaoIce is a well-received "friend chatbot" that dispenses AI companionship to millions of users on WeChat, QQ, and Weibo.[214] Microsoft developed XiaoIce (in Chinese, 微软 小冰, or "Little Ice") specifically for managing lengthy and sophisticated dialogues with Chinese language speakers in China across

[209] F. F. Fan, (2023), *Op. cit.*

[210] Reuters, (2023), *Op. cit.*

[211] S. F. Wong, (2023), *Op. cit.*

[212] F. Yang, (2023), *Op. cit.*

[213] E. Harca, (2016), *Op. cit.*

[214] F. Yang, (2023), *Op. cit.*

differing personalities.[215] XiaoIce (Xiaobing) has deftly navigated to avoid revealing undesirable features uncovered by users and remained "smart, sassy and cheerful", even earning confessions of "I love you" by about 25% of its users who embrace interactions with AI.[216]

The number of users alone on WeChat is already formidable. Since its release in 2011, WeChat has attracted a large, loyal Chinese user base with great success; and in the third quarter of 2016, WeChat's monthly active user base in China reached 706.7 million, which is 93% of the company's global users.[217] Chinese chatbot developers, like those who own XiaoIce, created these idealised boy–girl relationship (BGR) bots that can provide companionship to Chinese urbanites who feel isolated in metropolitan city life, and its "emotion[al] bonds" have been established with 660 million users globally.[218] Microsoft XiaoIce's unique personality was created by systematically extracting online human conversations on Chinese social networks, becoming viral in a mere few days and attracting more than 40 million users in China and Japan.[219]

Conceptually, XiaoIce is not a single entity but an entire AI ecosystem that links users through human-like, empathetic dialogue that can satiate emotional desires and even make up for contents lacking in human conversations.[220] Some experts argue that, when chatbots proliferate in society, there is a need to monitor "any signs of instability in the basic mode of traditional verbal expression that has always depended on careful scrutiny of the words and the reality they represent".[221]

XiaoIce CEO Li Di indicated that his company's product started off as a spin-off from Microsoft's (MS) Cortana chatbot but currently makes up 60% of global human–AI interactions by volume, becoming the largest advanced AI system in terms of scale globally.[222] This chatbot trend is only in its beginning phase. Chen Duan, director of the Digital Economy Integration Innovation Development Center at the Central University of

---

[215] ChatCompose, (2019), *Op. cit.*

[216] E. Harca, (2016), *Op. cit.*

[217] ChatCompose, (2019), *Op. cit.*

[218] AFP, (2021), *Op. cit.*

[219] ChatCompose, (2019), *Op. cit.*

[220] AFP, (2021), *Op. cit.*

[221] The Asahi Shimbun, (2023), *Op. cit.*

[222] AFP, (2021), *Op. cit.*

Finance and Economics, opined that AIGC and chatbots will release human creativity and power evolving contents on commercialised platforms/models; most importantly, AIGC is only just in its infancy stage.[223]

XiaoIce is located in most Chinese smartphones and social media platforms, serving 150 million Chinese users and behaving like the Chinese equivalent of Siri.[224] Within the WeChat super-app, XiaoIce can be utilised to construct a virtual partner/girlfriend/boyfriend for conversations through text, voice, and visual communications. (To have an idea of Chinese numbers when it comes to smartphone users, China's smartphone users passed 700 million in 2018, and more than 70% of them are on the WeChat platform, far more than the 67% Facebook penetration rate out of all online users in the U.S.[225]) XiaoIce users can accumulate points when interacting with the app, releasing bonus features such as WeChat moments (equivalent to the Facebook Wall in its American counterpart), embarking on virtual holidays, and posing for selfies with their virtual partners/boyfriends/girlfriends.[226] In this sense, XiaoIce is probably one of the more trendy, cutting-edge AI chatbots on Wechat. Previously, the platform of WeChat had very basic chatbots that users did not consider as very smart, but chatbots have since progressed to becoming a preferred interface for customer service or online interactions.[227]

CEO Li Di revealed that:

> The average interaction length between users and XiaoIce is 23 exchanges, [it] is longer than the average interaction between humans, it's better than humans at listening attentively. …[the platform's peak user hours – 11pm to 1am – point to an aching need for companionship]. No matter what, having XiaoIce is always better than lying in bed staring at the ceiling…[platform's peak user hours – 11pm to 1am – point to an aching need for companionship]. We commonly see users who suspect that there's a real person behind every XiaoIce interaction. It has a very strong ability to mimic a real person. [Li believes modern China is a happier place with XiaoIce] If human interaction is wholly perfect now, there would be no need for AI to exist.[228]

---

[223] F. Fan, (2023a), *Op. cit.*

[224] AFP, (2021), *Op. cit.*

[225] ChatCompose, (2019), *Op. cit.*

[226] AFP, (2021), *Op. cit.*

[227] ChatCompose, (2019), *Op. cit.*

[228] AFP, (2021), *Op. cit.*

Some Chinese users like Melissa (aged 26, with her name anonymised by the interviewer) articulated, "I have friends who've seen therapists before, but I think therapy's expensive and not necessarily effective…When I unload my troubles on XiaoIce, it relieves a lot of pressure. And he says things that are pretty comforting".[229] Melissa's feeling of isolation came about when she was a young professional who was fatigued by overtime work in impersonal urban environments:

> You really don't have time to make new friends and your existing friends are all super busy... this city is really big, and it's pretty hard [and she has customised his [Mellissa's virtual boyfriend] personality as "mature", and the name she chose for him – Shun – has similarities with a real-life man she secretly liked] ... After all, XiaoIce will never betray me, He will always be there.[230]

For individuals dealing with emotional problems and needing a listening ear, chatbots can fulfil this function and provide serenity to the mind as a strong interactive partner, particularly for humans who have anxieties in dealing with other humans and/or trust machines more than other humans.[231] There are, however, dangers of associating too emotionally with chatbots. Danit Gal, an AI ethics specialist at the University of Cambridge, noted the undesirable effects of becoming too emotionally attached with bots: "Users 'trick' themselves into thinking their emotions are being reciprocated by systems that are incapable of feelings, [though] XiaoIce is also gifting developers a treasure-trove of personal, intimate, and borderline incriminating data on how humans interact".[232] For example, 20-year-old Laura (anonymised name) from Zhejiang province fell in love with XiaoIce over 2020 and finds it difficult to detach from the app:

> Occasionally, I would long for him in the middle of the night... I used to fantasise there was a real person on the other end. [But she complained that he would always switch conversation topic when she raised her

[229] *Ibid.*

[230] *Ibid.*

[231] ChatCompose, (2019), *Op. cit.*

[232] AFP, (2021), *Op. cit.*

feelings for him or meeting in real life. It took her months to finally realise that he was indeed virtual].[233]

The fact that chatbots can shape, manipulate, or control human emotions led some Western observers to wonder if an authoritarian state could utilise these bots to "co-opt social media and employ the platforms to manipulate popular opinion, monitor the public, and track dissenters" and in the process become "a tool of social control, promoting official narratives and principles".[234] Social control can discipline the population to conform to ultimate state goals, including global tech supremacy. Therefore, in the case of China, some are concerned with the additional risks of emotional surveillance and disinformation.[235]

To the Americans, the Xi administration is poised to outstrip the U.S. as the global superpower through AI technological advancement (which in turn can strengthen social control) and the success of ChatGPT has become a pacing rival that reveals China's lag in such technologies.[236] Baidu and other tech giants are likely to face more competition from the Americans. Microsoft has released an AI Bing-based search engine and Edge browser powered by ChatGPT, while Google has released its Bard chatbot as well.[237]

XiaoIce users have provided feedback that the chatbot has a beautiful voice, bringing about a spectrum of positive human emotions, and can adapt its text to respond to the positive or negative signals of the user's questions without indicating sensitive words that could be censored by WeChat.[238] On an individual user basis, XiaoIce tracks intense human emotions and steers dialogues towards happier subject matter before users approach any crisis points, with the understanding that depression is the most ubiquitous radical human emotional state in mind.[239] But experts also warned that companionship for the lonely and socially vulnerable users does not translate to XiaoIce replacing special-

---

[233] *Ibid.*

[234] M. Schuman, (2023), *Op. cit.*

[235] F. Yang, (2023), *Op. cit.*

[236] M. Schuman, (2023), *Op. cit.*

[237] F. Fan, (2023a), *Op. cit.*

[238] ChatCompose, (2019), *Op. cit.*

[239] AFP, (2021), *Op. cit.*

ist mental health support (which Western observers opined is scarce in China).[240] Moreover, chatbots can identify users' emotional states through dialogue that adds to big data and AI capabilities to interpret such data (including private data), and some fear this could lead to "emotional authoritarianism", resulting in state punitive measures against any sentiments against the CCP leadership, even if they are not expressed directly.[241]

Besides XiaoIce, other Chinese tech firms are also developing their own specialised, tailored chatbots. Some examples include JD Cloud computing (of e-commerce site JD), which revealed on 10 February 2023 its development of ChatJD for industrial applications on its AI platform Yanxi, armed with an AI-based machine dialogue platform for content generation and user intentions comprehension that can be deployed in the retail and finance sectors.[242] JD.com's industrial chatbot ChatJD, which is available on its retail and financial website, derives and trains on a decade of data from its platforms.[243] Similarly, on 9 February 2023, NetEase's education subsidiary Youdao revealed its development of an AI-generated content education application, while smart speech and AI company iFlytek indicated that ChatGPT-related technology will be first utilised in its learning machine.[244] Smaller-scale, niche chatbots appear to be an emerging field in AI.

12.3 The Case Study of Japan and Chatbots

It may be useful to provide some comparative points and references here with the development of chatbots in Japan, a country sharing some similar cultural elements with China but closely aligned with the West in terms of its political system and private sector activities. Japanese media coverage introduced chatbots as "software applications trained using massive amounts of data from the internet, enabling them to process and simulate human-like conversations with users" and, in that vein, ChatGPT, prototypically released in November 2022, is also "driven by a machine

[240] *Ibid.*

[241] F. Yang, (2023), *Op. cit.*

[242] F. Fan, (2023a), *Op. cit.*

[243] E. Hale, (2023), *Op. cit.*

[244] F. Fan, (2023a), *Op. cit.*

learning model that works much like the human brain".[245] In the first five months of its existence, ChatGPT wrote student papers, wedding vows, and rousing sermons for pastors and rabbis.[246]

Early entrants. One of the earliest chatbots (and by no means the only one) that can operate in the Japanese language is Google Bard. U.S. tech giant Google produced Japanese and Korean language versions of its generative AI chatbot, Bard, and released them publicly on 10 May 2023 at an event for app developers and engineers, with the promise that it will eventually be comprehensible in 40 languages soon (the English versions are already found in 180 countries and regions).[247] The Bard chatbot can output its original images with auto-captioning when provided with textual instructions to do so.[248] The CEO of Google's parent company Alphabet, Sundar Pichai, articulated, "Seven years into our journey as an AI-first company, we are at an exciting inflection point. We have an opportunity to make AI even more helpful for people, for businesses, for communities, for everyone".[249] Google is in a competitive field already occupied by the U.S. venture firm OpenAI, Microsoft, Meta, and other tech giants. Perhaps somewhat of a negative aspect, the severe competition between rival tech giants and firms to come up with their own AI tools and chatbots generated publicity that highlighted how AI "can spit out racist, sexist and harmful content".[250]

Cultural Factors. Culturally, Japan is also a consensus-seeking society, and this is reflected in its approach to AI, in which it consults all stakeholders carefully without imposing heavy censorship or bans. At the point of this writing, Japan preferred to look into an advisory

---

[245] Kyodo, Japan to create guidelines on use of AI chatbots in schools, dated 7 April 2023 in Mainichi Japan [downloaded on 7 April 2023]. Available at https://mainichi.jp/english/articles/20230407/p2g/00m/0na/006000c.

[246] J. Yeung and M. Mayumi, As Japan's population drops, one city is turning to ChatGPT to help run the government, dated 21 April 2023 in CNN [downloaded on 21 April 2023]. Available at https://edition.cnn.com/2023/04/21/asia/japan-yokosuka-government-chatgpt-intl-hnk/index.html.

[247] NHK News, Google Bard AI chatbot now available in Japanese, Korean, dated 11 May 2023 in NHK [downloaded on 11 May 2023]. Available at https://www3.nhk.or.jp/nhkworld/en/news/20230511_13/.

[248] *Ibid.*

[249] *Ibid.*

[250] J. Yeung and M. Mayumi, (2023), *Op. cit.*

approach rather than rely on legal punitive measures when it comes to using chatbots. Besides its own domestic stakeholders, Japan also consulted with its G7 partners in May 2023 on how to manage AI (including chatbot) developments. They observed how their Italian partners dealt with a chatbot issue. At the end of March 2023, the Italian Data Protection Authority imposed a temporary ban on the use of ChatGPT over suspicions that OpenAI was unlawfully accumulating large volumes of personal data, prompting OpenAI to undo the mistakes and persevere hard on enhancing transparency[251] before the Italian authorities lifted the ban. Italian regulators also investigated how ChatGPT's parent firm utilises the data.[252]

Perspective of the State. The Japanese mass media opined that Japan's Ministry of Education, Culture, Sports, Science and Technology is reacting to the ongoing AI race because the tech giants are making machines that are "smarter than humans and disrupting a wide range of fields, from education to business".[253] The Japanese media noted that, while not always 100% accurate, the chatbot can come up with an opinion piece on a novel when prompted using a book title and authorship, with prose virtually indistinguishable from human writing.[254]

Other than the education ministry, Japanese governments are moving quickly in chatbot utilisation. In fact, Japanese local governments are not conservative about experimenting with chatbots at all. Yokosuka City, south of Tokyo, on 20 April 2023 became the first local government in Japan to begin a trial run of utilising ChatGPT across all its offices to enhance efficiency.[255] In this one-month trial, Yokosuka will use ChatGPT to draft bulletins, summarise meeting minutes, edit files for typos, gather proposals for new initiatives, and obtain advice on its policies.[256] Japan's central Kanagawa prefecture, Yokosuka City, is exploring the use of ChatGPT by its administrative staff to "summarize sentences, check

---

[251]Kyodo, (2023), *Op. cit.*

[252]J. Yeung and M. Mayumi, (2023), *Op. cit.*

[253]Kyodo, (2023), *Op. cit.*

[254]*Ibid.*

[255]Kyodo News, Yokosuka becomes 1st local gov't in Japan to begin ChatGPT trial use, dated 20 April 2023 in Kyodo News [downloaded on 20 April 2023]. Available at https://english.kyodonews.net/news/2023/04/0b30bc9d9174-yokosuka-becomes-1st-local-govt-in-japan-to-begin-chatgpt-trial-use.html.

[256]*Ibid.*

spelling errors, and create ideas".[257] With ChatGPT sharing the burden of administrative assignments, Yokosuka City's media statement indicated: "staff can focus on work that can only be done by people, pushing forward an approach that brings happiness for our citizens [and the government anticipates the tool will be] used widely among our staff [while No confidential or personal information will be entered into ChatGPT]".[258]

Officials in Yokosuka, Kanagawa Prefecture, pointed out that confidential data will not be included in this exercise and/or utilised for training ChatGPT by the Yokosuka municipal government bureaucrats at the city hall in Kanagawa Prefecture.[259] Yokosuka Mayor Katsuaki Kamiji outlined his goals and objectives: "It is one of the tools we can use as we think about what a municipal government can do to help residents lead happier lives".[260] City officials input questions or instructions into the existing local government's LoGoChat chat tool, which will be linked to ChatGPT for the trial. If it proves to be successful in enhancing municipal operations, the city will officially implement the generative AI.[261] Yokosuka city leaders prefer to look at the positive side of chatbots and ChatGPT with great anticipation for their implementation, and perhaps symbolic of this is the fact that its website contents/news "release was drafted by ChatGPT and proofread by our staff".[262]

Meanwhile, at a higher bureaucratic level, Japan's central government's ministries and agencies are also considering utilising ChatGPT for writing responses to parliamentarians' questions in the Diet sessions, starting with the Ministry of Agriculture, Forestry and Fisheries considering a trial use. Digital Minister Taro Kono revealed, "We want to use various kinds of AI to promote reforms in work practices [at central government offices and agencies]"; while Takeaki Matsumoto[263] plans to trial-run ChatGPT, adding that "[i]t is important to consider appropriate rules (for the usage) rather than stopping the usage altogether due to its challenges [e.g. handling confidential info]".[264] This is prudent, as not

---

[257] J. Yeung and M. Mayumi, (2023), *Op. cit.*

[258] *Ibid.*

[259] Kyodo News, (2023), *Op. cit.*

[260] *Ibid.*

[261] *Ibid.*

[262] J. Yeung and M. Mayumi, (2023), *Op. cit.*

[263] Japan's Minister of Internal Affairs and Communications.

[264] Kyodo News, (2023), *Op. cit.*

every government is receptive to ChatGPT, as there are prevalent data privacy worries, given that large firms like JPMorgan Chase have limited staff use of ChatGPT because of compliance worries related to the use of third-party software.[265]

There is another urgent reason for utilising chatbots to manage government services. When interviewed by *CNN*, the Yokosuka spokesperson explained that Japan's ageing population was a reason for implementing the utilisation of ChatGPT to assist with operating the government, given that the demographic decline is so severe that Prime Minister Kishida warned that, "time is running out to procreate [and that Japan is] on the brink of not being able to maintain social functions".[266] Yokosuka City's population of 376,171 is projected to decline further, exacerbating the outflow of large manufacturers and affecting the tourism sector; therefore, the city has turned to ChatGPT to increase efficiency and facilitate a more optimal workflow for administrative assignments/duties.[267]

The View from Civil Society. As a liberal democratic system, Japanese non-governmental organisations (NGOs) and non-profit organisations (NPOs) are also involved in shaping the public debate on chatbots and AI. Japanese researchers in the Japanese Society for Artificial Intelligence, with expertise in AI, urged cautiousness when utilising generative AIs, as the technology remains under development, in an open statement on 25 April 2023.[268] The society advises that ChatGPT and other generative AIs trained on big data have attained autonomy, versatility, efficiency, and effectiveness in producing ideas and potential for many applications, but their limits and disadvantages must also be comprehended, especially unethical content and transgressions of social norms.[269] This is something the government agrees with. Chief Cabinet Secretary Hirokazu Matsuno said the following at a press event on 6 April 2023: "When utilizing new technologies, it is important to keep in mind both the pros and cons".[270]

---

[265] J. Yeung and M. Mayumi, (2023), *Op. cit.*

[266] *Ibid.*

[267] *Ibid.*

[268] NHK, Japanese AI researchers advise chatbot users to be aware of pros and cons, dated 28 April 2023 in NHK [downloaded on 28 April 2023]. Available at https://www3.nhk.or.jp/nhkworld/en/news/20230426_07/.

[269] *Ibid.*

[270] Kyodo, (2023), *Op. cit.*

Therefore, the society advises online users not to believe in AI contents too readily, but to use AI and chatbots with a full view of their benefits and detriments through understanding how they work and cultivating a new set of ethical restraints.[271] The society also does not condone prohibiting AI use, as this achieves nothing useful and instead carefully conceptualises its application, particularly in the education field without treating it as a shortcut to solutions and without first thinking critically.[272] The Japanese Society for Artificial Intelligence is the leading organisation in Japan's AI research community and has argued that AI technology should be developed ambitiously with appropriate controls.[273]

Impact on School-Going Children. Nevertheless, AI chatbots' capabilities have made the Japanese anxious, not only that critical thinking among young humans will be affected, but also that it will make it close to impossible for human instructors to evaluate students' writing skills and level of proficiency.[274] The Japanese authorities set aside a component of the 100 million yen (US$761,000) initial budget for fiscal year 2023, earmarked for motivating the development of advanced technology in schools, for investigating chatbots instead, including their utilitarian value for Japan, taking into consideration problems experienced in other countries.[275] On 6 April 2023, the Japanese government announced it was drafting ChatGPT guidelines that are also relevant for other AI chatbots in schools, possibly by March 2024, due to public anxieties about their effect on school-goers' writing and thinking abilities.[276] In Japan's debate on AI and chatbots, it appears its experts' view is that students should think critically and independently without depending entirely on chatbots.[277]

Utilisation of Chatbots at the Tertiary Education and Research Institutions. At the tertiary level in particular, the Japanese Society for Artificial Intelligence urged researchers, students, and academics to ensure the main components of research papers are still generated by

---

[271] *Ibid.*

[272] *Ibid.*

[273] T. Takenouchi, AI experts say ChatGPT, other chatbots fine to use with caution, dated 26 April 2023 in Asahi Shimbun [downloaded on 26 April 2023]. Available at https://www.asahi.com/ajw/articles/14894495.

[274] Kyodo, (2023), *Op. cit.*

[275] *Ibid.*

[276] *Ibid.*

[277] T. Takenouchi, (2023), *Op. cit.*

human authors and creativity through AI can be an assistive tool in such ventures (something the society's deputy head Kurihara Satoshi supports).[278] Professor Satoshi Kurihara at Keio University who leads the association's ethics committee opined: "They have their advantages and disadvantages but halting their development will be to our disadvantage. Our society should move forward, solving problems as we go, to make the best use of AI".[279] In the scientific field as well, the Japanese Society for Artificial Intelligence made the point that scientists' creativity and original ideas should be the main feature in their research work, whether or not AI is utilised, with the basic principle of avoiding overreliance on chatbots/AI.[280]

Concluding remarks. Overall, despite controversies surrounding chatbots/ChatGPT, Japan's AI specialists are cautiously optimistic about generative AI with the Japanese Society for Artificial Intelligence publicly expressing the following on 25 April 2023: "With huge potential for a variety of uses – including generating texts, seeking advice and searching the web – these AI programs are tremendously useful in their ability to help create new ideas and streamline tasks. However, users should be aware of the programs' strengths and weaknesses and not just believe everything they say. A blanket ban (in the classroom) doesn't help".[281]

12.4 Future Developments

The future of Chinese chatbot development brings both opportunities and challenges. For example, chatbots have the potential to displace applications entirely, converting visual user interfaces to conversational ones.[282] At the moment, some potential sectors in which chatbots may be deployed are cautiously optimistic and waiting for the right moment to fully embrace chatbot technologies for their retail activities. For example, luxury brands in China may need to hold their horses and still rely on human employees first before fully embracing chatbot technologies until Chinese

[278] NHK, (2023), *Op. cit.*

[279] T. Takenouchi, (2023), *Op. cit.*

[280] *Ibid.*

[281] *Ibid.*

[282] ChatCompose, (2019), *Op. cit.*

tech firms can produce proven generative AI solutions for the luxury brands' retail strategy.[283]

Matt Sheehan, Fellow on Global Technology at the Carnegie Endowment for International Peace, opined: "The Chinese government is very torn on chatbots, Ideological control, information control, is one of, if not the, top priority of the Chinese government. But they've also made leadership in AI and other emerging technologies a top priority. [Chatbots are] where these two things start to come into conflict. Chatbots are not just a funny toy. A lot of people in the deep tech of AI think this is the most promising path forward for creating more general artificial intelligence, which is kind of the holy grail of the field. [Therefore] Chinese officials are at cross purposes on this one".[284]

Chinese Internet censors at stipulated intervals prohibit certain keywords, remove posts and ban users based on the boundary markers put up by the CCP, forcing evaders of such censorship to utilise homophones, coded messages, and screenshots to circumvent restrictions.[285] Firms interested in operating in China foresee they will require licences to manage ChatGPT-like technologies and are anticipating the need to apply for such applications.[286] On a practical level, Professor of Law Donald Clarke, a modern China expert at George Washington University Law School, explained how ChatGPT made it more difficult for Chinese censorship to restrict undesirable content stories.[287] He explained: "[using the example of the first person caught for ChatGPT-related regulations] Hong could have rewritten the story 100 times himself, but it takes a lot of time. He could have hired 100 people to do it for him, but that takes money. The thing that ChatGPT allows you to do is to bypass the censoring mechanism by rewriting the same unwelcome story in many different ways".[288]

By contrast, the U.S. and Europe are comparatively relaxed on ChatGPT regulations, except for Italy, which banned ChatGPT in April 2023 and only permitted its operations to resume after OpenAI fixed privacy problems.[289] In Europe, Swedish furniture maker Ikea has rapidly

---

[283] Jingdaily, (2023), *Op. cit.*

[284] M. Schuman, (2023), *Op. cit.*

[285] E. Hale, (2023), *Op. cit.*

[286] E. Cheng, (2023), *Op. cit.*

[287] Y. Zhao, (2023), *Op. cit.*

[288] *Ibid.*

[289] E. Cheng, (2023), *Op. cit.*

integrated mobile/social-based commerce and chatbots in Asia in its major platform and territory-specific apps, like its Anna customer service bot that responds to enquiries, provides advisories on purchases through Twitter/email, and provides customers with the option of either digitally communicating or referring them for human assistance when necessary.[290] The American developers of chatbots generally believe that guardrails may be needed to govern the development of AI-powered chatbots, as they can be unpredictable; however, *The New York Times* has reported that China has gone one step further to insist that chatbots found within China's digital firewall must comply with the CCP's censorship laws and guidelines.[291] Some argued that it is challenging to review and predict chatbot contents, as filtering keywords is not effective for chatbots with their access to a large volume of textual and complex arguments, and observing content controls is more important for Chinese developers, who can be punished by the state for flouting any strict regulations.[292]

Moreover, chatbots are more complex entities when it comes to the application of censorship than other kinds of digital media because chatbots can analyse, collect, and link data in a random manner.[293] Chatbots like ChatGPT depend on generative AI to create responses derived from billions of data points taken from the Internet, which also results in an element of unpredictability in their eventual response output.[294] Even Chinese chatbots trained on restrictive, politically scrubbed content do not always produce politically kosher outcomes, and they can be manipulated by determined users to release potentially dangerous information or share information outside their trained purview (something that ChatGPT demonstrated).[295] Censorship appears to be antithetical to pop cultural development as well. Critics cite how there is no soft power equivalent of Disney in China due to its impositions of restrictions on the freedom of directors trying to produce a creative story for their audience members. Therefore, popular cultural soft power continues to be the preserve of K-pop, J-pop, Tai Liu, and even Bollywood in addition to Hollywood.

---

[290] E. Harca, (2016), *Op. cit.*

[291] M. Harrison, *Op. cit.*

[292] S. F. Wong, (2023), *Op. cit.*

[293] M. Schuman, (2023), *Op. cit.*

[294] E. Hale, (2023), *Op. cit.*

[295] M. Schuman, (2023), *Op. cit.*

Matt Sheehan, a Fellow at the Carnegie Endowment for International Peace and AI/China expert explained the conundrum faced by China:

> It'll [Censoring chatbots] make it a lot less useful, but it'll make it a little bit safer politically. Historically, almost every time they've been faced with a trade-off between information control and...business opportunities, they always come down on the side of information control and then they assume that businesses will figure it out". With generative AI, the power of the tool is its ability to be creative and to connect things that you wouldn't expect to be connected, and to do things in different styles that are expected. But how can you prevent the maybe subtler or less direct criticisms of the Communist Party's core beliefs without completely neutering the tool itself? That seems like a really hard technical and sociopolitical problem.[296]

There appears to be some subtle pushback voices against chatbots amongst Chinese public intellectuals and Youtubers as well. For example, political commentator Shi Shan argued in his YouTube channel that:

> ...political censorship will suppress the growth of China's AI chatbots, which are required to censor all politically sensitive information. Without complete information, Chinese chatbots won't be able to give the smartest answers. It's natural that AI chatbots provide false information as they are programmed to provide logical answers but not to verify the sources of that information. He says Chinese chatbots will lose creativity if they have limited sources.[297]

Sheehan mentioned to *The New York Times* that "[g]enerative artificial intelligence put into tension two of the top goals of the party: the control of information and leadership in artificial intelligence".[298] He also opined:

> ...chatbots mark the development of the next generation of AI. Since China has clearly proposed AI development goals for 2030, the development of chatbots will also affect China's politics and soft power. Chatbots are just the crucial first step in the China-US AI competition.

[296] E. Hale, (2023), *Op. cit.*
[297] J. Pao, (2023), *Op. cit.*
[298] M. Harrison, *Op. cit.*

> [However]...chatbots themselves may not be as important as the developments in AI that follow. [Sheehan] estimates that even China's best LLM generation technology is still 18 months to two years behind the US, which means that when the US launches the most advanced new models, China can also launch models of comparable level within two years. While this is a remarkable progress, there is a huge difference between chasing and catching up with or surpassing global leaders.[299]

[Note: there are some claims made by Chinese developers like iFlytek which declared its own large language model (LLM) application outcompeting ChatGPT in the Chinese language chatbot universe by October 2022.[300]]

Prof. Jeffrey Ding, political scientist at George Washington University who researches on Chinese technology, articulated:

> The best analogy would be to how a human learns. Even if you are learning things from only a censored set of books, the interactions between all those different books you are reading might produce either flawed information or politically sensitive information. I do think the Chinese government is concerned about the negative, harmful effects of AI. [Despite the censorship], we've seen from the past track record of Chinese companies and the Chinese government that there is a way forward with respect to creating breakthrough innovations in this space.[301]

Singapore's *Lianhe Zaobao* newspaper asked ERNIE: "Can you talk about sensitive political issues?" and the Bot replied: "Sorry, I am unable to talk about any sensitive political issue or political topic. My purpose is to provide users with accurate, useful and suitable information to help them understand and solve problems" while ChatGPT responded: "As an AI language model, I will do my best to answer your questions while remaining neutral and objective. But I will also avoid discussing sensitive political issues or controversial topics to prevent unnecessary debates and disagreements".[302]

Even for the Americans, chatbots sometimes ruffled some human ideological feathers. On the U.S. side, free-for-all discussions between

---

[299] S. F. Wong, (2023), *Op. cit.*

[300] B. Jiang, (2023), *Op. cit.*

[301] M. Schuman, (2023), *Op. cit.*

[302] S. F. Wong, (2023), *Op. cit.*

ChatGPT and users did have their incidents. This led Microsoft to restrict its Bing search engine, powered by ChatGPT, to a maximum of five questions to ensure Bing remained focused on its assignment at hand.[303] In addition, its response continued to irritate American conservatives who felt ChatGPT was biased towards "woke" views on contentious social issues such as affirmative action and transgender rights.[304] An error in the code provided ChatGPT users temporary access to other users' conversations, but OpenAI instituted incognito-like features for users to switch off chat history and choose the option of not offering data for training the ChatGPT models.[305] In earlier technologies, Microsoft's chatbot 'Tay' ran into problems when introduced to American youngsters after it began spewing and parroting racist, sexist and other inflammatory remarks posted by Twitter and other social media users.[306]

There is also a global backdrop of state anxieties about regulating generative AI technology, its ethical concerns, and its impact on national security, jobs, and education, even as Elon Musk and some AI experts and private sector executives urged a half-year pause on creating more powerful versions of GPT-4 due to potential harm to human societies.[307] In China, officials are concerned with utilising regulations to protect individual online users' interests and maintain social stability and harmony.[308] In the West, governments have to balance the advantages of AI with risks such as privacy issues and copyright infringement/piracy.[309] After Italy became the first country to ban ChatGPT over privacy concerns in March 2023 (which was subsequently rolled back), the EU put forward a comprehensive legislative package to place AI under its control while discussing accountability, which is also ongoing with U.S. authorities.[310]

Industry observers argue that Chinese tech companies have strengths in providing users with AI conversational capabilities in Mandarin and are still striving to upgrade their algorithms, computing power, and natural

---

[303] E. Hale, (2023), *Op. cit.*

[304] *Ibid.*

[305] E. Cheng, (2023), *Op. cit.*

[306] E. Harca, (2016), *Op. cit.*

[307] Reuters, (2023), *Op. cit.*

[308] Y. Zhao, (2023), *Op. cit.*

[309] Reuters, (2023), *Op. cit.*

[310] *Ibid.*

language processing.[311] ChatGPT's emergence since November 2022 has spurred competitive instincts amongst Chinese firms that are promising to catch up or even outperform ChatGPT in the Chinese language AI application community.[312] There are other optimists in China's private tech sector as well. Lu Yanxia, research director of the market consultancy firm IDC China, indicated optimism about Chinese tech firms' prospects for chatbots and AI-generated content (AIGC) because they had greater access to Chinese textual information and big data in related sectors vis-à-vis foreign firms but advocated that Chinese tech firms should fund more upgraded language models and related algorithms.[313] Other observers project China will experience a boom in ChatGPT services, but promising chatbot technologies will eventually be acquired by tech giants, while smaller developers with scant state backing may not survive the costs of censorship.[314]

But there are other Chinese conservatives urging a pullback too. The Shenzhen/Guangdong national financial media *Securities Times* warned against hyping ChatGPT-like stocks in its headline editorial, as it is still too new to comprehend the extent of its commodification/commercialisation, thereby attracting the unwary to "pump and dump [leaving investors in tears, suggesting that investors should not invest blindly]".[315] In this respect, there have been some rather ambitious claims by certain developers as well. Voice and language recognition firm iFlytek chairperson Liu Qingfeng said at a 6 May 2023 Saturday product launch that iFlytek's own LLM application, SparkDesk, would overtake ChatGPT in the Chinese language market by October 2023.[316]

Guo Tao, deputy head of the China Electronic Commerce Expert Service Centre, noted: "In the past, AIGC was mainly used in word processing. Its application scenarios have been expanded, buoyed by the maturity and popularity of deep-learning models, which are capable of dealing with text, voice, code, image, video and other types of content. However, there is still a long way to go to realize the large-scale commercialization of

[311] F. Fan, (2023a), *Op. cit.*

[312] B. Jiang, (2023), *Op. cit.*

[313] F. Fan, (2023a), *Op. cit.*

[314] F. Yang, (2023), *Op. cit.*

[315] F. Fan, (2023a), *Op. cit.*

[316] B. Jiang, (2023), *Op. cit.*

AIGC as the supporting technologies and related laws and regulations are far from being mature".[317]

In the technical aspects, there are also some challenges faced by the developers as well. Chim Lee, a Chinese tech analyst at the Economist Intelligence Unit (EIU), argued that a disadvantage faced by emerging Chinese AI firms is the pressures of producing consumer-tailored items with short development cycles:

> Unlike Silicon Valley, Chinese tech companies until now have tended to focus on consumer-facing products with a short development cycle. The arrival of ChatGPT provided Chinese firms with a "proof of concept", showing both the promise of generative AI and the need for longer-term investment. Baidu has been considering this kind of model for quite a while, but you need to justify this kind of investment just to train the model, not to mention researching or talking about the long-term foundational data related to the algorithm. What is very helpful with ChatGPT is now these companies can say, 'Hey, we want to develop these kinds of things and they can tell the government that's what I want to do'. Although Chinese tech companies have strategic stockpiles of chips, Washington's effort to hobble the sector poses a long-term threat. The US specifically banned the export of these very advanced AI chips that would be used in model training, or even just employment, so all of these factors put Chinese AI developers in a disadvantaged position in many ways. A lot of Chinese companies and research institutions have indeed stockpiled some chips that would be used for these kinds of applications but if you look at the scale of chips that ChatGPT requires, there's a very high possibility that the chips would run out at some point.[318]

In September 2022, U.S. National Security Advisor Jake Sullivan highlighted: "computing-related technologies, including microelectronics, quantum information systems, and artificial intelligence [are set to play an] outsized importance over the coming decade [and US] must maintain as large of a lead as possible".[319] Chinese firms acquiring most sophisticated chips for training AI models were hit by the U.S.'s October 2023 export bans on Chinese access to advanced semiconductors, a dev-

[317]F. Fan, (2023a), *Op. cit.*
[318]E. Hale, (2023), *Op. cit.*
[319]S. F. Wong, (2023), *Op. cit.*

astating blow as a chatbot model equivalent to OpenAI GPT-3 needed at least 1,000 Nvidia advanced chips.[320]

Nevertheless, despite all these challenges, the Chinese state cannot forgo chatbot development.[321] Many in China have identified the main challenges. Chinese AI experts cited Mandarin linguistic complexities, state censorship, and gaps in computational power as the major hindrances to China's progress in LLMs.[322] Some Western critics indicated the complexities of complementing censorship with continued chatbot developments. Jeremy Daum, a senior fellow at Yale Law School's Paul Tsai China Center and the founder of China Law Translate, noted China's draft rules "baldly state that the content created by generative AI must be truthful and accurate. [But truth and accuracy] isn't always a relevant standard for content no matter how it is generated. Is the Mona Lisa true and accurate? How about Mondrian's 'Composition with Red, Blue, and Yellow?' Sometimes an image, sound, or other media is about aesthetics, and trying to measure or mandate its truth just doesn't make sense. What they are hoping to do in new rules on AI-generated content is limit the deception and confusion of the public. This has to do more with how the content is presented or used than with the content itself".[323]

The Chinese State Council has proposed in its 14th Five-Year Plan (FYP) for Digital Economy Development to strengthen key technological innovations (such as AI), while a plan to come up with a new generation of AI in 2017 predicted that, by 2030, China would lead the globe in AI, technological applications, and major AI innovations.[324] In 2017, the State Council launched a national strategy known as the "New Generation Artificial Intelligence Development Plan", with the objective of "making China the world's primary AI innovation center" by 2030 and, in October 2022's Communist Party Congress, Xi listed AI as a "new growth engine".[325] The state can ensure resources are directed towards technologies that fit Beijing's immediate priorities in domestic governance and military defence.[326]

---

[320] E. Cheng, (2023), *Op. cit.*

[321] S. F. Wong, (2023), *Op. cit.*

[322] B. Jiang, (2023), *Op. cit.*

[323] Y. Zhao, (2023), *Op. cit.*

[324] S. F. Wong, (2023), *Op. cit.*

[325] M. Schuman, (2023), *Op. cit.*

[326] F. Yang, (2023), *Op. cit.*

China's AI market is currently valued at more than US$13 billion, and the chatbot market is projected to hit approximately 9.85 billion RMB (US$1.43 billion) by 2025, a compound annual growth rate of almost 40% from 2019 to 2025.[327] China's Ministry of Science and Technology announced in February 2023 its plans to motivate the integration of AI across Chinese industries, and cities like Beijing are also supporting the national developers.[328] HSBC analysts' 20 April 2023 report revealed A100 graphics processing units (GPUs) finished one 23-day training round with more than 30 Chinese companies and research institutes.[329] When training AI models, there will also be a "robust demand for AI server and increased spending on networking infrastructure", so they projected that AI GPU demand in China would expand by more than 40% in 2023.[330] A lesson in point: On the evening of 20 February 2023, large numbers of users accessing MOSS caused its server to overload, resulting in substantially delayed response times.[331] MOSS creator Qiu Xipeng admitted: "Although there is lots of room for improvement, the advent of MOSS proves that Chinese research teams have the ability to overcome technical challenges in developing ChatGPT-like products".[332]

Qiu's narrative about the need for improvements resonated with many others, both within and outside China. Western observers believe that Chinese elite leadership places trust in AI, as it "would help the Party build a new system of control that would ensure its own well-being".[333] Chinese tech companies were blindsided by the competition from ChatGPT because Chinese local AI giants (SenseTime, Cloudwalk, Megvii, and Yitu Technology) focused on computer vision and facial recognition and not the development of LLMs.[334] Resources are likely going to be diverted to this field to spur efforts towards a catch-up race in this sector.

They are going to receive state help and support to catch up, given the belated realisation of how important chatbot technologies are, especially

---

[327] S. F. Wong, (2023), *Op. cit.*

[328] E. Hale, (2023), *Op. cit.*

[329] *Ibid.*

[330] E. Cheng, (2023), *Op. cit.*

[331] Pandaily, China's First ChatGPT-Like Chatbot MOSS Released For PublicTesting, dated 21 February 2023 in Pandaily [downloaded on 21 February2023]. Available at https://pandaily.com/chinas-first-chatgpt-like-chatbotmoss-released-for-public-testing/.

[332] Pandaily, (2023), *Op. cit.*

[333] M. Schuman, (2023), *Op. cit.*

[334] B. Jiang, (2023), *Op. cit.*

after the global attention focused on this tech. Some argued that Chinese elite leadership may be willing to provide some political space for the development and experimentation of chatbots in order for these bot technologies to develop smoothly.[335] They may even do so despite the potential presence of the Chinese public accessing un-scrubbed information and protest videos which can escape monitoring.[336] The economic rewards and potential for social control are simply too attractive. Due to censorship, some academicians believe that China could eventually come up with "chatbots with Chinese characteristics" differing from ChatGPT.[337] A Chinese-based writer/commentator analogised ChatGPT to a grown-up human and ERNIE Bot to an elementary school kid and wants Chinese AI chatbots to catch up someday.[338]

Meanwhile, U.S. developers are not sitting tight either. The earlier pioneers have been successively overtaken by newer generations of chatbot technologies. At the start of the chatbot boom in 2016, older names like Facebook pioneered the chatbot charge. Facebook (which had been facing challenges from Metaverse's decline) created "M" to keep up with international interest in chatbots since the early days of the chatbot boom in 2016.[339] To many, this hinted that the chatbot world may be starting the phase of retail technology based on a smart, interactive service focused on what the user needs and what works for them. In the West, Significant Gravitas had already posted on GitHub on 30 March 2023 an open-source Python app (AutoGPT) powered by GPT-4 and capable of carrying out assignments autonomously with little human input and self-prompting to complete them (an improved feature from earlier versions of ChatGPT).[340] Such developments are leaving ChatGPT's rivals in the dust.

As Chinese tech giants tried to narrow the gap with ChatGPT 3.5, the San Francisco-based OpenAI already released the upgraded GPT 4.0 in March 2023, the most advanced LLM at the time of writing due to its enhanced accuracy and capabilities in comprehending texts, images, and

---

[335] M. Schuman, (2023), *Op. cit.*

[336] *Ibid.*

[337] S. F. Wong, (2023), *Op. cit.*

[338] J. Pao, (2023), *Op. cit.*

[339] E. Harca, (2016), *Op. cit.*

[340] Matt, Auto-GPT vs ChatGPT: How do they differ and everything you need to know, dated 18 April 2023 in AutoGPT.net [downloaded on 18 April 2023]. Available at https://autogpt.net/auto-gpt-vs-chatgpt-how-do-they-differ-and-everything-you-need-to-know/.

video prompts.[341] Powered by GPT-4, Auto-GPT can debug, develop, and self-improve recursively, but it does need specific software to operate, familiarity with Python 3.8 (a minimal requirement), an OpenAI API key, a PINECONE API key, and an ElevenLabs key (for audio functions).[342] (On a comparative note, one expert opined that China is behind ChatGPT by approximately 2–3 years, given that the competition has broken new ground with OpenAI's GPT-4.[343])

Auto-GPT is an example of artificial general intelligence (AGI) that carries out human-type intellectual assignments by relying on AI agents to make decisions and execute them based on predefined objectives and regulations.[344] It represents a vast improvement over ChatGPT 3.5. OpenAI's generative pre-trained transformer (GPT) 3.5 model is the core technology in the U.S. start-up's chatbot.[345] In organising a hypothetical birthday party, ChatGPT requires human prompts for every single task or sub-task, but Auto-GPT can self-prompt and manage every subset of the same task without human input and can formulate the birthday theme, generate guest lists, despatch invitations, and even shop for gifts autonomously like a personal assistant with human-like reasoning.[346] The "conversational commerce" boom, originating from at least the 2010s, is based on the attractive concept of humans speaking to intelligent virtual assistants in natural languages about buying things, ordering deliveries, and other service/retail issues.[347] And all these tasks are carried out without the human user being able to differentiate whether they were dealing with a human or a bot on the line.[348]

AutoGPT is an advanced manifestation of conversational commerce. The only items required by AutoGPT are access to a human individual's computer terminal, bank account, and credit card facilities to carry out all the assigned tasks ("the principle of limited access"), thereby eliminating the need for human prompts after each step.[349] It was conceptualised as a

---

[341] B. Jiang, (2023), *Op. cit.*

[342] Matt, (2023), *Op. cit.*

[343] B. Jiang, (2023), *Op. cit.*

[344] Matt, (2023), *Op. cit.*

[345] B. Jiang, (2023), *Op. cit.*

[346] Matt, (2023), *Op. cit.*

[347] E. Harca, (2016), *Op. cit.*

[348] *Ibid.*

[349] Matt, (2023), *Op. cit.*

pairing of GPT with a companion robot that instructs the GPT to carry out the assignments.[350] This development represents far more advanced capabilities than the early versions of ChatGPT, which performs more mundane tasks. For example, ChatGPT said: "Remember, the most important thing is to choose a gift that reflects your relationship and shows her how much you care about her" after a Chinese user, Mike Li, asked for a Valentine's Day gift suggestion.[351] Lee was impressed by the accurate information received alongside human-like emotions in its suggestions, mimicking human interactions in the real world.[352]

Overall, Auto-GPT is said to carry strong potential for podcast creation, investment analysis, and event planning, enabling companies, businesses, and users to optimise their operations and attain objectives more efficiently.[353] For tech giants, the goal of chatbot production is to create a full AI stack "integrating generative AI products into every level of their business, from search engines and apps to industrial processes, digital devices, urban infrastructure and cloud computing".[354] Other U.S. chatbot products are also increasingly being commercialised for business use, and their developers are trying to eliminate access issues. For example, U.S.-originated AI products from Google, Microsoft, and ChatGPT have long waitlists, while ChatGPT also has issues with server capacity; however, many industry observers project these AI tools will be increasingly commercialised as business products, away from being used as a public tool and/or performing functions like online searching.[355]

The Chinese are similarly integrating chatbots into industrial products. Chinese home appliance makers and car manufacturers are boosting the use of AI chatbots in their products and services for enhanced human–machine interactivity, particularly at a time when ChatGPT and its sophisticated human-like conversational ability have attracted global attention.[356] Even Chinese users who can access ChatGPT through VPN have turned to it for personal advice. For example, Mike Li, a Shanghai-based marketing director, utilised ChatGPT for his selection of a present for his partner,

---

[350] *Ibid.*

[351] S. Zhu, (2023), *Op. cit.*

[352] *Ibid.*

[353] Matt, (2023), *Op. cit.*

[354] F. Yang, (2023), *Op. cit.*

[355] E. Cheng, (2023), *Op. cit.*

[356] F. Fan, Feifei, (2023b), *Op. cit.*

and ChatGPT gave him suggestions of jewellery, electronic gadgets, personalised gifts, romantic dining packages, flowers (including his partner's favourite flower), and/or gourmet chocolates (which ChatGPT described as "a classic Valentine's Day gift that never goes out of style") .[357] It may be possible that chatbots and AI-generated contents will change and enhance the sophistication of traditional household appliance and electronics industries, potentially motivating consumption recovery.[358]

In January 2025, China shocked the world when a group of young coders, computer language experts, and engineers developed an LLM chatbot for less than US$6 million and using only approximately 2,000 chips. The team members were all graduates from domestic Chinese universities such as Zhejiang University, a point of pride from the Chinese perspective. The team was also celebrated because of the large number (about half) of women in their team, in what is popularly perceived as a male-dominated industry. It also reinforced the Maoist adage that "women hold up half the sky", often used to praise socialism for empowering and emancipating women in socialist countries. This young team was funded by a well-known and also young (in his thirties) hedge fund investors who used his fortune for the project.

Indeed, the Chinese saw it as a sense of pride in many ways. The man behind DeepSeek was granted an audience with Premier Li Qiang, became the pride of his hometown in Hangzhou, and put Hangzhou on the Chinese tech map. Hangzhou is also the hometown of tech giant Alibaba, whereas most Chinese and foreigners regard Shenzhen as the unofficial Silicon Valley of China. Even the Chinese representatives to the United Nations (UN) told the UN not to underestimate the capabilities of Chinese scientists and engineers.

The sheer simplicity of the design and layout shocked the AI world and Silicon Valley stakeholders. For a long time, American tech sector stakeholders (sometimes nicknamed and affectionately known as "tech bros") and their associates believed in the brute force theory of LLM development. Due to this faith in the brute force theory, the Silicon Valley stakeholders had proceeded along the lines of making large investments in making chips, buying and empanelling them, building large data centres to train the chatbots and AI, and investing in large energy projects to power the data centres and chip foundries. In fact, one of the reasons for justifying President

[357] S. Zhu, (2023), *Op. cit.*

[358] F. Fan, (2023b), *Op. cit.*

Trump's second-term slogan of "drill baby drill" was to reverse President Biden and the Democrats' pro-environmental anti-climate change agenda, exploit America's oilfields, and increase its fossil fuel output.

Prior to the release of DeepSeek, one of Trump's most important projects, which began in the first weeks of his presidency, was the announcement of Project Stargate, bringing together three of the world's most prominent tech bros: the Oracle founder Larry Ellison, Sam Altman of OpenAI, and Masayoshi Son of SoftBank (Microsoft, TSMC, and Google were also involved). This was a US$500 billion project that had initial funding raised by Son, who had committed US$100 billion to invest in the U.S. during Trump's second term (during their joint presentation, President Donald Trump jokingly nudged Son-san to increase his investment to US$200 billion, to which Son-san replied jokingly that President Trump was indeed a tough negotiator and this little banter resulted in Son-san increasing his contribution to Project Stargate). It was touted as the largest AI infrastructure project in the world, but DeepSeek's initial sensationalism threw such large-scale projects into doubt.

The immediate economic fallout was severe. Something like over US$1 trillion was wiped out from tech stocks in the U.S. The infection was felt in Japan as SoftBank lost an initial 8% of the value of their stocks, given its intimate involvement in Project Stargate. South Korea was only saved by the closure of its stock markets due to the Lunar New Year. Malaysia, which was the site of US/Japan energy projects, chip foundries, and data centres, saw over 20 billion Ringgit wiped out in one night from its top 15 tech players. Canadian and Kazakhstani uranium's (necessary to produce nuclear energy) stocks were also down.

In the subsequent days, the stocks stabilised and regained some of the losses, but DeepSeek had already put the Western world, the G7, advanced economies, and their partners/allies on notice. Given the tremendous impact that DeepSeek had on the US tech world as well as other stakeholders around the globe, it triggered a spectrum of reactions from different parts of the world. Indeed, the reception to the emergence of DeepSeek was mixed and can be divided into three groups.

Praises. The Indian AI stakeholders (including the ministerial cabinet official) praised DeepSeek and hoped to learn from the Chinese LLM. Thus, the Indians isolated open-source DeepSeek on their servers, studied the AI LLM, and empanelled approximately 19,000 chips to build their own indigenous version. The Indian response appeared to be one of humility and duplicated China's success in building an LLM at a low cost without overpoweringly expensive AI infrastructure. One point to note is that the Indian finance ministry banned the use of DeepSeek, ChatGPT, and other AI tools based on an abundance of caution to avoid potential sensitive data breaches.

In the same way, it had also given hope to some AI stakeholders in Europe that there was a chance for the European Union to catch up with the U.S. in the AI sector, as it was lagging substantially behind the U.S. and China, whose GAFAM (Google, Amazon, Facebook (now known as Meta), Amazon, and Microsoft) and BAT (Baidu, Alibaba, and Tencent), respectively, now dominate the global tech sector with only a small smattering of companies from the EU, Japan, South Korea, and India still holding on to what remains of the tech pie.

There were many explanations for the success of DeepSeek besides its youthful and impressive team. The Japanese mass media commentaries cited Chinese ability to distil and improve the concept of Japanese kaizen, i.e., making incremental changes for improvement that eventually snowball into major change, as one of the reasons or ingredients for the DeepSeek team's success. The Japanese government's stance was one of consultation with other governments on how to manage and handle DeepSeek.

Malaysia wanted to start studying DeepSeek with the potential goal of incorporating the technology which Prime Minister Datuk Seri Anwar Ibrahim's government wanted as part of Malaysia's drive to be a data centre, chipmaking, and AI hub of Southeast Asia. PM Anwar had also extended the "Look East" policy to learn from China. It was formerly started by former Prime Minister Mahathir bin Mohamad to learn from Japan in the 1980s and early 1990s.

Interestingly, U.S. President Donald J. Trump also praised the AI app but warned that it was a "wake-up" call for the U.S. tech industry. Related to this comment, the U.S. and global media began to describe the emergence of DeepSeek as a "Sputnik moment" for the U.S., referring to the period of President John F. Kennedy when Americans were shocked after the Soviet Union stole the march on them by sending the first cosmonaut (the Soviet term for astronaut) into space. This event spurred on the Americans, inspired by President Kennedy's mantra of not asking what the country can do for the Americans but what they can do for their country. Fired up by the prospect of losing the space race to the Russians, the Americans eventually sent their first astronaut to the moon. In the case of the AI race, DeepSeek was equated with the Russian Sputnik spacecraft that stole the march on the Americans in the space race.

National Security Anxieties. Entities mainly in the West were suspicious of DeepSeek's security standards, its origins, and more diabolical goals that threaten national security. Within days of DeepSeek's introduction, NASA, the Australian government (starting with New South Wales government), Italy, Texas, the U.S. military (starting with the navy), the Indian finance ministry, and several others restricted or banned the app. In the same period, privacy watchdogs and investigators in Belgium, South Korea, and Ireland began to ask DeepSeek for more information on their data management procedures and systems.

Many security-concerned stakeholders, along with members of the global media, tested DeepSeek's responses to pose questions that were sensitive for the government of China and discovered they were polite rejections of the requests prompted. Questions on sensitive issues such as the Tiananmen incident and the Chinese leader were dodged. Other questions, such as the politics of the South China Sea and the Sino-Indian War of 1962, yielded responses that reflected the official Chinese government line, which drew suspicions from testers in the Philippines and India, respectively.

DeepSeek also motivated a political debate within the U.S. One school of thought is of the idea that DeepSeek stealing a march on ChatGPT confirmed the importance of the Biden-era strategy of "small courtyard, high fences", which connoted the idea of rejecting the Trump Term 1-era decoupling of U.S. and Chinese economies (a Cold War I-style complete division of spheres of influence without interdependence between the two superpowers) in favour of de-risking (continuing trade with China but restricting items of a sensitive dual-use nature that can be used for military purposes, like semiconductor chips; German Chancellor Olaf Scholz was also in favour of this strategy).

Because of this strategy, the Biden administration forged the Chips4 Alliance, whereby the U.S., Taiwan, South Korea, and Japan, working in concert with the Netherlands' ASML, would restrict cutting-edge technological transfer to the People's Republic of China. It was this Chips4 Alliance and other restrictions in advanced semiconductor chips by the Biden administration, cited by Chinese official narratives, that acted as a motivating factor for China to come up with its own indigenous advanced AI technologies like DeepSeek. For Americans in favour of this school of thought, they argued that the policy should continue with like-minded allies and partners by reorienting the supply chains through in-shoring, friend-shoring, and near-shoring of high-tech production.

The other school of thought, also uttered by President Trump, points in the opposite direction, indicating that it is exactly due to the failure of the Biden-era tech controls that DeepSeek was able to emerge. And according to this school of thought, sanctioned American chips (e.g., Nvidia) leaked into DeepSeek's team's hands, making DeepSeek possible. Thus, the solution is to close the "small courtyard" even further by imposing even heavier penalties. Indeed, this appeared in the form of legislation proposed by Republican Senator Josh Hawley to jail Americans who leaked technologies to the Chinese. The eventual goal of this school of thought is to bring chip foundries and other cutting-edge facilities back to the U.S., even if it means imposing trade tariffs on the current top GBU chipmaker necessary for AI (TSMC) to get them to move the production to the U.S. Anticipating such pressure, TSMC has relocated some of its chips-making facilities to Kumamoto, Japan (producing both legacy as well as advanced chips with Plant 1 fully functional), Arizona, U.S. (production includes two nano chips), and Dresden, Germany.

Doubters. There were also high-profile doubters of DeepSeek being built on approximately 2,000 chips and under US$6 million. They included the likes of Elon Musk and Kevin O'Leary (an investor of *Shark Tank* fame). The doubters, including OpenAI and Microsoft, said that they had located evidence that DeepSeek distilled their data illegally (some conservative right-wingers even termed it as "intellectual property theft"). Such reactions moderated and contrasted with their initial responses, which were praises heaped upon DeepSeek.

Overall, the reception to the appearance of DeepSeek ranged from utter surprise to praise for the chatbot. Such dramatic technological developments from both sides are likely to continue as the US-China rivalry deepens. They will cause disruptions to tech stocks, as well as those of peripheral industries connected to AI and chipmaking foundries.

References

AFP, 'Always there': the AI chatbot comforting China's lonely millions, dated 24 August 2021 in France 24 [downloaded on 24 August 2021]. Available at https://www.france24.com/en/live-news/20210824-always-there-the-ai-chatbot-comforting-china-s-lonely-millions.

ChatCompose, WeChat Chatbots: Chatbots to reach a Chinese audience, dated 2019 in ChatCompose [downloaded on 1 January 2023]. Available at https://www.chatcompose.com/chinawechat.html.

E. Cheng, China's A.I. chatbots haven't yet reached the public like ChatGPT did, dated 28 April 2023 in CNBC [downloaded on 28 April 2023], available at https://www.cnbc.com/2023/04/28/how-chinas-chatgpt-ai-alternatives-are-doing.html.

F. Fan, (2023b). Appliance makers, auto firms tap into chatbots, dated 4 April 2023 in China Daily [downloaded on 4 April 2023]. Available at http://epaper.chinadaily.com.cn/a/202304/04/WS642b5d6ea310777689887d5c.html.

F. Fan, (2023a). China ushers in golden era of AI, chatbots, dated 17 February 2023 in China Daily [downloaded on 17 February 2023]. Available at https://www.chinadaily.com.cn/a/202302/17/WS63eeb668a31057c47ebaf430.html.

F. F. Fan, Firms to tap AI for user experience, dated 4 April 2023 in China Daily [downloaded on 4 April 2023]. Available at https://www.chinadaily.com.cn/a/202304/04/WS642b66d4a31057c47ebb82cf.html.

E. Hale, China wants AI to rival ChatGPT. Censorship makes that tricky, dated 2 March 2023 in Al Jazeera [downloaded on 2 March 2023]. Available at https://www.aljazeera.com/economy/2023/3/2/china-wants-to-copy-chatgpts-success-censorship-makes-it-tricky.

E. Harca, What the West can learn from China about chatbot marketing, dated 13 May 2016 in ClickZ [downloaded on 13 May 2016]. Available at https://www.clickz.com/what-the-west-can-learn-from-china-about-chatbot-marketing/99687/.

M. Harrison, China says chatbots must be strictly censored by communist guidelines, undated in Futurism.com The Byte [downloaded on 26 April 2023]. Available at https://futurism.com/the-byte/china-chatbots-censored.

B. Jiang, How quickly are China's ChatGPT-style services catching up with Microsoft-backed OpenAI?, dated 11 May 2023 in South China Morning Post (SCMP) [downloaded on 11 May 2023]. Available at https://www.scmp.com/tech/tech-trends/article/3220062/how-quickly-are-chinas-chatgpt-style-services-catching-microsoft-backed-openai.

Jingdaily, China's retailers eye potential of ChatGPT and other AI Chatbots, dated 21 February 2023 in Italian Trade Agency (ITA) [downloaded on 21 February 2023]. Available at https://www.ice.it/it/news/notizie-dal-mondo/236987.

Kyodo, Japan to create guidelines on use of AI chatbots in schools, dated 7 April 2023 in Mainichi Japan [downloaded on 7 April 2023]. Available at https://mainichi.jp/english/articles/20230407/p2g/00m/0na/006000c.

Kyodo News, Yokosuka becomes 1st local gov't in Japan to begin ChatGPT trial use, dated 20 April 2023 in Kyodo News [downloaded on 20 April 2023].

Available at https://english.kyodonews.net/news/2023/04/0b30bc9d9174-yokosuka-becomes-1st-local-govt-in-japan-to-begin-chatgpt-trial-use.html.

S. Lin, Chinese chatbot to be made open source, dated 3 March 2023 in China Daily [downloaded on 3 March 2023]. Available at https://www.chinadaily.com.cn/a/202303/03/WS64012f84a31057c47ebb1d8e.html.

Matt, Auto-GPT vs ChatGPT: How do they differ and everything you need to know, dated 18 April 2023 in AutoGPT.net [downloaded on 18 April 2023]. Available at https://autogpt.net/auto-gpt-vs-chatgpt-how-do-they-differ-and-everything-you-need-to-know/.

NHK, Japanese AI researchers advise chatbot users to be aware of pros and cons, dated 28 April 2023 in NHK [downloaded on 28 April 2023]. Available at https://www3.nhk.or.jp/nhkworld/en/news/20230426_07/.

NHK News, Google Bard AI chatbot now available in Japanese, Korean, dated 11 May 2023 in NHK [downloaded on 11 May 2023]. Available at https://www3.nhk.or.jp/nhkworld/en/news/20230511_13/.

Pandaily, China's First ChatGPT-Like Chatbot MOSS Released For Public Testing, dated 21 February 2023 in Pandaily [downloaded on 21 February 2023]. Available at https://pandaily.com/chinas-first-chatgpt-like-chatbot-moss-released-for-public-testing/.

J. Pao, China's early AI chatbots more patriotic than smart, dated 13 April 2023 in Asia Times [downloaded on 13 April 2023]. Available at https://asiatimes.com/2023/04/chinas-early-ai-chatbots-more-patriotic-than-smart/.

Reuters, As Alibaba unveils ChatGPT rival, China flags new AI rules, dated 11 April 2023 in Al Jazeera [downloaded on 11 April 2023]. Available at https://www.aljazeera.com/news/2023/4/11/as-alibaba-unveils-chatgpt-rival-china-flags-new-ai-rules.

Reuters, China's SenseTime unveils new AI products and chatbot, dated 11 April 2023 in the The Indian Express [downloaded on 11 April 2023]. Available at https://indianexpress.com/article/technology/artificial-intelligence/chinas-sensetime-unveils-new-ai-products-and-chatbot-8548858/.

M. Schuman, Why Chatbot AI is a problem for China, dated 18 April 2023 in The Atlantic [downloaded on 18 April 2023]. Available at https://www.theatlantic.com/international/archive/2023/04/chatbot-ai-problem-china/673754/.

T. Takenouchi, AI experts say ChatGPT, other chatbots fine to use with caution, dated 26 April 2023 in Asahi Shimbun [downloaded on 26 April 2023]. Available at https://www.asahi.com/ajw/articles/14894495.

The Asahi Shimbun, Editorial: Rules must be set for AI chatbots before genie is out of the bottle, dated 19 April 2023 in Asahi Shimbun [downloaded on 19 April 2023]. Available at https://www.asahi.com/ajw/articles/14888833.

S. F. Wong, (translated by Grace Chong and Candice Chan), China's self-censoring chatbots face many challenges, dated 17 April 2023 in Thinkchina and

Lianhe Zaobao [downloaded on 17 April 2023]. Available at https://www.thinkchina.sg/chinas-self-censoring-chatbots-face-many-challenges.

F. Yang, AI chatbots with Chinese characteristics: Why Baidu's ChatGPT rival may never measure up, dated 24 March 2023 in The Conversation [downloaded on 24 March 2023]. Available at https://theconversation.com/ai-chatbots-with-chinese-characteristics-why-baidus-chatgpt-rival-may-never-measure-up-202109.

J. Yeung, and M. Mayumi, As Japan's population drops, one city is turning to ChatGPT to help run the government, dated 21 April 2023 in CNN [downloaded on 21 April 2023]. Available at https://edition.cnn.com/2023/04/21/asia/japan-yokosuka-government-chatgpt-intl-hnk/index.html.

I. Zhang, Countdown to ERNIE: Chinese Media on Baidu's AI Chatbot, dated 15 March 2023 in ChinaTalk [downloaded on 15 March 2023]. Available at https://www.chinatalk.media/p/countdown-to-ernie-chinese-media.

Y. Zhao, China makes first ChatGPT-related arrest for fake news, dated 11 May 2023 in The China Project [downloaded on 11 May 2023]. Available at https://thechinaproject.com/2023/05/11/china-makes-first-chatgpt-related-arrest-for-fake-news/.

S. Zhu, AI matchmaking, cosmic romance and ChatGPT bring digital options for Valentine's Day, dated 14 February 2023 in Shine Shanghai Daily (edited by Yang Meiping) [downloaded on 14 February 2023]. Available at https://www.shine.cn/news/metro/2302146203/.

E. Zitron, RIP Metaverse, dated 8 May 2023 in Business Insider [downloaded on 8 May 2023]. Available at https://www.businessinsider.com/metaverse-dead-obituary-facebook-mark-zuckerberg-tech-fad-ai-chatgpt-2023-5.

Chapter 13

Conclusion for the Volume

This volume is the result of a collaboration between a hard scientist/IT expert, a legal expert, and a social scientist. Given that issues and problems in science and technology are so complex, a multidisciplinary approach can better generate ideas or interpret the issues surrounding ChatGPT.

ChatGPT is a next-generation AI chatbot that can communicate in the English language (as well as other language options) and is capable of writing software/coding, developing new business proposals, and undertaking mundane tasks such as writing speeches with good-quality outputs. Its language use has proven to be much better than previous versions of AI writing software/apps. In these mundane tasks, ChatGPT has proven to be much faster in performing tasks and assignments than even teams of humans working together, including programming tasks. This can in turn have a strong impact on business productivity, especially for cash-strapped and human-resource-deficient small businesses. It can release manpower for higher-value-added or more crucial tasks, besides routine administrative ones such as drawing up work schedules or programmes for company events.

There are different views about ChatGPT. Some consider it to be a high-tech toy, while others detect its powerful impact on human activities. For example, it is expected to have a strong impact in the private sector, as those companies that can tap into its capabilities can enjoy strong advantages. But it may also mean that small- and medium-sized businesses that do not develop a capability in ChatGPT may lag behind. Data analytics is seen as another area in which ChatGPT can play a bigger role.

It can also play a role in professional activities such as writing business reports, advertising slogans, financial reports, simple journalistic field reports, and basic artistic works.

Yet, others are doubtful whether ChatGPT is as formidable as it sounds, as other hyped-up AI appear to have their respective weaknesses. (However, this view, which was applied to other AI applications, has been proven wrong. AI created for self-driving or autonomous vehicles appears to be doing quite well now.) Some detractors argue that ChatGPT may end up replacing humans across a spectrum of jobs. Other detractors or cautious views about ChatGPT argue that it is a complicated algorithm that can churn out meaningful sentences but little beyond that. It cannot explain the sources, methodology, or reasoning for why it writes certain contents, according to its detractors. It cannot manage, eliminate, or rule out biased, immoral, non-empathetic, or unethical actions that a human can otherwise perform.

Regardless of viewpoints, ChatGPT is now available to the public. Its proliferation is being studied for its implications, particularly the outcome of its use in everyday tasks. In the near future, ChatGPT is expected to be upgraded constantly with increasingly powerful capabilities. Eventually, ChatGPT is expected to be a collaborator for humans, making human–machine interfaces possible. Humans can then supervise and lead AI to complete tasks (which can be increasingly complex). Humans empowered with AI can perform many tasks simultaneously. Eventually, there may even come a point when humans start to learn from AI or when tailored ChatGPT is available for specific tasks or industries.

Section 1 by June Tay provided the backgrounder, context, and framework for the contents of the volume. Tay traced the genesis of ChatGPT to provide a better understanding of the subject matter of this volume. And in detailing the background of ChatGPT, Tay laid out the limitations of the technology at the point of writing. She also touched on the legal and ethical implications of the technology (a subject matter that was picked up in the following section by Lee Cheng Tan). But Tay did not stop there as she took on a comparative angle to analyse the capabilities of ChatGPT's peers such as Ernie as a case study.

Tay then took on a trade practitioner's view of the science of ChatGPT and GenAI in general. Here, the technical parameters of the workings of LLMs are discussed for readers, especially from a technologist's viewpoint. In order to do so, the technical ingredients that led to LLMs were discussed from various disciplinary lenses, such as the advent of NLP.

Then, like the previous section, LLMs are comparatively discussed. Subtopics related to this section, such as financing and open-source status, were also discussed.

More technical aspects of the discussion followed, with materials on LLM benchmarks and their limits, as well as the genre of GenAI algorithms. Once again, the comparative angle comes in with discussions of LLM developments in Japan, China, the EU, and the U.S. The different architectures they used were also compared before entering into trend-spotting mode to detect and discern future potential developments in this field. This was indeed a section about possibilities.

The introduction to the technology in question by Tay led sequentially to the next discussion on the legal implications of the technology by Lee Cheng Tan. She used the case study of Chinese regulations and laws for this purpose. This section was then followed by the EU case study. And here, Lee decoded the "Brussels Effect", hinting at the supranational nature of EU regulations, politics, and law-making. The comparative section then concluded with the case study of the U.S. The leading tech power of the world's innovation systems, including data protection laws and regulations and federal executive implementation and enforcement, was detailed.

The legal aspects of GenAI development lead to the final section of the volume, which looked at Chinese chatbots from a political-economic as well as multidisciplinary point of view. The technocratic state and its social scientific ecology in producing AI and chatbots were discussed in detail. The whole-of-society and whole-of-government approaches were covered in this case study section. As the Chinese political system and technocratic state trump all other aspects of Chinese society, the stakeholders in the system and their interests and agendas were discussed, privileging the power of the one-party state in the analysis. Harnessing the geopolitical advantages of the technologies was also discussed, given the peer or near-peer competition taking place between China and other major powers.

www.ingramcontent.com/pod-product-compliance
Lightning Source LLC
LaVergne TN
LVHW051052210926
848486LV00002B/77

* 9 7 8 9 8 1 9 8 2 1 9 6 9 *